I had started writing my book, *Hack The Buyer Brain*, and I'd hit a wall. I wasn't sure if what I had done was the right thing, or if I was just writing a bunch of crap in a crappier format. I'm the kind of person who does a lot of research on how to do things (bit of procrastination in there).

I'd looked at tonnes of resources, and none of them were any good. The things that were for business books were awful, and the fiction book advice wasn't applicable. I just really needed help to get unstuck, and out of my own way.

## I Wanted A Good Book!

If Vicky had even remotely been like any of the other resources, spouting nonsense about a business book just being the best business card you'll ever have and that no one will read it anyway—I would have run a mile.

There is so much rubbish advice out there about the positioning a book will magically give you, even if the book is crap. The fact of the matter is, your book needs to be good too. It's not enough to just have a book, it needs to be worthwhile, else you're never going to get clients.

Instead, not only did Vicky give me a brilliant bit of advice that got me unstuck and writing again, but she helped me make my book a good book. She held my hand every step of the way.

She validated my ideas, and saw through my fears and concerns to give me the insights, advice and kicks up the bum I needed. She made my book a good book.

But more than that, she gave me the confidence to feel good about my book. I have that confidence now not because she's built me some kind of false ego like some wanky coaches do, but because she helped craft something I can be truly proud of. I have a good book—and that's all Vicky's fault.

## No Justification Required

Weirdly, the thing I love the most about this process is that

I never had to justify myself. Sometimes you have to explain why you're riddled with anxiety, or that yes I know I'm procrastinating but it's because it's part of my routine and and and...

When other people don't get that you're just a bit odd, and they have never been where you've been, you fall into an awful lot of justification behaviour. Vicky gets it. She knows, and she has all the little tricks and tips to help get you unstuck. She's also immensely knowledgeable and talented, helping me navigate through all the intricacies of getting a book published and out there. I would have been lost without her.

## Time, Money, And Sanity

I saved huge amounts of time by getting help from Vicky. She was able to redirect me in a fraction of the time it would have taken me to figure it out myself. And the end result is 10x better than it would have been.

Going through this process also actually saved me money. If I had wasted all my time trying to do it all myself without direction, it would have been productive time down the drain. It would also have meant way more down-time being used up; I have precious little spare time as it is. To be able to spend that time on things that are important to me and allow me to function best at work, is priceless. It saved me buying all the courses out there that are awful, and stopped me from buying all the books...

And of course, there is the sanity it gave me. I can't quantify the emotional aspect, aside from to say that Vicky gave me the confidence to launch. And that alone is worth 10x the price I've paid.

## She Knows Her Shit

I can wholeheartedly recommend Vicky, her book, her workshops, her course, and her services. I have recommended her to other authors and I will do time and time again. The financial, time and emotional return on investment I have had has been phenomenal.

She knows her shit and she'll help you craft a book worth being proud of.

## Phenomenal Results In Just Two Months

The help that Vicky has given me in getting Hack the Buyer Brain together has meant that for three months I've had nearly two interviews a week about the book. I sold enough books on my prelaunch to pay for the first print run. I sold out of my first print run within a month.

Within two months I sold over 300 copies—most authors will only sell 250 in their lifetime. I did my first book signing at an event I was invited to speak at, where people queued for 45 mins to have their copy personally signed, and sold out of all copies bought.

I have two brand new clients who have come directly through the book—both of whom came to me within a day of reading the book. I have consistent 5-star ratings and reviews so far, and I know of two groups that have used the book as a book club read.

I've recently won an award for Outstanding Contribution to my field as a result of the content of the book—which officially makes it an award-winning book. It's also been made required reading for the Content Marketing Academy, as well as part of the syllabus for two universities in the UK.

I get consistent compliments and messages from readers who have said it's changed everything for them. People are starting to get results from the book's content too.

And as a result of all this, I cannot rave enough about what Vicky has done.

**Kenda Macdonald, Automation Ninjas, Author of** *Hack The Buyer Brain*

# The Fastest Read I've Ever Had

I'm in a little hotel in the middle of nowhere with 90 per cent of my first draft done—and thanks to having read your draft book from cover to cover today (since 9 am, it's 3.30 pm now), I have another great boost of confidence, and notes and Post-Its coming out my ears.

My compliments, you really have perfected the art of asking.

One a-ha moment I genuinely did experience myself while reading is that I want to help people to understand my business.

It's probably the fastest read I've ever had, and it's set me up nicely for my week of finishing *The Big Hairy Green Book* all about artificial grass, and the adventures of a man who made it big in the Emerald Isle. Which already has lots of grass.

**Mark O'Loughlin, Sanctuary Synthentics, Author of** *The Big Hairy Green Book*

## This Book Is Da Bomb!

I **LOVE** this book. It has totally made me want to write a book (I didn't start out thinking it would!)—so now I need to start mulling over my why and my big idea. The beauty of your system is that rather than floundering around, wondering where to start, and then giving up because it's all too complicated and overwhelming, I now have the steps to follow. It feels infinitely more do-able.

And on a personal note, your writing style is a delight—readable, empathetic, with interesting stories and good data to back things up.

This book is da bomb!

**Tanya Smith-Lorenz, More Business Buzz, Conversion Copywriter and Future Author**

## So Engrossed I Lost All Feeling In My Leg

I hopped across the room and crashed into the cat. I'd just finished my second read-through of your book, stood up, and the pins and needles in my left foot were so intense I was delirious.

Engrossed? First time, naturally. You're a damn fine writer. But so engrossed that on my second reading I'd sat on my leg until I lost all feeling? Doesn't happen often.

Anyone serious about writing the best business book they're capable of should read this and follow your beetle steps. It's bloody marvellous, because:

- While the world's full of snake oil sellers and gurus saying they have an 'easy' way to write a book, you never pretend it's easy. That's not your schtick. You show people it's worth doing it right, and that's damn hard work, but so much better.

- You then break it down into digestible chunks. It's less daunting. Each feels doable.
- You're real and relatable-to. And honest about mistakes.
- It's proven. You've done it. Dom's done it. Your clients have done it.
- It makes sense. It's for people who are do-ers. It feels like you've got readers' backs. It's not a shitty cynical sales tool. If people read it and take the beetle steps they'll have a book written. And a book they can be proud of.

Despite being in your Superheroes world for a while, in which you've previously given brilliant and practical advice about, for instance, outlining/writing with clarity/being more bloody interesting/editing/etc. I still felt I learned a mahoosive amount from reading this. And the beetle steps will make the process of writing (which I love, and love to learn about)—including outlining, writing, polishing, so much less daunting for readers.

It also grabbed my interest immediately and held it all the way through. No filler.

**Jamie Veitch, Jamie Veitch Consulting, Author of** *The Social Entrepreneur's Guide To Winning Tenders*

## Cheering Me On

I feel like now that I've read your book, I'm equipped to get on and start! I felt like you were a friend cheering me on.

And I love the end chapter! I feel like you're pumping me up in a really good way and I feel psyched to get started. I loved it!

**Abby Popplestone, Adventurer and Future Author**

## Writing A Book Is Possible For You...

*How the Hell do you Write a Book?* is very obviously the work of an expert. Not just because of her research, although she has clearly studied her subject in considerable depth. Her expertise is reflected in how much she has learned from writing her first book, *Business for Superheroes*, several ghost writing projects, and indeed the writing of this book.

*How the Hell do you Write a Book?* makes very clear that writing a book is possible for someone who is sufficiently determined. This book also explains why writing a book is not easy and the serious challenges which will present themselves. This book is the work of someone who has already written several books and is maturing as a writer, both in terms of becoming confident in her own voice and having served her apprenticeship as a copywriter.

If someone is seriously thinking of writing their own book then they should read this one first. This is a realistic and totally practical account of what it takes to create a business book. The existence of the book itself proves the author knows what she is talking about. This book makes clear the effort required and challenges that will be faced in writing a book. The various stages that will have to be gone through are outlined in detail. The reader is left in no doubt about the help that is going to be needed to get from initial idea to published volume. Vicky did not write her book alone and neither will you.

Writing a book is a challenge but not an insurmountable one: Vicky Fraser has confronted and triumphed over that challenge many times now. This book will guide you in taking on this challenge yourself. Vicky does not pretend that writing a book is easy but she does prove that it is possible.

**Graham Butcher, Ice & Fire**

# How The Hell do you Write A Book?

# How The Hell do you Write A Book?

**Unleash Your Inner Author & Write Your Business Book
One Simple Step At A Time**

First Edition

Vicky Fraser

How The Hell Do You Write A Book: Unleash Your Inner Author &
Write Your Business Book One Simple Step At A Time
First Edition (2019)

ISBN: 978-1-912713-87-5

Published by Moxie Books (Vicky Fraser Ltd.)
www.moxiebooks.co.uk

Cover design: Julia Brown, Brown Owl Design
www.brownowldesign.com

Feather pen icon made by EpicCoders from www.flaticon.com. Beetle
icon made by Freepik from www.flaticon.com.

Printed and bound by Elite Publishing Academy
www. elitepublishingacademy.com

This book is produced from independently certified FSC paper to ensure
responsible forest management.

*For mum and dad, who never refused to buy me a book or take me to the library, and who always made me believe I could do anything I set my mind to. I'm still working on telekinesis.*

*"No one is actually dead until the ripples they cause in the world die away…"*

*Sir Terry Pratchett*

# Contents

Why write a book. Your excuses demolished. A story from *Star Trek*. I've heard all your nonsense because it's my nonsense too. The best time to write.

Space. Time. Harnessing space-time. You're a collection of bad habits. SMART goals and stupid goals. Beating procrastination before it smacks you in the face.

The worst thing that can happen during a pole dancing competition. Living large with the creators of *South Park*. Identifying your Inner Dickhead. Why are you doing this? The nature of humanity. Fail better.

Yelling at you for your own good. Coming up with ideas. Thinking sideways. Radical notion: talk to people. Collect stories. Create your hook. How to play.

Writer's block is a myth. Crashing out of your comfort zone. How to kill your book. The Blank Page of Doom. Loosening you up without gin.

The Chicken Bomb. Why are they reading? Why are you writing? Burrowing into brains: yours and theirs. Asking the right questions. How to use your Weirdo Profile.

Recycling for the win! Starting from scratch. The hybrid method. Genre & purpose. Cobbling it together and polishing it up.

Front matter. Main body. Back matter. Structural integrity: how to keep your book from falling apart.

# Foreword

Vicky Fraser is one of those rare creatures who can and has done, and also knows how to teach you how to do it.

Moreover she is peculiarly well fitted to do so, because the writing she started her career with is perhaps most difficult of all: Persuading people to buy things.

You will find plenty of books that suggest how you can write well, and successfully.

But the thing that really stands in the way of you and what you want to write is fear. Fear you're not up to the job.

You lack the confidence you need; you don't know where to start, or for that matter how to carry on. How to gain and keep your reader's attention.

This book is not just about these technical challenges. It builds your morale, makes you feel better about your ability. It gives you what you need to believe in yourself and get started.

And after it's done that it takes you by the hand and leads you, step by step, to success. Nobody can give you talent but Vicky shows you how to make the best of what you have.

But Vicky adds something extra. She is funny. You cannot be bored into learning. She makes it fun.

Good luck with your book!

**Drayton Bird, July 2019**

# The 10 Commandments
# Of Writing A Book

1. If you write, you are a writer. You can do this.
2. Do not edit as you write: write freely and write fast.
3. Create a detailed outline before you start writing.
4. Protect your writing time and space fiercely.
5. Embrace the Shitty First Draft.
6. Do not sit and wait for inspiration to strike. Go out and grab it.
7. Understand whom you're writing for and crawl inside their head.
8. Give yourself permission to be wholly and unapologetically yourself.
9. Pay attention to the details: you're not an amateur, don't act like one.
10. Take criticism with grace and gratitude, and use it to become better.

# On Not Writing

*"I was taught that the way forward was neither quick nor easy."*
Marie Curie

I wrote my first book when I was in middle school—when I was maybe nine or ten years old.

It was a mini-masterpiece, that book, in my memory.

It had chapters. Pictures. A story.

It even had covers and a binding, of sorts.

My first book started as an assignment in my English class. We'd been told to write a story…and as usual, I went extra and wrote an entire book.

In creating that somewhat overblown story I discovered, before I'd ever heard of the wonderful Sir Terry Pratchett, that writing is the most fun you can have by yourself.

I have no idea what happened to that book, and I can't even remember what it was about now, but I do know this: it kicked off a lifelong love affair with writing. Obviously, then, I didn't write another book for more than twenty-five years.

I spent a lot of time *thinking* about writing a book and *talking* about writing a book, and *not* writing a book…

Until, one day in 2015, I stood in front of a roomful of other business owners and boldly declared, "I will write a book all about my business and how I can help my customers. And not only that, I will write it in ninety days! Hiiiiiiii-ya!"

(Imagine me performing an overenthusiastic karate chop, and beaming like an elephant with a hosepipe.[1])

Funny thing about saying stuff in front of people you respect and admire—you kind of have to deliver on it or risk looking a total twit.

Three months later, after more ups, downs, twists, and turns than an over-caffeinated rollercoaster, I turned up clutching my shiny new book in my sweaty little hands—which is when the *real* work began.

Because, my fine feathered friend, we're not in the business of writing books for the sake of it. I'm not writing this book *only* to help you "get published" (although it is pretty gorram[2] amazing when your books arrive with your name on the front).

Nope; I'm writing this book because I know if you write *your* book, and use it to its fullest potential, it could change your world.

Words change worlds.

Books change lives.

I've adopted the word moxie[3] for my business and for this book because it perfectly sums up what a book can do for you and to you. My favourite definition of moxie is "force of character, determination, or nerve". To write and use a book successfully for your business, you'll need moxie. The act of creating your book will help give you moxie, that I promise.

I want to help change your life for the better when you write your book, and I want to help you transform your clients' lives for the better, too. That might sound like a tall order, but if you have happy

---

1    Note to reader: elephants love hosepipes. Look: http://bit.ly/moxie-elephant

2    If you watched *Firefly* (may it rest in peace), you'll get this semi-sweary reference.

3    Did you know the word moxie became popular in the 1930s as the name of a fizzy soft drink? It's still popular today in New England and Houston, Texas. It came to mean "courage" because, in 1876, it was patented as a medicine called Moxie Nerve Food.

clients, you're already doing this. You're already changing lives, whether you believe me or not. Your book will help you change more lives and do bigger, better things.

Remember, great deeds begin with one word and one step.

And great books start with one word and one sentence.

Changing the world doesn't always mean the act of stopping a war (or starting one). It doesn't mean solving world poverty *right now*. It doesn't mean changing an unjust law overnight.

All those things do transform the world, for sure—but they start with just one tiny beetle step. Like Rosa Parkes, who refused to give up her seat on the bus to a white passenger, kickstarting the Montgomery bus boycott, and becoming the "first lady of Civil Rights". Or Facebook, which started as one nerd's way to keep in touch with fellow students on his Harvard University campus—and mushroomed into the software and social media giant it is now.

Maybe something magnificent will start with a book something like the one hibernating inside your head.

Maybe by changing one person's life in a small way, you can set off a chain of events that'll change the world in a bigger way.

What do you think?

Worth a try?

I reckon so.

Start here. Start today. I've got your back, grasshopper.

# Writing With Moxie

*"Writing is the most fun you can have by yourself."*

*Sir Terry Pratchett*

O H GOD WHAT AM I DOING?!"

This is a perfectly legitimate reaction to the idea of writing a book. But guess what? We're not going to write a book today. I'm not going to sit here and pretend you can do the impossible, because that's not fair. You're (probably) not a seasoned writer; you're a business owner who wants to write a book.

I am a trapeze artist, and I can tell you—no trapeze coach would order a first-timer to hop up and knock out a performance-worthy routine, right now, *today*. And, as your writing coach, I won't urge you to sit down in front of your computer and write a book, right now, *today*.

If I did that, you'd give me the finger and go and do something else. Quite rightly, too.

Instead, let's do this: find your Big Idea, hatch a plan, make an outline, and build your book step by tiny beetle step, bite by bite, word by word.

Let's do something simple that won't explode your brain and have you hurtling in the opposite direction at breakneck speed.

Let's take you from "ohshitohshitohsit I have no idea how to do this" all the way to "YAY I'M AN AUTHOR BABY!"

Before we do, though, I want you to understand something about writing books: it's *not* easy... but it's definitely easier than you think. Anyone can become an author... but not everyone should and most people won't because it's bloody hard work. It will almost certainly make you cry tears of rage and frustration at least once. However, writing a book will also bring you joy because writing truly is the most fun you can have by yourself. You will get a huge kick out of your achievement, especially when people start reading and passing your book around.

I believe in you. You can do this.

So let's start at the beginning with this question: do you have a book in you?

Then let's ask two more: can you write a book? *Should* you?

I'll help you answer those questions in painful detail during the first few chapters but think about it now. You're reading this book because you want to write your own book... But why do you want to write it?

While you're pondering that, let me explain what you won't be doing.

## Snapping at J.K. Rowling's Heels

Let's get one thing straight: if you're reading this, you're probably a business owner who wants to write a book of some kind. You're not looking to become the next J.K. Rowling or Stephen King. You're not hoping for the type of £34 million royalty cheque the creator of Harry Potter receives.

Right?

Good. Because chances are, your book is not going to make you rich in and of itself. The chances of you writing the next *Eat, Pray, Love* or *Think And Grow Rich* are slim. Not impossible, and I'm rooting for you, of course. But becoming a financially successful author with mass global appeal in your own right is the exception, not the rule. That's not what this book is all about.

I want to manage your expectations here—the purpose of your business book is not solely to catapult you to the top of the literary world and make you rich and famous. That may happen as a byproduct, and I hope it does—but there's a more profound purpose to the book trying to claw its way out of you.

You're writing a book because you have an idea or a story you need to share. Or the glimmer of an idea. You're writing it because you know your skills, knowledge, and expertise can improve people's lives. What difference are you trying to make in the world through your business? *That's* why you're writing a book: to help you fulfil your purpose. It's the most important reason you're writing a book. But there are other benefits, too, as you'll discover in Chapter 1.

## How To Use This Book

I've divided this book into three parts:

1.   Part I: Laying The Foundations
2.   Part II: Build Your Book Step By Tiny Beetle Step
3.   Part III: The Finishing Touches

You won't start actually writing your book until Part II but I want you to be patient, grasshopper. You may be tempted to skip ahead—and you can do if you want, I'm not the boss of you—but I urge you to work through Part I first.

It's all very well starting to build your walls, but if you don't have strong foundations, the whole lot may come tumbling down[1]. Do the preparation in Part I because without it—without nailing down your Big Idea and getting to know your ideal reader—you will not be able to write your book.

In Part II, we'll go through all the elements of your book and how to write them in great detail. This will be much easier if you do the work from Part I.

---

1 I know this because I am renovating a 17th-century cottage. It's a little… shaky in places.

11

And in Part III we'll put the finishing touches on and get your book ready for print and publication.

My beta readers told me they read through the book once, then sat down with a notepad and a pen to work through it properly. You may find it helpful to do this too: read the book in one go and get a feel for what you're doing, then come back and work through it piece by piece.

You may find yourself flipping backwards and forwards through this book as you write, so in Appendix I you'll find a chart to help you find what you're looking for. For example, if you were looking for information on how to tell a story, you'd go to Chapter 15. Speaking of what you'll get, I have two important notes for you.

First, there is more than one way to write a book. My approach is not The One True Way. This is my take on things; the way I write my books, the way I ghostwrite my clients' books, and the way I teach my students to write their books. You might find a better way, and that's okay. Do what suits you. I want you to write your book in the best way for you, not struggle along with a system that may not fit you.

Second: despite what certain sections of the internet might like you to believe, most of us cannot (and will not) write a book in a weekend. Not a substantial, meaningful, valuable book, at any rate. There is a way to write a book super-fast, and I'll explain in Chapter 7... but, really, this is about how to write a book the "hard" way.

Throughout the book, you'll find action points in the shape of Tiny Beetle Steps—and directions for where and how to download the resources you'll need to help you write and publish your book. Please use them, because they'll help you take action—and action is the only way you'll reach your author goal.

In the appendices are notes and examples you may find useful as you read and write. You'll also find a bibliography of fantastic books that have helped me over the years.

From scrawling your Shitty First Drafts and overcoming the

Blank Page of Doom to fun-sheets that set out how to write your introduction, conclusion, and middle chapters, all the way to how to avoid looking like an amateur, and ultimately publishing your work, you'll find everything you need between these covers.

## Why Me? How Can I Help You?

Chances are you picked up this book because you know something about me already, but just in case you don't, here's why I'm qualified to help you write and independently publish your book: I understand the exquisite agony of writing a book.

I know what it's like to have a book inside you that you can't dig out. I know what it's like to make excuse after excuse as to why you can't do it. I know what it's like to find 3,597 other tasks you absolutely must do right now or the world will explode—instead of writing your book. And I know—oh, how I know—how successful your Inner Dickhead is at sabotaging you.

I have a small pile of half-finished books gathering digital dust on my hard drive. Some of them, I'll finish; others will probably fade away. You may think that's nothing to shout about, but I am shouting about it because those half-finished projects mean I understand you. I see you. I know all your excuses, because they're my excuses, too.

Despite all that, when I wrote my first book, *Business For Superheroes*, I did it in around ninety days. Since then, I've been showing other business owners how to write their books, much faster and better than they thought they could.

I understand why some books die a sad little death before they're ever published, and how to make sure you're writing the right one from the start.

I understand why writing stalls, and why it can sometimes feel impossible to get started again—and I know how to make sure you do start again. I know how to keep you going so you don't abandon your book because everyone has something important to say. Everyone's story can change someone's world, even if only in the tiniest way. And that tale deserves to be published.

And by the beard of Zeus![2] I'm gonna help you do it.

I learned from those who came before me. I took systems and processes and adapted them and made them my own. I tweaked and tinkered and tested—and found something that works for me and my clients. Now I'm sharing it with you.

It's not just my own books I've written and published, either; I've also ghost-written or heavily edited eleven books for clients (at the time of publishing this one). I've been through the process laid out in this book many, many times, refining it and improving it each time, learning from every mistake and making things better. I've coached or taught more than twenty-five authors to write their own books using variations on this method. And I improve my methods all the time based on my clients' feedback and suggestions.

Perhaps most important of all, though, is this: I am still doing what I teach. I am still writing books for myself and my clients. I keep up with the latest in the indie-publishing world, and I stay friendly with the best contacts in the industry. I love what I do, so I'll be writing and teaching other business owners to write for a long time. You're next. It's your turn. But remember…

## Don't Just Read, Act

It's not enough to read this book. I mean, reading is brilliant, obviously—in fact, it's essential if you want to be a good writer—but you have to *do*, too. If you want to write a book, I'm afraid you have to sit down and actually write.

Which is why, throughout this book, you'll find Tiny Beetle Steps to take at the end of each chapter. I call them Tiny Beetle Steps because sometimes even baby steps are too big. The Tiny Beetle Steps are tasks I'll set you. Small goals to reach, as part of your book-writing adventure.

Because it is an adventure, and I promise you'll have fun.

Please do these small tasks, because they'll help you write your

---

2 Yes, I am a massive fan of the movie *Anchorman*.

book and become a published author.

Before you start, remember this: Tiny Beetle Steps are enough. Don't worry about the long list or the big picture; just focus on the next thing you get to do. As Confucius said, "Every journey of 1,000 miles begins with a single step."

Are you ready for your first Tiny Beetle Step? Then let us begin with making a promise to yourself—and by declaring your intent to the world (or, at least, to me).

Email me right now at 1000authors@vickyfraser.com and tell me your Big Idea. Copy yourself in, so you promise yourself, too. Then set a monthly reminder in your calendar, so it pops up and asks you how your book is going.

Use this subject line: Great Odin's raven, I'm writing my book!

Then send me a message that says something like:

---

I have a Big Idea for my book, and it is this

_____

I may be afraid of failure. I may be a terminal procrastinator. And I may be an expert at inventing crappy excuses. But I am drawing a line in the sand, right here, right now: Enough.

I will crack on and write my book. I will block out time in my schedule and pick up my writing tools and write. I will find inventive ways to clamber over the obstacles writing will throw my way.

I have a story I need to tell, and by golly! I am going to tell it. I will have my book printed and in my hands by

_____

---

You got this. Now let's go.

# PART I

# Laying The Foundations

*"If you have built castles in the air, your work need not be lost; that is where they should be. Now put the foundations under them."*

*Henry David Thoreau*

# CHAPTER 1

# The Beating Heart Of
# Your Business

*"Great things are not accomplished by those who
yield to trends and fads and popular opinion."*

*Jack Kerouac*

Why do you want to write a book for your business? You may
have a single powerful reason, or more than one purpose.
Think about it carefully as you read this first chapter—and all
the chapters that follow. While you consider your reason, I'd like
to share this message with you. It came from a lady who read my
first book, then joined my tribe.

"Well I finally finished reading your book last night! And I
cried! Cried because you are a superhero that goes through shit
like everyone else. That makes me feel like I can and will succeed
at running my own business. I honestly don't know who when
or why but listening to your podcasts and reading your book has
pulled me out of a very long depression that I was in. I knew I
was bad but I didn't realise how bad but something has clicked
and I am now taking action and making decisions and plans for
my future!!"

She did take action, too. She's grown her business so much
she's fully paid off one debt and is making inroads into the others.
And she made enough profit to give her and her son a proper
Christmas with treats for the first time in years.

I've had a fistful of emails and messages from this remarkable lady over the past year or so, and most of them have had me in tears. The fact that my little book helped her out is astonishing and delightful to me (although she's done all the work).

This is my reason why: to help business owners believe in themselves so they can write the book that will change everything for them. The book that helps them create a business and life they love. There's more than one good reason to write a book, but the most important reason is to help people and make a real difference in someone's life. What's the thing you can do easily, but others struggle with? What struggles have you overcome that will help others do the same? How can you reach your hand back down the ladder and help people up behind you?

Your book is the perfect way to do it because books change lives. And there are other fabulous (and profitable) reasons to become a published author, too. Let me explain.

## Why Write Your Book?

I've seen "gurus" mushroom up from the depths of the internet, selling business owners a "canned book" or a "glorified business card"—and you know what? Good luck to them. To each their own. But that's not what I'm here for.

This isn't about making a fast buck, it's not just another marketing tick-box exercise, and it's not about grabbing a little fakespertise to shore up a struggling business. Writing a book is not a short-cut to expertdom. Writing your book is about putting the expert stamp on what you're already doing—and if you write it well, a whole host of cool benefits will follow naturally. You won't be creating an illusion of expertise; you'll be the real deal, getting your message out into the world and helping to improve people's lives in the best way you know how. And, of course, your book will help you grow your business.

My friend and client Kenda put it perfectly: done well, a book becomes the beating heart of your business. It's your core message, wrapped in your personality, tied with a ribbon of your values, to help the right people find you and work with you.

Once your book is published and out in the world, it can do all the hard marketing work for you. People can find out, in one neat package, who you are, what you stand for, and what it would be like to work with you. You market your book and your book markets you and your business.

There are more fantastic consequences to writing your book, too. Not least that you'll get a huge kick out of finishing and publishing your book. I cannot describe the excitement and joy you'll feel when your books arrive, and people actually start buying and reading them.

Writing a book will change the face of your business, elevating you above your competition and positioning you as the go-to expert in your industry. Your book will be one of the best sales tools in the world—the most fantastic relationship-building device there is, second only to spending real time, with real people, in real life. A top-notch book:

- **Shows everyone you're serious.** You've created something vast and lasting. You've gone the extra mile to produce a book people can keep, read, use, and pass on.

- **Makes you sticky.** What do you do with most business cards, leaflets, and brochures? Put them in your pocket, then peel them out of your pocket again once they've been through the washing machine. You read the leaflets and brochures once, maybe twice—then most people chuck them in the recycling bin. Your book is memorable. People do not throw books away.

- **Opens doors for you and boosts your credibility**, creating opportunities you may never have had before. Event organisers love authors, for example—so you'll be more likely to land public speaking gigs if you've written a book.

- **Is always there.** Your book is never sick, or on holiday, or taking a duvet day. It's your best salesperson, and it's working for you 24/7/365 so you can spend more time doing what makes you happy.

- **Lets you charge more for your services.** Look at Christine Hansen, AKA The Sleep Boss—she charges $25,000 per retreat. She wrote the book on sleep for overworked entrepreneurs and executives then used it to position herself as the industry expert. There is no reason on Earth why you can't do similar in your business.

- **Demonstrates your authority and underlines your expert status.** People like Tony Robbins, Oprah Winfrey, and Elizabeth Gilbert have all written books, and their books speak for them.

- **Endows you with a certain** *je ne sais quoi*: rightly or wrongly, people are still impressed by authors. It's a hangover from when only priests and society's elite could read and write. Books have gravitas—especially print books, which is why I make such a big deal of getting your book printed (despite the extra investment). People look at you and treat you differently when they know you're a published author. Not everyone can, should, or will write a book—so those who do are cloaked in a veil of awe.

- **Levels up your confidence:** there's nothing like writing a book to convince yourself you actually do know what you're talking about. You'll find your confidence increases as your writing progresses. It's like the best therapy ever.

- **Builds connections with people you'd otherwise never meet.** Books are global: they allow you to connect and build a relationship with people all over the world. You don't have to meet everyone in person to demonstrate your skills and knowledge—your book can do it for you.

- **Takes your business in a new direction**, one you've never thought of. When I wrote *Business For Superheroes*, I had no inkling it'd lead me down this path. Now, I do more of what I love: help other business owners write and use their own books.

- **Short-cuts relationship-building:** you don't have

time to explain exactly what you do, how you do it, and what your story is to large numbers of people. But your book can do it for you.

- **Generates high-quality leads** and attracts precisely the kinds of clients you want to work with. If someone's willing to read your book and they enjoy it, they've already invested a considerable amount of time in you. If you're a good fit, they'll get in touch. If not, neither of you will waste any more time.

- And—this is exciting in terms of ongoing income—you can **repurpose your book** into a whole smorgasbord of new products and services… at a far higher value to you (and your clients) than the book alone.

How does that sound? Like something you'd like to do?

Fabulous!

Now you know why to write a book and all the cool things that can happen after you've written your book and marketed it. But what about actually doing it? I know you'll have objections. I know all the excuses you'll make because I've made them too. Let's take a close look at them now.

## I've Heard All Your Excuses…

I've made all your excuses, too, including one that makes me feel sad: "I'm not really making a difference in the world."

You are. I promise you, you are. Even if you can't see the impact you're having right now, it's there. I want to share a story I first read in one of James Clear's regular emails[1]. It's a *Star Trek* story, which makes me happy (yes, I'm a Trekkie).

In 1967, at the height of the Civil Rights Movement in California, Lieutenant Uhura of the Starship Enterprise met Dr Martin Luther King, Jr. Uhura was played by Nichelle Nichols— and despite her role on one of the biggest TV series ever made,

---

1    James Clear writes wonderfully about habits. He's also written a book (surprise surprise!) called *Atomic Habits*. Writing is a habit.

Nichols was about to quit *Star Trek*.

Nichols' character, Lieutenant Uhura, was the Chief Communications officer on the Starship Enterprise and she was the first black woman on TV who wasn't cast in a role as a maid or servant. But her role had dwindled during the first season, and Nichols had decided to give Broadway a try instead. She had her resignation letter all ready—but she never sent it[2].

Dr King loved *Star Trek* and told Nichols he was her greatest fan. She thanked him and started to tell him about her resignation—but King stopped her. "You cannot," Dr King said. "You cannot leave. Do you understand? You have changed the face of television forever. Because this is not a black role. It is not a female role. Anyone can fill that role. It can be filled by a woman of any color, a man of any color. This is a unique role and a unique point in time that breathes the life of what we are marching for: equality. You have no idea the esteem we hold for you. You have no idea the power of television." He continued, "This is why we are marching. We never thought we'd see this on TV."[3]

Nichols truly did have no idea the esteem she was held in. She thought of herself as an actor with little impact, not a role model for people of colour. Until then, she'd had no idea of the importance of her role on the show.

Nichols went back to work on *Star Trek* of course and continued to play Lieutenant Uhura in every episode and movie for the next forty years. She made waves all through her career as she had the first interracial kiss on national television and acted in many roles that redefined black women in the eyes of society.

Without Nichelle Nichols as Lieutenant Uhura, the Civil

---

2   Paraphrased from StarTalk Radio with Neil DeGrasse Tyson: A Conversation with Nichelle Nichols. July 11, 2011 (www.startalkradio.net/show/a-conversation-with-nichelle-nichols/) Go and listen to this interview because it's fascinating.

3   StarTalk Radio with Neil DeGrasse Tyson: A Conversation with Nichelle Nichols. July 11, 2011 (www.startalkradio.net/show/a-conversation-with-nichelle-nichols/)

Rights Movement may have played out differently. And without her, we may never have seen Whoopi Goldberg on our screens. When Nichols and Whoopi Goldberg met, Goldberg said, "When *Star Trek* came on, I was nine years old. And I saw this show and there you were and I ran through the house saying, "Hey! Come everybody! Quick! Quick! Look! There's a black lady on television and she ain't no maid! I knew from that moment that I could become anything I wanted to be."[4]

You never know the impact you have on those around you. Do not underestimate the difference you make in the world now—and what a difference you could make if you write down your message in a book of your own.

Let's go through some of the other reasons people give me for not writing their own book.

## "I can't believe I have anything to say that is novel or unique on leadership and getting what you want in a career."

Leslie, one of my email subscribers, told me this when I asked my list what's stopping them from writing a book. Her field is leadership… but I've heard similar objections from business owners in many industries, and it always makes me smile because the business owners I talk to are so spectacularly skilled at underestimating themselves.

If one of your excuses—and yes, they *are* excuses—as to why you "can't" write a book is everything's already been said on your subject, and you have nothing new or exciting to say: listen up, Sunshine. I'm going to change your mind.

You say you don't have anything new or unique to say? I say *tosh*. It's not true. Oh yes, I can hop onto the internet and find a bazillion articles about your subject, but guess what's missing?

---

4    StarTalk Radio with Neil DeGrasse Tyson: A Conversation with Nichelle Nichols. July 11, 2011 (www.startalkradio.net/show/a-conversation-with-nichelle-nichols/)

YOU. You're missing.

Your take on your subject is missing. Humans don't learn with facts alone. In fact, they rarely learn effectively with just the bare facts. We learn everything we know from stories, from rich experiences told colourfully and persuasively. For humanity to survive, thrive, and evolve, we had to teach our descendants what we'd learned about the world.

This isn't just my opinion; neuroscience backs me up. As neuroscientist Antonio Damasio says: "The problem of how to make all this wisdom understandable, transmissible, persuasive, enforceable—in a word, of how to make it stick—was faced and a solution found. Storytelling was the solution—storytelling is something brains do, naturally and implicitly. Implicit storytelling has created our selves, and it should be no surprise that it pervades the entire fabric of human societies and cultures."[5]

Facts are fine and good and necessary, but they only make a difference when they're wrapped in a real person's experience, enhanced by their wins and losses, given context in your life.

Instead of thinking you have nothing new to say, think about how to say what you know. Think about how to tell your story, and how it will help your reader to relate to you, to learn from you, and to change their life for the better.

## "Why would anyone buy my book when they can just look on the internet? Everything's there for free!"

It's true, I can find anything I want to know on the internet. Google is a universe of facts, figures, stories, and funny cat videos—right at my restless fingertips.

But here's the thing: I'm a messy browser, and my tabs mount up. When I google for information, I open 793 tabs then freeze, because there's *too much*. I don't know where to start.

---

5   Damasio, A 2012, *Self Comes To Mind*, Vintage.

Do you know what I do then? I turn to my bookshelf. I dig out one of my books, the one that deals with the question I'm asking, and find the answer in there. Or I go to Amazon and find a book by someone I know, like, and trust—and buy it.

Google is a fantastic reference tool, but when you want to learn deeply about a subject, a well-written book is better. You, the author, can gather all the relevant information together in stories and essays and order it logically, so I don't have to meander aimlessly through the wastelands of the internet.

Make it easy for me to learn what I need to know.

The other problem with the internet is, any muppet can write an article that seems authoritative. Any old Johnny-come-lately can regurgitate other stuff from online—without fact-checking it—and claim it as their own.

There's so much information flying around for free, which is terrific... but it comes with its own problems. Like, how do I know the author of that article I've just found actually knows what he's talking about?

Unless it's someone I already know and trust, I can't be sure the writer knows what they're talking about. But if you've written a book, I *know* you're an expert. Even in these heady days where it's easy for anyone to write a book, I can still be pretty sure you're an expert. I can trust you.

After all, you wrote the book on it.

Speaking of trust: if you write a book, it gives me a chance to get to know you. The books I've written, for myself and for my clients, contain buckets of personality. I pour myself into my books because I know they're a window into my life. I include my stories, my joys, and my pains because my readers relish them. They help people to get to know, like, and trust me.

My readers read my books in bed, in the bath, on the toilet... and you don't get much more intimate than that. Your readers will take you to bed, too. Trust me when I tell you, there's no faster way of building a relationship.

I don't take Google to bed. Nor do your potential clients. I don't want to know about the faceless people behind random search results... but I want to know *you*. I want information from someone I can rely on, and so do your readers, so write your book. Let people get to know who you are, what you know, and where you come from. Then they'll let you help them.

## "I don't know enough to write a book. I'm not expert enough."

I bet you are expert enough. I bet you know more than you think. And you'll become more of an expert as you write, I promise you that. Here's another way of looking at it: you may not be the most experienced or the most knowledgeable person in your entire industry—but you're definitely more of an expert than your clients or people who are just starting out in your field.

Let me be clear: I'm not for one nano-second suggesting you set yourself up as an expert if you're not. That's wrong, unethical, and immoral.

If you're just starting out in your industry, here's an idea: write about your journey. I bet you wish there'd been a book about getting started in your industry, right? By someone who was actually going through it? Well, why don't you write that book?

That's pretty much what I did when I wrote *Business For Superheroes*. I wasn't pretending to be the all-knowing marketing expert; far from it. I was simply sharing my take on things from a few years into running my own business. What I'd learned. What had worked for me, and what hadn't. You do know enough. Just make sure you know whom you're writing for, and why.

## "I'm not interesting enough. Nobody wants to hear my story."

Yes, they do. Your readers don't want the bare facts. They want your experience of the facts—and here's why. We humans struggle with abstract concepts because we're creatures of the real world. We struggle to relate cold, hard facts to what's going on in our lives.[6]

If you can tell me the facts as you've experienced them and give me your story to follow, I can relate those facts to my own life. Perhaps I'm going through the same things you went through. Possibly I'm suffering the same problems you suffered. Maybe you started in the same place as I did—so I can relate to you immediately. I want to learn from someone who's been where I am now, and so do your potential customers and clients.

Write your story because there are many people out there who want to read it. You can help people other experts can't—not because they're not as good as you, but because they're not *you*. The people you can help may not be able to relate to those other experts, but they can connect with you. Don't shut them out.

You owe it to those people to help them. Don't let your fear of not being enough stop you from writing a book that could change somebody's world.

## "I don't have enough to say to fill a huge, weighty tome."

You have more to say than you probably think, but it doesn't matter because you don't have to write a giant weighty tome. There are no rules to say your book must be the *War And Peace* of the business world; in fact, it's probably better if it's shorter.

You'll discover more about this in Chapter 18 on editing, so let me just repeat something I learned from my first mentor, Peter Thomson: if you can speak eloquently on your subject for an hour, you have the basis of a book right there. Your book can be the book of your keynote speech.

If the book you write is simply one well-formed idea, that's fine. In fact, it's wonderful. Knowing this might help with the next excuse I hear—which is one of the most common reasons of all for not writing a book.

---

6    Cron, L 2012, *Wired For Story*, Ten Speed Press.

## "I don't have time to write a book."

Really? If you're not truly committed to writing a book and you don't want to do it badly enough, then no, you probably don't have time. You won't make time. If, however, you have a message you know will solve a problem or help people improve their lives, and you want to write your book, you do have time. You'll make time.

We all make time for the things that matter to us. You have the same amount of time in your day as I have in mine, as Richard Branson has in his, as Oprah Winfrey has in hers. How you use that time is up to you.

If you can carve out an hour a day, you can write a book. If you can set aside half a day a week, you can do it. In Chapter 2, I'll help you figure out how to make the time—and schedule it into your calendar, so you actually do the work.

## "My competitors will steal all my secrets if I put them into a book."

No, they won't. And even if they do, it won't matter. Nobody can offer exactly what you offer, in the way you offer it. All your competitors can hope to do is create a pale imitation of your products and services—and they won't be able to copy your personality, your skills and experience, and the experience you provide for your clients. Look around at the most successful business owners out there: they're generous with their knowledge and open about what they do and how they do it. Has it hurt them? No. Quite the opposite.

## "If I give away too much information in a book, nobody will pay me to do what I do."

Also not true. A minuscule percentage of people who read your book will take what you write and run with it, creating their own success. And that's great! Those people will be some of your loudest and most supportive advocates.

Most of your readers will not do it themselves. Many of them will read your book, love it, then do... nothing. It's the way of the world, and you can't do much about that. If you doubt me, think of your own experiences of reading a book. I've read loads of books on how to play the guitar—and I still went to a guitar teacher because it's better than trying to do it myself.

Some of your readers will read your book, love it, and want you to help them personally. Your book will convince them of your knowledge and expertise; and more importantly, it'll convince them you're the type of person they want to work with.

You don't want every reader to seek you out as a client—there's no way you could cope with that much business. Instead, your book will help to bring the best type of clients to you, in numbers you can cope with.

You cannot give away too much information, despite what the poverty-minded may claim. The more information you give people, the more likely they are to buy from you[7].

## "I'm not a writer!"

I think of all the excuses I hear for not writing a book, this is my favourite. Let me tell you something, my splendid friend: you are capable of so much more than you think you are.

Not-so-secret secret: writers write.

Do you think when Charles Dickens or J. K. Rowling were born, the doctors said to their mums, "Congratulations ma'am! You've just delivered a beautiful baby writer!"

No. Writers write. They practice, they fail, they start again, they get better. One of my best clients (and also one of my best mates) Dom Hodgson "isn't a writer". He's a pet business and doggo[8] expert. Oh, and he's written (at the time of publishing) four books of his own.

---

7    Sheridan, M 2017, *They Ask, You Answer*, Wiley.

8    Doggo is what dogs call themselves. True fact.

Dom is very definitely a writer.

If you're not comfortable sitting down with a blank piece of paper, and you think that makes you not-a-writer, don't worry. I can help you because there is more than one way to write a book—as you'll find out later.

I've covered all the main excuses people give me for not writing their books—have you ever said any of them? I hope you now realise they're just excuses, and if you let go of them, you can do this.

## The Time Is Now

It's never been easier to write and publish your own book, which is magnificent! No longer are we beholden to the big publishing houses and their business plans. No longer do we have to wait nervously for a stranger to decide, based on parameters that have nothing to do with us and our businesses and our goals, whether our manuscript is worthy of publication. We can do it ourselves. The floodgates opened a few years ago, and we're now reading brilliant books that would never have made it past the traditional book industry—which is a peachy state of affairs.

On the other hand, it's never been easier to write and publish your own book—which means it's never been easier to write and publish a crap book. I mean, there have always been terrible books. Publishers don't get it right all the time. It's just that now you can publish an awful book at the click of a mouse, without some pesky editor, agent, or publisher telling you your baby isn't good enough.

The deluge of crappy content written for quick clicks has threatened to drown the internet for years—and since the rise of self-publishing, guff has threatened to inundate the world of books, too. I don't want that to happen, because books are my life. You are not going to write a crappy book. You are going to write a fabulous book.

I read my first book when I was three, nearly four years old. I remember it. It had big colourful pictures and chunky letters, and it was about animals. It may have been *The Very Hungry Caterpillar*. I kept reading; my parents weren't particularly well-off, but they never said no to a new book or a trip to the library. I remember being frustrated when I went to school, and my teachers tried to hold me back with Peter and Jane when I was reading *The Magic Faraway Tree* at home.

Almost everything I'm interested in, understand, can do, and am good at started with a story or an idea from a book. You can immerse yourself in a book and live the story you're reading. It's active, not passive—you're not standing bewildered as a stranger firehoses information at your face; you're choosing to read and absorb the story, and you learn from it. Books shape us like nothing else can.

If I want to learn about something new now, I'll Google it, of course. I'll find articles. I'll watch videos. But ultimately, if it's something that means a great deal to me, you'll find me buried in a book because that's where profound knowledge and wisdom resides.

There's something about books: they're traditional repositories of knowledge. The vaults of human experience. Books marked the end of guesswork and misremembering, as we passed down skills and wisdom verbally. As soon as we learned to write things down and share them widely, we made knowledge available to everyone who could read—or listen to someone else read.

*We trust books.*

I wrote this book to help you write your own fantastic book.

## You've Got This

I hope now you understand why I want you to write your book—and I hope you now believe you can do so.

It won't be without its challenges, though: there will be setbacks. You'll have moments of crushing doubt, and you'll want to give up at various stages. But that's why I wrote this: to help get you through those moments of crushing doubt, and to help you leap (or clamber) over the obstacles writing will throw in your way.

You can do this.

I have your back.

Grab a piece of paper and a pen. Take your first tiny beetle steps below, then we'll set you up for success with some practical preparations—simple stuff you can do easily and quickly.

Ready?

## Tiny Beetle Steps

1.  What promise are you making to your reader? What will your reader have, do, be, and know by the time they've finished reading your book? (This may change as you write your book—that's fine. At this point, I want you to get started.)

2.  How do you help people in your business? What's the thing you can do, that your clients struggle with? Write it down and stick it in front of you. Every time you doubt you know enough, look at your note.

3.  Why are you writing this book? What's driving you? What do you want to achieve? (We'll come back to this in more detail in Chapter 6 so don't worry if you're not 100 per cent sure—just start thinking about it now.)

# CHAPTER 2

# Preparing To Write

*"Protect the time and space in which you write. Keep everybody away from it, even the people who are most important to you."*

*Zadie Smith*

Suspended upside down, hanging by my feet from the trapeze bar several feet above the stage, I have to trust my equipment. The space must be right.

The integrity of my skull depends upon it.

I'm a trapeze artist and pole dancer when I'm not writing and teaching business owners to write. Although what I do in the air may look preposterous, I take safety extremely seriously because I want to keep swinging around from my feet above a stage for as long as I can.

It's crucial to check the rigging, the ropes, the carabiners[1], and the strops[2]. Is everything secure and in place? You can bet your buttons I make damn sure it is.

I do something similar when I'm writing. Not hanging upside

---

1   A carabiner is a metal D-shaped or oval coupling ring with a safety closure. It's mostly used in rock climbing—but also when rigging aerial equipment like trapezes.

2   A strop—not strap—is a rope or nylon sling used to rig aerial equipment. It's also slang for a temper tantrum, which you will inevitably experience before you've finished writing your book.

down by my feet, of course; but making sure I have everything I need to make progress.

One of the biggest mistakes people make in any endeavour is diving in without putting in the proper groundwork. It's like painting your walls without stripping the previous surface off, sanding them, and washing them with sugar soap. You'll get a painted wall, but it'll look a bit crap.

The problem is, you can't see the results of the foundations until you've got the finished book, so it's tempting to skip the foundation work. Don't.

Please bear with me, dear reader, and do as I bid.

Before you start putting fingers to keyboard in earnest, we need to sort out your space, protect your time, and build some healthy habits. This may take a little while, but I promise it'll pay off later.

We'll start with a voyage into space and time, then look at writing habits (including some of the tools I use to help me write), and finally how to set goals and schedule your writing time.

First, though, a note on distractions. I am the world's most distractible human, and I struggle with the digital world. I find myself mindlessly scrolling Facebook and getting more and more agitated if I'm not careful. I play silly platform games on my iPhone and waste hours.

It doesn't feel good.

It feels awful.

As a consequence, I went digital minimalist. No more Facebook app on my phone, only on my desktop. No more computer games on my devices. And an app called Freedom on my laptop, so I can only access specific sites at certain times of the day.

I'll say no more on distractions, other than this: if you're serious about writing your book (or focusing on anything important to you), please read *Digital Minimalism* by Cal Newport. It may just change your life.

Right. Let's blast off into space.

## Space

Some writers will tell you real writers can write anywhere, and that may be true if it's what you do all day, every day, year on year. But you're not looking to become a full-time author (or so I assume), so pay attention.

To write, you need a space of your own. It doesn't have to be Ernest Hemingway-style heavy oak desks with leather tops and green lamps and fountain pens. (Although it can be if you like.)

Your writing room should be a pleasant, quiet place without distractions. A humble place, if possible.

There's only one unbreakable requirement: a door you can shut on the rest of the world.

Aside from that, I recommend your writing room is free of:

- Television.
- Video games.
- Telephones (put your mobile in another room on silent).
- Books (except those you need right now for your research).
- Anything else you reach for to distract yourself.

Experiment with music. I cannot write to music; I find it pulls me in and I lose myself... although I do my editing to classical music. Music might help you, though. Stephen King swears by music and apparently listens to heavy metal while he's writing.

Try different orientations for your writing desk. Some writers warn against putting your desk at a window because it's too tempting to daydream instead of actually writing. I find it helps me to think if I can see out of my window—but it has to be somewhere away from people and activity or I get distracted. My office window looks out at our garden and woodland, and that's perfect.

Some people write with others around, others require solitude. I mostly require isolation, but occasionally I seek out company at a café, or a writing retreat.

Perhaps you prefer to write outside if you're lucky enough to live in a warm, dry climate. (I'm writing this chapter from the shade of a palm tree in sunny Lanzarote—I came here specifically to write this book, for you.)

Whether you prefer your own office or a café or a dungeon or a beach or the top of a mountain, claim a nook as your writing space and make it your own. Set yourself up with everything you need—and get rid of everything you *don't* need (like your phone, your Xbox, and your TV).

## Time

Now we've sorted out your space, let's find the time you need. Are you a morning person or a night person? Do you feel more energised and creative when you've first woken up, or when everyone else is asleep?

You might not know right now, and that's fine. We'll find out. Spend the next few days trying to write at different times of the day, and see which suits you best. If you're wondering what to write as part of this test, it doesn't matter. Write anything. Get the thoughts that are inside your cranium out onto paper.

Are you a morning writer, or an afternoon writer? Or perhaps you're an evening or dead-of-night scribe. It took me a while to find out when I'm at my best. Many moons ago, when I was writing my first book, *Business For Superheroes*, I thought I was a naturally early morning person. I forced myself to get up at five in the morning every day for weeks. Oh, how foolish I was. It was awful because to get up early I need to make sure I get enough sleep—and I wasn't very good at going to bed early, either.

The thing is, I love being up early before anyone else is up. The world is quiet and fresh and new, and I can imagine I'm the only human on the planet. It's delightful. But the process of getting out of bed is horrific, and I will go to great lengths to avoid doing so.

I am, however, at my most creative and energised once I'm up and doing—and I've found I'm also pretty creative and motivated in the early evening, too.

There's no right or wrong time to write. There's only the best time for you, so experiment over the next few days and see what suits you.

Once you've discovered your optimum time for writing, set aside time to do it.

*This is crucial!*

Do not think that if you squeeze writing in as and when you get a chance, you will write a book. You won't. You'll write a few notes, swear a lot, decide it's impossible, and give up on the whole idea. Which is sad.

If you want to write a book, create time to do it—then protect your writing time as if it were a tiny, helpless kitten.

You might tell yourself you don't have time to write a book. It's a lie. You *do* have time; if you think you don't, your priorities are wrong. Remember, this is one book; it's not forever.

For the next ninety days, make time to write. But I don't want you to be miserable while you write your book, so here's what you're going to do.

Start by protecting your family time and your me-time. Don't sacrifice what's most important to you. Mark that time in your diary. For me, that's a date with Joe (my husband), working on our home renovation, and training trapeze and pole at the aerial studio. Those times are in my calendar, and they never shift. Not for clients, not for my book.

Then squirrel away time for client work and any appointments you know you can't change. Mark the time in your schedule. I keep Tuesdays and Thursdays for client work; perhaps you could set days aside too.

Now for your writing time. I'd like you to keep a diary for the next few days and find out what you do with the rest of your time. Record what you do and how long you spend doing it. I have an app called Moment on my phone, which tracks how long I spend with my device. It's shocking and eye-opening how much time I wasted on social media before I downloaded that app.

Maybe you like to have a regular Netflix binge on a Monday

evening for three hours? Knock it back to one hour, and spend two hours writing. The extra hour or so in bed on a Sunday? Use it to write, instead. Can't miss *Strictly Bakeoff*? Video it, and catch up when your book's done. Make it your reward.

If you honestly want to write your book, make writing it a priority—at least for a little while. You'll be surprised how much you can get done in an hour.

When you're blocking out time to write, remember everyone works differently: I like to write in blocks of three or four hours, punctuated with short breaks to move around. Maybe you'll write better in one-hour stints or thirty-minute chunks.

I recommend setting aside at least eight hours a week to write. Eight hours is a decent chunk of time: enough to make real progress on your book, but not so much you'll struggle to put the time aside.

Divide your writing time however you like—maybe four hours on a Wednesday morning, two hours on a Friday, and two hours on a Sunday. Or perhaps one hour every weekday and three hours on a Saturday.

How you break it up isn't important. The important thing is that it becomes a habit: "From 9.30 a.m. until 12.30 p.m. on a Saturday, I write my book."

"Between 8 a.m. and 10 a.m. on Mondays and Wednesdays, I write my book."

Write a declaration setting out your writing intentions. Print it out and stick it up where you'll see it every day—if you can see it, you'll be more likely to stick to it. You need to make it so if you *don't* write at the allotted time, you feel wrong and weird, like something's missing. Like you've forgotten to brush your teeth, or you've gone out without pants on.

When you've decided when to write, block out the time in your calendar as if it were a meeting with your best client. I want you to think of your book as your best client because if you do, you'll be far less likely to flake out on it. Would you let a client down? No, of course not. Don't let yourself down, either.

If you don't block time out as if your book were a client, you won't keep to your schedule, and you won't make progress. I know you won't because whenever I work with coaching clients who struggle to make progress, it's *always* because they don't do as they're told: they don't treat themselves as their own best client. If you're not willing to do this, you will struggle to write your book.

Are you willing? Good! Then put a sign on your door, so your family, friends, neighbours, employees, and colleagues won't disturb you—even if the zombie apocalypse is going on outside. If you're worried about your family/friends/dog needing you, don't be. I don't want to rain on your parade, but they can cope without you for an hour or so.

Make your writing time sacrosanct. Protect it fiercely. If you don't, you won't write your book.

## Building Good Habits

Even with the right space and time set aside to work on your book, it'll still be tough—so I want to help you build good writing habits. These good habits will help you in all areas of your life and business, by the way, so this is an extra-valuable chapter.

I'll start with a book recommendation: *The Power of Habit* by Charles Duhigg. If you understand how our brains work and why habits are so crucial to success (or failure) in any endeavour, you'll find it easier to build and maintain your own patterns.

Start by removing any friction—by which I mean, make it as easy as possible to sit down and start writing. Create a routine.

Here's my routine. Every evening, I map out the next day, so I know exactly what I'm doing in the morning. I get out the notes or books I'll need to start on my first task, so I don't have to worry about anything. I don't faff around writing lists and getting ready to work. Lists and information-gathering are friction—do them the night before. Every morning, I step out of bed and into my running clothes. They're laid out ready for me on the chair in our bedroom, together with my writing clothes.

(If I had to go and dig my running clothes out of the drawer, I'd never get out of the house—it would cause friction.)

When I'm dressed, I get out into the village before my body has time to realise what's going on. I don't run far; twenty minutes or so. It's my version of meditation and solitude to start clearing my brain of the clutter that will cause friction when I sit down to write. I come back and stretch, then write my Morning Pages (more on those in a moment) to scrub my brain clean, have a hot shower to scrub my body clean, get dressed in the clothes I laid out last night, make a cup of tea, and start writing.

I've done this routine so many times now, it's become a habit. It's almost automatic.

Finally, I set rules for myself, because even with all these preparations and habits, I'm still a champion tangent-taker. I'm incredibly easily distracted. I learned my main rule from Neil Gaiman: I am allowed to write or do nothing. No reading, no talking, no cleaning the house or feeding the chickens. No stretching, no television, and definitely no mindless scrolling of social media.

Write—or nothing.

It works well, because it's less draconian than screaming, "WRITE OR ELSE, MO-FO!" at myself. This rule gives me the illusion of choice. There's only so long you can do nothing at all before you get bored, and writing suddenly seems more fun.

## SMART Goals

Right then. If you've got your space sorted, worked out a schedule, and started building good habits, it's time to set SMART goals. Without Specific, Measurable, Attainable, Realistic, Time-bound goals, all you have is a vague plan that almost certainly won't come to fruition.

"Make progress on my book" is not a smart goal. It's a stupid goal. "I will write one chapter of my book by 7 p.m. on Friday" or "I will write 500 words today" is a smart goal. Make smart goals.

Because this is a business book we're writing, I'd like to start at the end. When do you want to print your book? For argument's sake, let's set a ninety-day goal (that's three months)—it is possible to write your book in three months, I promise. I've done it. Some of my clients have done it.[3]

Your primary goal is to have your book at the printers in ninety days. Now work backwards from your printing date. Here's an example timeline:

- November 30: Send manuscript to printer.
- November 25: Final manuscript checks.
- November 11: Send manuscript to proofreader, then indexer (if you're having an index). Check their timeframes, but if you book them in plenty of time, a week for each should be sufficient. If you're not having an index, you can move this task back a week.
- October 28: Final edit. Do not underestimate how long this will take, especially if you're editing your own work. If you're hiring an editor, check their availability and turnaround times. Good editors get booked up months in advance.
- October 21: Send an advance copy to your beta readers. Give them at least a week to read your draft and send you suggestions.
- October 7: Edit your work, after you've looked again at your Shitty First Draft (see Chapter 18).
- September 30: Put your Shitty First Draft in a drawer and walk away for at least a week. Don't think about it.
- September 29: Finish your Shitty First Draft.
- September 6: Write your Shitty First Draft.
- September 3: Write your detailed outline (see Chapter 9).
- September 1: Nail down your Big Idea (see Chapter 4).

---

3  You do not have to write your book in three months! If that scares you, or you know it won't be possible, choose your own timeframe; one that works for you.

This book walks you through this entire process, starting with a few exercises to get you used to writing. Build a few odd days in at the start of your timeline to accommodate these. You'll see how and why this works as you read on through the book.

Adapt this timeline and stretch it out to suit you. It's absolutely fine if it takes longer than 90 days; it takes most people longer than 90 days. The crucial thing is to set SMART goals, give yourself deadlines, and do your best to stick to them. Without deadlines, your book will balloon into a massive project you'll struggle to complete.

## Voyaging Into Space And Time

You can't start writing until you have a suitable writing space and you've set aside time to write. Do that before you move on, and start building healthy writing habits, so you write regularly. Dedicate a room to write in, and make sure it contains only the tools you'll need to write your book.

Set aside time to write. Treat yourself as your own best client—this is critical. If you don't, you'll find excuses not to write. Schedule writing time in, and stick to it.

Making SMART goals will help you do this. If you book other professionals to help you write your book, those deadlines will spur you on.

Some people tell you to write every day. Others tell you to write when you feel like it. I say: find some middle ground. What conditions make it easy for you to write? When you get into a flow, how did that happen? Make notes—then replicate those conditions so you can write whenever you like.

All this is easy to write and easy to intend to do... but tricky to actually pull off. How many times have you decided to do something, but struggled to follow through? If you're anything like me, loads of times. I get it. And I want to help. In the resources section of my website, you'll find a webinar to help you do all this stuff I've just been talking about.

Finally: I mention many tools throughout this book. I thought about including them in this chapter, but I didn't want to break the flow—so you can find my Writer's Toolkit at the back of this book, in Appendix I. Choose the ones you think will help you write your book most easily.

Now, take the Tiny Beetle Steps below before we move on. In Chapter 3, we're going to sort out your (dick)head.

## Tiny Beetle Steps

1.  Find a space you can write in, and turn it into an impenetrable fortress of creativity.

2.  Block out writing time in your calendar and don't let anyone or anything destroy it. Watch my productivity webinar at www.moxiebooks.co.uk/moxie-book-resources.

3.  Develop habits and routines to help you write consistently. Do you write best in the morning or evening? Monitor yourself. Check out *The Power of Habit* by Charles Duhigg and *Atomic Habits* by James Clear to help you do this.

4.  Visit Appendix I at the back of this book and choose the best tools to help you write.

# CHAPTER 3

# Sorting Your (Dick)Head Out

*"Grant me the serenity to accept the things I cannot change; the courage to change the things I can; and the wisdom to know the difference."*

*Reinhold Niebuhr*

Silence. Sudden silence. The kind of velvet silence that soaks up every whisper. The only sound in your head is the bass-beat of your panicked heart… and all eyes are on you.

What's the worst thing that can happen during your competition pole dance performance? Wardrobe malfunction? Nope. It's pole dancing, everybody'll cheer.

You fall over? Nope. You can make that look like it's part of the routine, and carry on regardless.

Your music stopping halfway through your dance? And they can't get it started again?

Yep, that'll do it…

I tell you, nothing's bloody simple, is it? I was smashing out the best performance of my life until the music just… stopped. Time was, I'd have gone to pieces. Rushed off the stage. Cried in a corner.

How humiliating, right?

Well, not this damn time. Not after all that hard work.

As I stared, wide-eyed and frozen in panic, someone broke the silence and yelled, "You carry on, girl!" and I thought "Screw it. I will!"

The audience cheered, then someone started clapping a rhythm—and everyone joined in. I finished my routine. It wasn't perfect—how could it be? I had no music—but I put my entire soul into it. The judges asked if I wanted to do it again... but I said no, thank you. I didn't think I could do a better job than that, in that place, on that night, and they were happy to score me on the dance I did.

Let me tell you something, dear reader. There is nothing—*nothing*—like the feeling of a roomful of people who've got your back. Who are willing you to do your best and carry on in spite of a technological failosaurus.

Total strangers who come up and give you a hug and tell you how freaking amazing you are because you stuck two fingers up to technology and carried on anyway.

I have tears running down my face right now because of the love in that room. Does that sound cheesy? Yeah. Do I care? Hell NO. Because it's true.

Everyone in that room was putting themselves out there, doing their best, and having a whale of a time. And everyone watching was loving it. What. A. Night.

Oh, what's that? You want to know who won?

I'll tell you at the end of this chapter. But first, I want to talk about two funny cartoonists...

## Living Large

Matt Stone and Trey Parker—creators of *South Park* and *Team America*—give no fucks. This one time, they dropped acid then put on dresses and went to the Oscars. As you do.

Nothing is off-limits to them: their sole aim in life is to be funny, so they go at their careers all-in. They do the outlandish. They talk about the untouchable ideas. And they do it in dresses, while the rest of Hollywood looks on in bemusement.

Bemusement, because most of us simply won't behave that way. We're too scared about what other people think, which is amusing because the biggest single thing standing between you and that moment of elation when you hold your book in your hands is you. Or, to be more precise, your Inner Dickhead. He[1] lives in your brain, and his sole purpose in life is to stop you doing anything that might lead to Greatness because Greatness is risky.

Ask anyone who's reached the heady heights of Greatness, and they'll tell you there are many towns called Failure along the way. If you want to achieve great things, you have to be willing to fail a few times—which is where your Inner Dickhead comes in.

He hates failure. It's unacceptable to him. To your Inner Dickhead, failure at writing—or dancing or painting or a relationship—means failure as a human being. (Not true. You are not your failures.) Looking stupid in front of other people is a failure in the eyes of your Inner Dickhead and that, too, is unacceptable to your nasty little inner voice.

Before we start writing, here's what we're going to do: identify your Inner Dickhead, and set up a few defences and countermeasures, so he doesn't stop you writing this great book of yours.

## Identify Your Inner Dickhead

I'm not a psychologist or a counsellor; I want to get that out right now. But I am horribly well-acquainted with my Inner Dickhead. The sadistic little toe-rag.

Not a day goes by when I don't hear something like: "I'm shit. I'm shit at writing, and nobody is going to read this. Look at all those other writers who are so much better than me. Why am I bothering?"

It clangs loudly in my head, that voice, and it used to paralyse me. I hear it more softly now, but it's still there. How do I ignore it?

---

1 Don't ask me why, but my Inner Dickhead is a dude. I don't know why there's a man in my brain.

It's taken practice, that much is true. The first thing I learned to do was acknowledge the voice and identify it. Don't try to ignore it totally because it'll sit there and eat away at you like a rat in the loft insulation. Accept its presence and minimise it.

Try this: whenever you hear your Inner Dickhead say something poisonous, substitute "You" for "I" and say it out loud to an imaginary person standing in front of you, so you can hear how you'd sound if you spoke poison to someone else. My Inner Dickhead's statement would become: "You're shit. You're shit at writing and nobody is going to read this. Look at all those other writers who are so much better than you. Why are you bothering?"

How horribly mean is that? Would you ever say those words to someone else? Of course not. So why would you say it to yourself?

And while we're on the subject of other people, here's something else to stop doing: comparing yourself unfavourably to others.

"Comparison is the thief of joy," according to Theodore Roosevelt. It's true. I mean, it's possible to compare yourself to someone and aspire to improve, but let's be honest: you are never comparing yourself to someone else on a level playing field, are you? You look at all your bad points and compare them to someone else's good points. As well-known wise-owl Rob Lowe once said, "Never compare your insides to someone else's outsides." We only see of other people what they want us to see.

When I started my research for this book, I was wracked with self-doubt—partly because I have a book by a woman I'm in awe of. I have a proper writer-crush on her. Her name is Ann Sheybani, and the way she writes makes my brain tingle. I wish I could write like her.

There's the problem: I'm not her, I'm me. She has a Masters in Creative Writing from Harvard University, and I... don't. And that's okay. Because I am a good writer, too. I am writing a different book, for a different purpose, for different people. Comparing myself to Ann, and wailing and gnashing my teeth, is doing me no good and paying her no respect.

I'd like to pass on a little advice my coach, Mark, gave me. Instead of getting sad because I'll never be "as good as" someone else, reframe the thought. Recognise that other people have written books to help us. Oh, they want to make money, too—but they also want to help. Let them. Embrace their writing, their advice, and their knowledge and expertise, and approach your reading in a learning mindset.

Ask yourself, "What can I learn from this fine person? How can I apply what they've taught me, and frame it within my own experiences?" This reaction frees you to learn from them and to write your own truth, without fear of comparison.

Look at your Inner Dickhead's statements logically. Start by listening to Shakespeare, who said: "There's nothing either good or bad but thinking makes it so." What you think about yourself determines who you become. Do you want to be a negative, fearful person who never achieves anything tremendous? Or do you want to soar? If you allow your Inner Dickhead to pipe up and throw shade[2] at you whenever he wants, you'll struggle to write. You'll struggle to do anything at all, in fact.

Whenever a negative thought gallops across the landscape of your mind, throw up a tripwire. Pick it up and examine it. Is that thought true? Really? Almost certainly not.

Look for examples to prove to you it's not true. Remember a time when someone told you something you wrote is good. Dig out something you feel particularly proud of and read it again. Pull out testimonials from your best clients, the ones telling you how you've changed their lives for the better. Show the evidence to your Inner Dickhead and tell him to piss off.

And in case you're worried about crossing the line into arrogant, this isn't about building your ego; it's about countering your distorted view of yourself and bringing a little reality back.

Don't feed the troll. Banish it into the dark, dingy corner where it belongs, and muffle its voice.

---

2   Throwing shade: "subtle, sneering expression of contempt for or disgust with someone—sometimes verbal, and sometimes not" according to the Merriam-Webster dictionary. I first heard it on *RuPaul's Drag Race*.

This is about how to ignore your Inner Dickhead, not banish him. You can't silence him, and there's no point in trying; listen to him only rarely, because he's a destructive little sod. Almost everyone has an over-developed Inner Dickhead, and if you give him half a chance, he will crap all over your writing.

Don't let him.

## Go Back To Your Why

Let's revisit your WHY. Why are you reading this book? Why do you want to write your book?

Yeah, yeah, we want to grow our businesses and make mo' money, yadda yadda yadda…

But ultimately, we want to help people, don't we? I do. I want to help you write your own book—a book that will lift your business, boost your confidence, and enable you to reach and help many more people than you do right now.

What's your message? How do you want your book to help others? You might not know for sure yet, and your deeper why might be something you find out as you write your book—but you must have some idea, or you wouldn't be reading this.

If you're writing your book to help people improve their lives, it would be unconscionable—nay, spiteful—to withhold that book from them.

If you can help someone improve their life, don't you have a duty to do so? I believe I have a duty to help people, which is what keeps me writing when my nasty little inner voice tries to stop me.

Write your WHY down. Stick it somewhere you'll see it every day you write. Look at it when your Inner Dickhead rears his ugly snout and let it remind you why writing your book is so important to you.

Your WHY will lift you up and carry you along.

When you feel like, "Ugh, I have to go and write the next chapter of my book now," reframe it. Instead of saying "have to", say "I get to". Sit up straight—or, better, stand up—and say,

"Yay! I get to go and write more of my book now. I get to share my message, my skills, my knowledge, my expertise with people who need it."

It sounds silly and trivial; how can such a small thing make a difference? Try it, and you'll be amazed at how much more positive you feel about the stuff you "have to" do.

## Don't Self-Censor

When you actually do start writing, be warned: your Inner Dickhead will try to get you to censor yourself:

"Don't write that, you'll sound stupid."

"People will laugh if you share that with them."

"You don't know enough to make that claim."

Do not censor yourself during your first draft. Be yourself, in bright technicolour and surround sound. If you want to know how to do this with gusto, I highly recommend watching *RuPaul's Drag Race*. These queens have dealt with other people's crap, and their own crap, for their entire lives; they are done with censoring themselves.

Your first draft is you bleeding all over the keyboard. Get those ideas out and down on paper then worry about tidying it up later.

Don't show it to anyone yet. Do not give your Inner Dickhead a chance to second-guess you. Do your outline. Then write.

I'll talk about this in more detail later, but this is your editing process (cribbed from Stephen King)[3] in simplest terms:

1. Say it. (Splurt your words out with the door closed, for your eyes only.)
2. Say what you mean. (Revise it for your readers with the door open, then give it to someone to read.)
3. Say it well. Polish it. This is your final draft.

This process helps you get past the Blank Sheet of Paper, and it helps you sidestep your nasty little Inner Dickhead.

3   King, S. 2012, *On Writing*, Hodder Paperbacks

## A Note On The Nature Of Humanity

You may be reading this and thinking something along the lines of, "Well, that's all very well, Vicky, but what if people actually are laughing at me?" Fair enough. I worry about this all the time. So I'll share a few little diamond ideas with you—and in Chapter 19, you'll find a lot more about dealing with criticism.

Brené Brown gives us a fantastic tool to cope with criticism in her wonderful book, *Daring Greatly*. Here's what we do:

1. Take a small piece of paper. A Post-It note is good.

2. Write down the names of people whose opinions truly matter to us. People we love and admire. There isn't much room on this piece of paper, but that's a good thing: most of us only have a small number of people who fall under this category.

3. Stick your small piece of paper somewhere in your workspace.

4. Next time someone says something that upsets you, check your Post-It note: is their name on there? If not, why are you upset? Why does it matter to you? Move on.

5. If their name is on the paper, perhaps they had a point—in which case, reframe what they said as a learning experience, and talk to them about it. Fix the problem. Improve your writing.

I have two pieces of paper: one for personal stuff and one for business stuff. There are only around six names on each.

It's a funny thing, the human brain. We spend an inordinate amount of time and energy worrying about what others think of us when mostly others aren't thinking about us at all. They're fretting about the same stuff we are. Isn't that daft? Almost nobody has the time or mental space to waste mocking you and your efforts. Remember that.

Remember, too, that most people want you to succeed. People will have your back. When my music stopped, and I was all alone on stage, face on fire and teetering on the edge of shame, nobody laughed at me. Everyone cheered me on. I wasn't kidding about the love in that room. There's love in your writing room, too. Be open to it.

## Try Again, Fail Better

So, who won that pole competition I took part in? That would be me. I won my category. I was through to the finals.

Let me ask you something: do you think I'd have won if I'd stopped? Walked off? Tried it again later when I'd sorted the music out? Maybe. Maybe not. I don't think so. I think I'd have been too tired and too nervous and the fear would have defeated me. Sometimes you only get one shot that matters. Take it.

Next time you feel like something might be a little too scary, please remember my story. Next time you look at your manuscript, and your inner voice tells you this is too hard, you're not good enough, and you can't do this, remember my story. Picture the horrified look on my face as the music stops and fails to start again. Then picture me giving it fierce and doing it anyway.

Because if I can, you bloody well can, too. And you'll have all your clothes on.

It's not an easy thing to let go of your fears and doubts and do the scary thing you want to do. If something is scary, it's a sure sign you ought to do it anyway. You don't have to be fearless in life to succeed; I don't believe anyone is truly fearless. The secret is to feel the fear and do it anyway—despite your Inner Dickhead's attempts to sabotage you.

While you're worrying about what everyone else thinks of you, everyone else is worrying about the same thing. Focus on your goal: writing your book. Focus on making it as good as it can be, so your inner critic fades into the background.

Accept that on the way to success, you will fail a few times— and that's okay. The important thing is, you get back up and try again. Fail better.

And remember, when you're comparing yourself to others,

that it's not a level playing field. You don't know what's really going on in their lives. You can't see underneath their surface. All you can do is compare today's you to yesterday's you—and try to be a little better.

You only get one shot at this life. Being afraid is fine. I'm afraid all the time. Just don't live a half-life, perpetually terrified of what others think, allowing your fear to hold you back.

Take these Tiny Beetle Steps, then we'll talk about the flash of inspiration you're waiting for.

## Tiny Beetle Steps

1. Gather your best testimonials and your favourite pieces of work and the achievements you're most proud of, and build them into a protective fort. Bring them out when your Inner Dickhead gets going.

2. Write your WHY on a piece of paper and stick it somewhere you'll see it every day you write. Let it remind you why writing your book is so important to you.

3. Watch *RuPaul's Drag Race* and read RuPaul's book *Workin' It!: RuPaul's Guide to Life, Liberty, and the Pursuit of Style*.

4. Do Brené Brown's Post-It note exercise: write down the names of people whose opinions matter to you. Stick it up where you can see it, and every time someone upsets you, check that note. If their name isn't on the list, don't allow them to mess with your head.

# CHAPTER 4

# The Flash Of Inspiration

*"Amateurs sit and wait for inspiration, the rest
of us just get up and go to work."*

*Stephen King*

Isee you, sitting there, staring out of the window, waiting for a
spark of inspiration to sleet down out of the ether and ignite
you into heroic action. I see you procrastinating.

I see you because I've *been* you.

But, grasshopper, I have bad news for you: the flash of
inspiration ain't gonna happen. It is a myth; a myth that has
stopped good writers from writing since humans first scratched
their shopping list on the cave wall. If you want inspiration to
strike, you need to create it yourself.

That's the bad news, if you want to see it that way. Here's the
good news: you are as creative as you want to be. Which means
you're in control of whether or not you have good ideas.

One of the most common excuses I hear for not sitting down
and writing a book is, "But I'm not creative enough! I'm not a
writer!"

Well, pickle, guess what? Writers write.

Don't just expect your "muse" to show up. He won't. He's a
bastard. You gotta put the work in.

We're *all* creative. You think creativity is solely the preserve of artists, musicians, and poets? Think again. The biggest problems in the world have been solved through creative thinking. The biggest advances in technology, science, and engineering have happened because of creativity.

You do have a creative mind, I promise you.

Perhaps you just need to wake it up.

Let's start by giving your book a working title. Don't spend any more than five minutes on this—it is not your final title. It is important to call your book something, though, so it feels real. For most of the time I was writing this book, it was called *The Book Book*, which worked fine for me. Give your book a name.

Then we'll move onto your Big Idea. I'm going to help you throw a virtual bucket of ice-cold water onto your brain—starting with a book recommendation.

## Coming Up With Ideas

Get and read James Webb-Young's splendid (and super-short) *A Technique for Producing Ideas*. It's only around twenty-five pages long, but I'll summarise it here for you.

There's no such thing as a brand-new idea; ideas happen when we combine old bits and pieces into new concepts. The ability to do this depends on how good you are at seeing relationships.

All new ideas come from a simple, five-step process:

1. Read lots. About all kinds of subjects. I'll come back to this later.

2. Get your brain working on all the material. Chew it over, swallow it down, and make like a sheep and chew it over again.

3. Walk away. Literally, if you can. Leave the problem behind, go for a walk, do some pole dancing, take a shower, have sex. Whatever. Just stop thinking about it.

4. Let your subconscious mind bring new ideas back to you.

5. Release your idea into the wild and see what happens. Then test it, tweak it, and adjust it based on the feedback you get.

Here's another super book: A Whack on the Side of the Head by Roger von Oech. Dip in and out of it. It's full of puzzles, anecdotes, exercises, questions, cartoons, stories, and quotations to help you break down mental blocks and "unlock the mind for innovative problem solving and creativity".[1]

## Thinking Sideways: An Example

I'll share some other techniques for coming up with ideas in a moment, but before I do, I have a tale to tell you. A tale of a folk music duo and the book they're writing (it may be out now).

Jay and Jon are Ninebarrow, and they make beautiful music together. Jay's mum is a friend of mine, and she was telling me all about their business plans—big plans which will be totally alien to most musicians. Ninebarrow don't just want to sell CDs and play gigs. They want more, and they want to build a business that doesn't just rely on them swapping time for money. As part of their dream, they're writing a book—and their Big Idea is magnificent.

Jay and Jon walk—a lot. They explore the Dorset countryside and coast, and while they're out walking they come up with ideas for songs. The book they've written is called *Ninebarrow's Dorset*, and it's filled with their walks and the stories behind the songs they write. When you're a fan of a band or a writer or an artist, you want as much of them as you can get—so writing this book is a stroke of genius.

If you're thinking something like, "All the books on my subject have already been written, and I can't come up with an original idea" try thinking sideways instead.

What's your backstory? What's the origin of your business? You don't have to write a how-to book or a self-help book. You

---

1    von Oech, R. 2008, *A Whack On The Side Of The Head*, Business Plus Imports.

can write anything you want—as long as your ideal reader is interested in you. I promise you: if you have customers who love what you do, they are interested in you. The more of yourself you give to them, the more they'll want and the more loyal they'll become. I know this because I've done it. This isn't theory gobbled up from someone else's blog, chewed over, and spat back at you. This is my life; my business.

Perhaps you're not ready to share your origin story yet, though, and that's okay too. Because I have another idea for you...

## Talk To People

Radical concept, I know, but... have you considered talking to—or rather listening to—your finest clients? Ask them about the hairiest problem you solved for them. What pain did it cause them? How did you fix it? Ask them what makes you different from your competitors. What makes you better. Why they chose you in the first place. Get them to tell the story of their suffering before they found you—and how you helped them change their life for the better.

Send out a survey to your customers and to your email list (if you have one—if you don't, start building one!) and include three simple questions—no more than three:

1. **What's your biggest challenge** [relating to your industry]?

2. **What pain is it causing you**, and how is it negatively affecting your life?

3. **If you could sit down with me for half an hour** over a glass of wine or a cup of tea, and ask me any two questions, what would you ask?

In Chapter 9: Outline Like A BOSS, I explain how I used these questions to create my book-writing course and write this book. There are diamonds in the answers you'll get. Ask the questions, then sit back, shut up, and listen. If a great idea for your book doesn't come out of that tête-à-tête, I'll eat your shoes.

## Become A Collector

Now I'd like to share my secret creativity weapon: I collect stories. Not just books; but articles, blogs, podcasts, snippets of conversation, pictures, photographs, radio shows, songs, films, TV series...

Any time I see, hear, or read something that captures my imagination or sparks a thought relating to my business (or anything else I care about), I grab it and file it away in Evernote (a piece of software—kind of like a digital scrapbook on steroids).

If I read a story about bravery, I'll tag it with "bravery"—but I'll also tag it with "cowardice", "struggle", and any other related or opposite ideas I might want to write about sometime.

If I hear a great podcast, I'll snip it and save it.

If I see a piece of art or a photograph that speaks to me or inspires an idea, I'll photograph it and save it and tag it.

If I manage to record an interesting conversation, I'll upload it to Evernote and tag it accordingly.

You can do the same. Collect stories—any type of story. You never know when they might come in useful, or spark off a great idea. Then, once you have a vague idea, get specific.

## Honing Your Big Idea

You might already have an idea for your book—but I'll wager it's a little woolly at the moment, which is a problem.

If you read the non-five-star book reviews on Amazon, a common complaint from readers goes something like, "Yeah, there were some good ideas, but this book could have been written in half the pages, and it would have been better. Too much filler."

I think this happens for two reasons.

Firstly, the writer mistakenly believes a book should be big. Big and thick and stuffed full of 200+ pages. Well, that's nonsense. Your book should be long enough to cover everything, and short enough to be interesting—which might be 50 pages or 500 pages.

Secondly, the writer isn't focused enough. They come up with a great idea… but then try to cram every thought they have on the subject into their book, even though it's not relevant to the core message.

I don't want that to happen to you. I want you to come up with a fabulous Big Idea, then get super-specific about it. Let's look at a few famous examples.

*Oversubscribed* by Daniel Priestley is all about "how to get people lining up to do business with you." The book covers the author's seven principles for creating demand that outstrips supply, so you have a waiting list of customers.

Jay Levinson's famous (and brilliant) book *Guerrilla Marketing* is a marketing book… but marketing is a massive topic, covered everywhere. If he'd chosen to write about "marketing", it'd be a bloated monstrosity of a tome. Instead, Levinson wrote a book specifically for small businesses with tiny budgets. The subtitle is "easy and inexpensive strategies for making big profits from your small business."

This book you're reading now could have been all about writing and publishing fiction novels, poems, short stories, memoirs, biographies, non-fiction, historical books, quote books, and every other type of book under the sun. It's not. This book is about how to write and self-publish a book to help you grow your business—and how you can do it in just ninety days (if you want).

I might have included a bazillion strategies about how to launch and market your book, then use it in sales campaigns, and how to get traditionally published, and on and on. And this book, too, would have swelled and strained and exploded under the weight of Too Much Information. There's a place for comprehensive books covering entire topics… but I urge you to keep your writing tight and fluff-free, or there's a danger you'll never finish it. (Not to mention the risk that nobody will want to read it.) Choose your Big Idea—then narrow it down.

Maybe you're a photographer who wants to help people take better photographs—but photography is a terribly big topic. If you're anything like me, a book filled with technical instructions about shutter speeds and apertures will have you reaching for Terry Pratchett's Discworld novels faster than the .303 bookworm[2] can eat through a shelf-full of magical books.

Instead, how about a short book on how to take photos in low light conditions? Or a book on how to take great portrait photographs? Or how to photograph landscapes so they don't look boring?

If you're a graphic designer, you don't want to create a book about the whole history of art and graphic design—that's already been done. And done. And done. Instead, focus on the problems you solve for your clients. Like... how to use design to increase sales from marketing materials. Or how to work effectively with a designer to get the results you want.

Go into real live bookshops and research your niche. Find around ten books similar to the one you want to write—or which are aimed at the same type of reader. What are others writing about? Is there a gap you can slide into with your Big Idea?

Go online, and find books on Amazon—then note the sub-categories on the left of the page which tell you where the book is in the online store. Click into the sub-category, and find similar books in the same niche. This type of research will help you narrow down your Big Idea.

For example, if you wanted to write a science book to get children interested in science and technology, you might search for "experiments for kids" within the category "Scientific, Technical & Medical". If you did, you'd find:

- *Geology Lab for Kids*
- *50 More Stem Labs—Science Experiments for Kids*
- *Make: Electronics*
- *The Geek Dad Book for Aspiring Mad Scientists*

The results you find can give you an idea of what's selling, what's not, and whether there's a topic you can put your spin on.

---

2   The .303 bookworm is the second fastest animal in the Discworld universe. Because magical books are often dangerous, this bookworm evolved to eat at incredibly high speeds.

## Turn Your Idea Into A Hook

Once you've got your Big Idea, and your portrait of your ideal reader, think about baiting your hook. What's going to draw your reader in, hit them between the eyes, and make them scream, "I have to read this book!"

To find your hook, we need to dig into decision science and look at how our brains work[3] so you can understand how our brains decide what to pay attention to. Nobel Prize-winning psychologist and economist Daniel Kahneman identified two systems of thinking: System 1 and System 2.

System 1 integrates perception and intuition and, according to Kahneman, it "never sleeps". System 1 makes fast, automatic, intuitive actions without thinking and without using up much energy—and it kept you alive back when the rustle in the bushes may have been a sabre-toothed bear that wanted to eat your face.

System 2 is slow, deliberate, and takes tons of energy. It allows us to reflect on what we're doing and thinking and make purposeful decisions.

We don't notice those systems at work; we think we're making thoughtful, rational decisions all the time. We're not. Often, we're reacting to something we've barely noticed—and it's that part of the brain we need to hook with the Big Idea for our book.

If you want to stop someone in his tracks, put dog poo there. Let me explain. I'm not for one second suggesting your book is dog poo. Instead, consider this: you could be walking along the street, nose buried in your iPhone, paying little or no attention to what's going on around you—and yet you don't step in the dog poo. Why?

Because System 1, the part of your brain on the lookout for danger, won't let you. It notices the poo and gently steers you around it—often without you even noticing.

Ask yourself: what danger is your reader facing? What do they stand to lose without your book?

---

3    If you're fascinated by all this, read *Thinking, Fast and Slow* by Nobel-prize-winner Daniel Kahneman.

How can you make it needle-point specific?

*That's* your hook. Your Big Idea.

Want a couple of examples? No problem.

*Perennial Seller* by Ryan Holiday isn't just about creating art and writing a book. It's about how to create work that matters and lasts in a world that champions fleeting, flash-in-the-pan successes. The danger his reader is facing is being forgotten. Creating stuff that doesn't matter and nobody cares about. Without his book, his readers stand to lose their legacy.

*The Easy Way To Control Alcohol* by Allen Carr offers freedom from life with alcohol. He promises an easy, fast, and pain-free way to end a relationship with alcohol. Without his book, his readers will continue to struggle with drinking, stopping and starting and retaining the psychological dependency. Without his book, his readers will never be free and in control of their lives.

The vague ideas for these books were "write books" and "stop drinking". The needle-point specific Big Ideas are "write books that matter and will continue to matter in years to come" and "how to stop drinking without a struggle and be happy about it".

Working out what really matters to your potential readers so you can think up your Big Idea is a much faster way than waiting for the flash of inspiration. It lets you get on with the important business of writing. It doesn't matter if your book is smaller and slimmer than you might like it to be. Your reader will thank you for it. Can you solve one problem, and build a relationship at the same time? Do it.

Don't try to solve *all* your customers' problems in one single book—you don't need to. After all, you can always write another book, can't you?

## Cultivating Creativity

Creativity is at the heart of writing a great book, even if you don't yet believe it. Just because you're not writing fiction, doesn't mean it's not creative.

When's the last time you did something creative for the sake of it? When was the last time you *played*? Maybe it was last weekend when you made cakes. Or last winter, when you built a snowman. Or when you decorated a bedroom, or painted a picture, or folded some paper, or made up a story on a walk.

If you don't let it out and use it, your creativity will wither—or suffocate, or burst out inappropriately while you're at a funeral or a wedding.

Make space to create. To play. Because creating and playing is good for the soul and your book will be better if you plan creativity into your world.

If you allow yourself to play, you'll find coming up with ideas happens naturally. Mix playing with talking to people, collecting stories, and researching similar ideas, and you'll be surprised at how creative you are.

You'll have your Big Idea in no time.

One final word on inspiration. Action doesn't come from motivation. Motivation comes when you act. So sit down and start.

Before you move onto Chapter 5, where we'll take some simple steps to get you oiled up and comfortable with the idea of putting words on paper, take these Tiny Creative Beetle Steps.

## Tiny Beetle Steps

1. Give your book a working title because naming your book will make it feel real. (Don't panic: you're allowed to change it later.)

2. Arrange a play-date with yourself every week. Perhaps you'll go for a walk in the nearby countryside, or join a drawing group, or learn to play an instrument. It doesn't matter what it is; just make sure it's creative and fun and just for you.

3. Talk to your best clients and find out all about what led them to you and how you helped them. You'll find helpful questions to ask your clients in the resources area on the book website www.moxiebooks.co.uk/moxie-book-resources.

4. Open an Evernote account and start collecting and organising stories. Visit www.bit.ly/Moxie-Evernote.[1]

5. Narrow down your book ideas to one tightly focused Big Idea. Your Big Idea should solve your reader's biggest, most painful problem or offer them an answer to the question eating away at them.

---

1   This is an affiliate link. If you use it, you'll get a month's free Evernote Premium, and I'll get points to put towards my Premium fees.

# CHAPTER 5

# Embrace The Shitty First Draft

*"I'm writing a first draft and reminding myself that I'm simply shoveling sand into a box so that later I can build castles."*

*Shannon Hale*

Come closer. I have a little secret to tell you. Are you ready? *Writer's block is a myth.*

It's a condition invented by people who aren't willing to sit down and Do The Work. It's a syndrome concocted by those who believe in the Inspiration Fairy. It's a malady suffered by those who aren't initiated into the Secret Way of the Writer.

Are you ready to learn the Secret Way of the Writer?

Excellent. I'd like to introduce you to the Shitty First Draft.[1] You're going to get well acquainted, and this concept will change everything for you.

Shitty First Drafts aren't just inevitable; Shitty First Drafts are vital if you want to make a good book. There are no great books in existence that didn't pass through the Shitty First Draft stage; that, I promise you.

Get comfortable right now with the idea that your first draft is going to be crappy—and because of that, your finished book will

---

1    I first heard about the Shitty First Draft when I read *Bird By Bird* by Anne Lamott (brilliant book).

be magnificent. Remember: in the history of all awesome things, there was a time when those awesome things were total crap. Ask Edison and his eleventy-million lightbulbs.

We're harder on ourselves than anyone else ever is. We don't allow ourselves to fail or to make mistakes. We hold ourselves to impossibly high standards. And we don't understand how creativity works (although I hope you have a better idea now you've read Chapter 4).

You won't give yourself permission to screw this up, so I'm giving you permission to screw it up. And I will allow you to do a bunch of things when you sit down to write your book:[2]

- Make mistakes. As many as you like.
- Be indecisive about what to include.
- Have a little cry if you feel like it.
- Be honest. Really, brutally, painfully honest—even if it might upset someone.
- Change your mind. Then do it again.
- Ask for help. It might be the bravest thing you ever do. (Amanda Palmer wrote a great book about the importance of letting others help you. It's called *The Art of Asking*.)
- Be imperfect, because none of us can be anything else.
- Be yourself! Fully, 100 per cent yourself.
- Be vulnerable because vulnerability is attractive.
- Be confident, because confidence is attractive (and confidence is not the same as arrogance).
- Be selfish. For a few hours a week, while you're writing this book, give yourself time to write and guard it jealously. That time is yours. You deserve it.
- Be wrong from time to time.
- Allow yourself to say what you're scared to say.
- Have a strong opinion—and own it.

---

2   I got this idea from the brilliant Ann Sheybani, who, in her book *How To Eat The Elephant*, gave me permission to do a number of similar things when writing this book, and sparked these ideas for me to share with you.

All these behaviours are good for your brain, and they'll help you write a fabulous book via your beautiful, imperfect, and wholly necessary Shitty First Draft.

Before you start on your actual book, though, I want to get you used to the idea of writing and letting go of some of your inhibitions and facing some of your fears. That's what this chapter is all about. It's playtime.

## A Note On Your Comfort Zone

To write a fantastic book, you will need to voyage out of your comfort zone. Waaaaay out. The reason is simple: your comfort zone is wonderfully comfortable, but it's a barren desert. Nothing grows there.

Later in this chapter, I've shared some of my favourite writing exercises with you. Before you get to them, though, I want to share something else: I am not a natural dancer. Yes, I am a trapeze artist and a pole dancer, but that's different. I am strong, and I love hanging around upside down from my feet. Put me on the floor, though, and ask me to dance and I sweat and shake and hyperventilate.

Of course, my reaction to boogying meant I had to learn to dance because if it scares me, I must master it. I found a dance class. At my dance class, the first thing the teacher told us to do was find a space and close our eyes. She put on some music and asked us to move. Eyes closed. No looking at anyone else. Then she gave us cues: be angry. Be sad. Be joyful. Be a cat. Be a jellyfish. Be a toilet roll (I know, that baffled me, too).

We moved hesitantly at first, eyes slitted, pretending we weren't looking.

I felt like a total muppet... but so did everyone else. None of them looked like muppets, though... so perhaps I didn't, either. I kept going. The more I moved, the less of a tit I felt. Then something weird happened: I didn't care anymore if I looked like a muppet. I loved dancing. Loved moving. And knew the only way to improve was to keep going.

71

This is a book on how to write a book—but here's a suggestion: do something that makes you feel daft every day. Just on your own to start with. Get used to feeling uncomfortable. Get used to feeling like a bit of a muppet. Pay attention to how, the more you do it, the less of a muppet you feel.

Then remember your feelings when you sit down to write.

You don't look daft. Soon, you won't feel daft, either.

And anyway, looking daft doesn't matter right now, because nobody will ever see the first things you write...

## How To Kill Your Book Dead

If you want to kill your book before you even get started, all you have to do is reject the Shitty First Draft. Embrace your lifelong perfectionism, and refuse to let it go.

People often say, in job interviews and suchlike, with a wry grin and a chuckle, their "biggest flaw" is they're a perfectionist. Said in such a way that the interviewer should understand you don't really mean it as a flaw; in fact, you mean it as a backhanded compliment. Because, as we all know, perfectionism is a virtue.

Getting things right the first time is to be applauded.

Failure is—well—failure.

Look: it's not your fault. Our entire society and education system is set up to make you want to avoid failure at all costs. We're encouraged to get everything right first time. We're taught that putting our hands up and getting the wrong answer is shameful (oh yes, we are—teachers and parents might tell kids it's okay to fail with a small "f", and they might want to believe it... But actions speak louder than words, and when we see vicarious embarrassment on the faces of people we look up to when we screw up, we internalise the idea that we must not speak up for fear of "getting it wrong".)

All this is a sure-fire recipe for Failure—with a capital F. Because if we're not willing to be wrong, and risk embarrassment, we are never going to create anything worthwhile.

Do you think it was easy for me to sit down and write this book? If you do, think again. Just because I'm a writer, doesn't make writing easy. It's not the *act* of writing that's tough, understand; it's getting started. Then putting it out here into the world for you to read when I'm done. Permitting myself to create something that may attract criticism—even hostility.

And that's scary.

You understand that because you feel it too.

But we step out onto the ledge anyway. We get on with it, because to succumb to perfectionism and the fear hiding behind it, is the real failure.

Perfectionism is also arrogance. The idea that we can sit down and create something perfect, right now, without any slips or trips—the notion that there's nothing else we can learn from what we're doing and failing at—is a special kind of arrogance wrapped up in extreme self-doubt and low self-esteem. Perfectionism stops you creating, learning, improving. And it will kill your book. You deserve better than that. You *are* better than that.

Here and now, I want to pause and direct you towards Brené Brown again. I love her, in a way that would probably make her back away into a bush, Homer Simpson-style. She wrote a book called *The Gifts of Imperfection*, and I implore you to buy it and read it right now. Buy and read *Daring Greatly*, too.

For now, though, I'll leave you with her wise words:

"Perfectionism is a self destructive and addictive belief system that fuels this primary thought: If I look perfect, and do everything perfectly, I can avoid or minimize the painful feelings of shame, judgement, and blame."

I'll leave a little advice of my own, too: don't show anyone your Shitty First Draft. Keep it to yourself. You *know* there's going to be a lot of work to do in the edit; having someone point out all the flaws you already know are there will upset you. Instead, write your Shitty First Draft, then put it away in a drawer for a week or two. Show someone your manuscript after your first self-edit.

Speaking of self-editing…

## Thou Shalt Not Edit As You Write

This is Vicky's Second Commandment of Writing.

If you edit as you go along, you will become an angry person who throws newspapers at flies and yells at technology. It's the most frustrating way to write. Instead of getting into a flow, all you'll see is typos, spelling mistakes, and words you could beat into better words. Editing as you write kills your creativity, your motivation, and your energy—and you'll hate what you're doing.

Confession: I find it monstrously tough to write without editing, so I feel ya. I really do. It takes practice to write freely. If you struggle with writing freely, try this: drape something over your screen so you can't see what you're doing. If you can touch-type, this will be relatively easy once you convince your brain the world won't explode.

If you can't touch-type—learn! I first learned to touch-type in college using Mavis Beacon software. I was astonished to find out Mavis Beacon still exists[3]. Other touch-typing lessons are available.

If you're not into typing, you could dictate your book. Nuance Dragon[4] is very good, or you could use a service like rev.com, which charges $1 a minute for transcription and has a lightning-fast turnaround. My point is: write first, edit later.

Stopping to correct a typo, or sort out the layout, or "fix" that paragraph you don't like, will harsh your buzz, man. It'll dam your flow, and you'll lose the essence of your message. Typos don't matter. Spelling mistakes don't matter. Awkward wording does not matter. Not at this stage.

What matters is the message you want to share, and the flow you want to get into. If you're able to manoeuvre yourself into a zen writing zone, you'll experience something akin to euphoria. Even if you're "not a writer" (and you are, because writers write, dammit), you can experience this for yourself.

---

3  I only just discovered Mavis Beacon is not a real person. One of our hens was called Mavis Peacock, as a shout-out to Mavis Beacon.

4  Nuance Dragon used to be called Dragon Dictation.

Getting into a state where your words tumble out of your head and onto the page, where your voice rings out loud and clear like a holy trumpet, is magnificent. But you won't get there if you permit yourself the indulgence of editing as you go along. (And make no mistake, it is an indulgence.)

How do you do avoid editing as you go along? It takes practice and self-awareness. I still struggle with editing as I go along. I literally just went up and changed the subheading at the start of this zen flow chunk. It's okay, though, because my little transgression jolted me back to reality and reminded me editing as you go is a fool's game.

Practice. Editing as you go along is second nature; it's an unconscious habit. Be aware of what you're doing at all times, check yourself, steer yourself back to the task of writing—and you'll begin to change the habit.

## The Blank Page of Doom

The final nail in perfectionism's coffin is beating the Blank Page of Doom. I call it that because I always feel a little like Frodo approaching Mount Doom: it's so big and scary and intimidating, I can't see any way up. Your blank page is a little like that, isn't it?

Even with a detailed outline, even with our books substantively written and planned out, we still have to face the dreaded blank page when we sit down to actually write.

You'll face the blank page a lot. Seriously. *A lot.* Even writers who write for a living sometimes feel like the words won't come. Yesterday was a day like that for me. It was a real struggle. You'll face those struggles too.

Guess what: you know how to deal with it already because the Blank Page of Doom isn't limited to writing. The Blank Page of Doom is a creative block, and it crops up all over the place. I'm sure you're familiar with it outside of writing your book.

Take trapeze, for example—which is pretty much my favourite thing to do, after writing. I might be working on an arduous new trick combination and feel like I'm getting nowhere. I'm stalled.

Instead of sitting on the floor and stewing over it, I go back to basics. I do some exercises I know I can do, which are the foundations of the advanced moves I want to master. The key is action. Take action—any action—and progress will happen.

My advice to you is: just flippin' WRITE.

But that's not terribly useful advice on its own. Instead, I'll give you three cool writing exercises which will help you get out of your own way. They'll help you beat your perfectionism and your Inner Dickhead's desire to produce a perfect first paragraph right away, so you get started fast.

Think of these writing exercises as your warm-up. I wouldn't get on a trapeze without warming up. You wouldn't start a workout in the gym without warming up. Don't start writing without warming up. You can do these exercises at the start of every writing session if you like.

## 1. The "Modernist Poetry" Exercise

Let's start with a little creative writing exercise that'll have you penning some bonkers modernist poetry. Stick with me; it'll be fun, I promise. Open a blank page—either on paper or on your computer. Write the first word that comes into your head. It could be anything.

Write another word. This is hard because it must be a random word, disconnected from the previous one. Your perfectionist Inner Dickhead won't like it, but your Inner Dickhead is a douchecanoe so ignore him and write the random word anyway.

Then write a third word. Then a fourth. And carry on.

Play with your words! Listen to the sounds they make, rather than their meaning. Think *Jabberwocky* by Lewis Carroll and Edward Lear's nonsense rhymes. Make up new words. Come up with the most random nouns you can think of. Turn nouns into verbs and vice versa. Break all the rules of grammar you ever heard. Don't use punctuation—unless you make it fun.

Don't be embarrassed, it's meant to sound absurd. And you don't have to show it to anyone (although I'd love to see it if you want to share).

How's this for a silly poem:

*Socks on trivet*

*Glowstick hides in Earl Grey tea*

*Halo the spatula and bromate the Sally*

*Petrichor on the palanquin*

See? Daft. But fun. You'll come up with words you never knew you knew.

This is a good game for exercising your creative muscles and letting go of your need to get things right. It's a good activity for loosening you up. Have a play, because playing is what this exercise is all about.

The next one is good for practising writing without editing. Are you ready?

## 2. The "Writers Write" Exercise

I learned this exercise from one of my mentors, Jon McCulloch—and he tells me he got it from a chap called Steve Manning. It's a splendid activity. Have a go.

Get a timer and set it for five minutes.

1. Get a piece of paper and a pen. Write down these three words: flamingo, cheese, pyjamas.

2. Pick one of those three words as the first word you write. It must be the first word of the first sentence you write.

3. Start your timer and begin writing. Write as fast as you can and don't stop to edit. Write anything that comes into your head.

4. The other two words must appear at least once in your first paragraph.

5. Write for the whole five minutes. Don't stop to think. Don't stop to edit. Don't stop, full stop!

6. When the timer stops, look at what you've written. I think you'll be pleasantly surprised at how high quality it is.

If you're stuck on a chapter and can't get started, try this exercise with keywords from the chapter. You will almost certainly need to throw away the first paragraph or two, but you betcha boots you'll end up with something useful. Fix the typos later; they don't matter.

# 3. The "Mundane Story" Exercise

A great way to start writing is to find a story and link it to your topic. This is why I collect stories.

Let's take an email I wrote about one of the things that's wrong with most business homepages. I could have droned on about how they're confusing, but that's dull.

Here's what came out:

\* \* \*

Dammit where is that egg timer? I know I've seen it somewhere.

In the kitchen. I last saw it in the kitchen.

Oh, no…

I think it might have been in…

\*cue B-movie dramatic horror music, thunder, and dimming of the lights\*

*The Kitchen Drawer of Doom*

That place where everything from pliers to birthday candles to napkins to old batteries to random spoons lurk forgotten and abandoned.

I don protective clothing and take a swig of gin. I'm going in. Wish me luck. Five minutes later, and I'm buying the thing I need from Amazon instead.

Funnily enough, it's also how I feel when I land on far too many websites. I have no idea what to do or where to go next, so I leave.

\* \* \*

Instead of agonising over the best boring way to start, the Kitchen Drawer of Doom popped into my head and reminded me that's what a lot of homepages are like: cluttered and confusing. So I told that slightly exaggerated but hopefully amusing tale about losing stuff in the kitchen. Then I flipped it into the topic I wanted to talk about.

By telling a story we can all relate to (because we all have a kitchen drawer like that) I was able to get and keep attention. Then I connected it to cluttered homepages—a connection my reader might not make by himself.

Look: the Blank Page of Doom won't ever disappear for good. But it doesn't have to be insurmountable. All you have to do is start. In this chapter, I've given you three ways to get words on paper, which is the most important thing of all.

When you do start, keep going—without editing as you write.

In the next chapter, we'll build on your creativity and refine your Big Idea by getting to know your weirdos. Do your Tiny Beetle Steps, then we'll meet your ideal reader.

## Tiny Beetle Steps

1.  Acknowledge your perfectionist nature and give yourself permission to make mistakes. Write this down and stick it somewhere visible in your writing room: I am allowed to screw this up. Everything good starts with a Shitty First Draft.

2.  Do one or all of the writing exercises in this chapter. Note how they make you feel, and what they can lead you towards in your book.

3.  Resist the urge to edit as you write—if necessary, drape something over your computer screen so you can't edit as you go along.

# CHAPTER 6

# Find Your Weirdos

*"In nearly every case, trying to lead everyone
results in leading no one in particular."*

*Seth Godin*

Almost everything you've experienced in your life up to now has been geared towards making you "normal". Making you fit in. Making you average. Ever since the industrial revolution, we've been in the age of mass: mass production, mass marketing, and mass media—generalised products, services, and messages aimed at everyone and no-one.

That won't work anymore, and the only reason it worked in the past was we didn't have a choice. There were only so many breakfast cereals, so many cars, so many life choices to make. Now, we know more. The internet has opened our eyes and ears and given us infinite choices about almost everything— so companies can no longer get away with generic marketing scattergun-splattered at the masses.

We are all weird, as Seth Godin points out in his book of the same name. We all have our quirks, and we're all drawn to people and things for specific reasons. You're reading this book because something about it—and me—appealed to you. You had other choices; there are plenty of other books on this topic. But you chose me. (Thank you.)

If you try to write a book to appeal to everyone in your market, you will appeal to nobody. If, as Godin says, you try to lead everyone, you will lead no-one. What you need to do is find your weirdos and give them what they want.

Before you write anything substantial in your book, before you even outline it, you must decide whom you're writing it for—and create a vision of your reader in glorious technicolour detail. I call this your Weirdo Profile.

This chapter will help you do so. Let's begin.

## The Chicken Bomb

I want you to pretend to be a chicken. No, really. Stop giving this book the side-eye and unleash your inner feathered velociraptor.

Are you chickening around the place? Marv.

Now then: you're still a chicken—okay?—but now imagine a bomb is about to drop on your town. What do you do?

Go on. Do it.

Are you... running around, flapping your arms, squawking like a fox is after you? I bet you are. Go on, admit it. If so, you're making a whopping mistake—one you don't want to make when you settle in to write your book.

Let me explain. Way back in the 1940s, fabled acting coach Stella Adler devised an exercise called The Chicken Bomb. Legend has it, she had a class of students pretending to be chickens, all flapping around like loons at the thought of getting nuked.

Well, all except one. One student strutted into a corner and pretended to lay an egg. Adler asked him why, and he said: "I'm a chicken—what do I know about bombs?"

BOOM! (So to speak.)

That student was Marlon Brando, and he was the only one who got what it was all about: the yawning gulf between "be a chicken" and "mimic a chicken". You might be wondering why I am going on about chickens. I'll tell you: in this tortured metaphor, the chicken represents your ideal reader. To understand your ideal reader, you need to climb inside their head and rummage around.

It is imperative—compulsory—inescapable for you to figure out whom you're writing for before you do any actual writing, or your book will be... not good. We're not going to write a mediocre book, you and I. We're going to write something people actually want to read—something they won't be able to put down because it will, in some way, change their lives for the better.

If you want to write a book that will captivate your readers from start to finish and enable you to build a lasting relationship with them, you need to crawl inside their heads and understand them. Too many business owners assume they know their ideal customers and clients well.[1] They are often wrong. Do not think you know what's in your readers' heads already.

We start with your reader... because if we don't start with your reader, your reader isn't going to want to read your shit.

Whom you're writing for will influence everything about your book: your message, your content, your style, and even your layout. We need to dig deep inside their heads and figure out what makes them tick—and that means going *way* beyond the standard internet marketing "avatar".[2]

In other words, we're not just going to imitate a chicken. We're going to be the chicken. We're going to become your ideal reader. Are you ready?

## Why Are They Reading?

Start with why your reader would read your book. Why do people read non-fiction at all? It's not for the same reasons they read fiction. How does this relate to your Big Idea?

---

1   This exercise to find your weirdos won't only be valuable for writing your book. It'll be worthwhile for your whole business.

2   An avatar is a representation of a real person. In marketing, we use the term to mean "ideal client or customer". In this book, it's your Weirdo Profile.

Remember, non-fiction readers usually want an answer to a specific problem, which is why so many weight-loss and self-help books are sold every January. What particular problem will *your* book solve?

Non-fiction readers are deeply interested in a particular topic and tend to buy lots of books on the subject. I have so many books on writing I could build an igloo out of them. I have almost as many books on ancient Egypt. If there are lots of books on your topic, you're probably onto a winner.

Sometimes readers of non-fiction are simply fans of the writer, which is why anyone with a large platform will probably get a book deal. The most recent example I can think of is that cleaning influencer (yes I just wrote that) from Instagram: Mrs Hinch.[3] Her fifty-bazillion followers hoiked her up the social media ladder and got her a book deal with Michael Joseph.[4] Good for her.

Whether you want to nab a book deal or not, if you have an audience, people will buy your book and read it. Do you have an audience already—large or small? If you do, what do they want from you? Do they want to learn a new skill? In which case, you'll be thinking about a "how to" guide—steps your reader can take to learn something new and become something more. Something like this book, in fact. Does your reader want inspiration? You could write stories about people like them, who overcame similar challenges and turned their lives around. Or you could produce a book of quotes, like Robin Sharma's *Daily Inspiration*.

Perhaps your reader wants to learn more about your area of expertise, in which case your book will be a kind of introduction to your subject—and an introduction to you. *The Copywriter's Handbook* by Robert Bly is a solid example of an introductory book.

Or maybe your reader simply wants to be entertained. There

---

3  Hinch, S. 2019 *Hinch Yourself Happy*, Michael Joseph. I recommend you buy her book, because it is a little masterclass in how to give your tribe exactly what they want, and put your personality into your writing.

4  Michael Joseph is an imprint—a trade name—of Penguin Books.

are plenty of business owners who wrote books to entertain as well as inform—like *Creative Mischief* by Dave Trott or *Marketing Insights and Outrages* by Drayton Bird. Of course, a reader may want more than one thing from your book. I hope this book entertains and inspires you, as well as shows you exactly how to write a book of your own.

Most readers have a specific reason for picking up and reading a new non-fiction book. Their reason will determine the type of book you write, and it'll be linked to your purpose for writing it.

## Why Are You Writing?

Now let's turn to you. What do you want? Why are you writing this book of yours? What do you want your reader to get, do, have, and be after they've read it? This is important because together with your reader's reason for reading, your reason for writing will inform the type of book you create.

Do you have something vital to say? A story you must share, or it'll burst out of you? Something you know will change people's lives if only you can get your message in front of them? Perhaps you want recognition from your peers and clients as the expert at the pinnacle of your industry mountain. Maybe you want to tell your story, so your book helps to build relationships with more people than you could possibly meet face to face.

Some writers want to solve a specific problem with a simple, straightforward "how to" guide; others want to change lives and perhaps even change the world with a teeth-rattling tome. Still others simply want a brilliant marketing tool—something that enables them to focus and does much of the heavy lifting in their marketing.

There's no right or wrong answer to the question "why are you writing this book?" All the reasons I mentioned—and any number of other reasons—are perfectly valid.

The crucial thing is to be clear in your own mind about why you're writing it because, until you are, you'll find it almost impossible to sit down and do the work.

## What's In Your Head?

Before we dig into other people's heads, let me ask you something. Are you your ideal reader? By which I mean—are you writing a book you wish you'd been able to read when you had a problem? I wrote my first book, *Business For Superheroes*, because when I started out, I couldn't find the exact book that would have helped me. So I wrote it for baby business owner me. I was my ideal reader.

When I sat down to plan *How The Hell Do You Write A Book?* I started with myself, too. This book is all about my experiences writing books for myself and my clients. What problems did I face? What was missing from the other books I'd read on the subject? Why did I struggle to get started? Why did I struggle to finish? I answer those questions first, for myself.

Then I moved onto my best clients.

If you're your own ideal reader, start with a little light navel-gazing. What's in your head? How did you feel when you had the problem you're writing about? What pain did it cause you?

Scribble notes. Speak into a voice recorder. Draw a picture. Whatever it takes to sort through your thoughts and feelings.

In my experience, most of my clients fit their own Weirdo Profiles, to a greater or lesser extent, so don't be afraid to use what you know of yourself. Then move onto other people...

## The Penthouse Of The Brain

Let's start up top, on the roof, with the bare and boring facts (known in the marketing industry as "demographics"). What industry is your reader in? What age? Is your reader a she or he—or another identification altogether? Gay, straight, somewhere in between?

How about ethnicity? What's their income, and where do they live? Are they married with kids, a dog, three sheep, and varying numbers of chickens?

What are the facts?

You can find these facts from all over the place. Look at existing market research. Look at your own current clients—they're all unique, of course, but there will be some common themes. Seek out people on social media who are talking about the problem you solve: what are the facts about them?

Facts are a sound place to start because they give us a jumping-off point. Instead of starting with the whole planet—7.7 billion people at the time of publishing—we can narrow the seething mass of humanity down to (for example) middle-class women with kids in the south of England.

These demographics will help you dig a little deeper because a drag queen from rural Herefordshire faces vastly different challenges in life than a straight white female shop owner from Leamington Spa, who has wildly different experiences than a rich black male lawyer from London.

## Going Down

Now let's take the elevator down a floor and unearth what's hidden. Who is this reader of yours, really? What are their worries, frustrations, and fears? What motivates them? What do they need? And, crucially, what do they *want*?

Let's say you're a photographer who specialises in branding photoshoots for female business owners. The demographics are easy enough: she's probably aged between twenty-five and forty-five and has owned her own business for at least three years.

Maybe she's married, and they have two kids and a dog. She lives in a city or a big town in the south of the UK, and she has enough disposable income to invest in a high-quality photoshoot.

But here's the thing: she feels guilty. She shouldn't be spending money on herself when there are two kids and a husband who need looking after. She never puts herself or her business first. All she does, she does for her kids.

She's frustrated because she's shit-hot at what she does, but her branding is amateur hour. It doesn't reflect who she is, which damages her chances at finding the best clients and charging top-shelf prices. She's stuck working with customers who don't appreciate her and who make her life difficult.

Added to all that is the sure and certain knowledge that somewhere between the mirror and the camera lens, the gods of photography replace her face with that of a misshapen troll. She's not photogenic (or so she believes), and she will cut you if you attempt to take a photograph of her and then post it on Facebook.

## Dig For Pain

Now get specific. Even in that quick pen-portrait about the photographer's client, there's a lot of information.

What problem are you solving for her? What pain is it causing her, and how will that pain slowly destroy her life, her business, her self-esteem, and her ambitions? There's no one right answer. This particular book you're writing now might focus on one big pain... but there's no reason why you can't write another book focusing on another of her significant pains.

The crucial question is: what's causing her to Rage Google[5] *right now*? What's the micro-moment of realisation that leads her to pick up your book, screech, "OMG YES", and read it?

It might be: "I hate my face! How can I make it look good in photos?" (And, yes, there's a chance I may have typed that into Google myself in the past.)

Or perhaps: "Why do photographers make me look ugly?"

Possibly: "Why are clients always trying to smash me down on price?"

Or even: "Why does my hair look like feathers?"[6]

---

5  Rage Google: the moment something pisses you off so much you Google a very specific and very angry phrase. Like "why the fuck is Amazon Video not working when I need to watch *Game Of Thrones* Season 7!!!!" complete with rage-induced typos and multiple exclamation marks.

6  Yeah, I've Googled that too.

Take their Rage Google Moment and expand it. What are the consequences of your reader's pain?

Sticking with the photographer's client, the consequences might be deteriorating self-esteem. Loss of confidence. A tendency to hide her face behind her hair, so nobody can see her expressions properly (which doesn't exactly engender trust). Reluctance to stand up in front of potential clients, to teach, to build relationships, to sell. A website and branding that doesn't reflect her true self, so she doesn't attract the best clients.

Loss of income. Loss of business.

*Loss of identity.*

Do you see what I've done here?

These are only a few lines, but I haven't sketched a quick, surface-level reader. I've spent time in her head. There is a lot of information here, and I've barely started. This is the difference between imitating a chicken and being a chicken. This is finding your weirdos.

Get to know your clients. Discover what wakes them up in the dead of night, shaking and sweating. Listen to what their nasty little Inner Dickhead whispers to them in the dark.

Tap into that, and use it to help them. Use it to discover why your reader is reading your book. What do they need? What do they *want?*

## How To Burrow Into Brains

All this theory is fascinating, but I bet you're thinking something like, "Well, fine. That's easy for you to say, but this is super-difficult. Digging around and finding out what makes people tick is not easy. How the bloody hell do I do it?"

You're right. It's not easy, and it's not quick. But it is fascinating and enlightening, and I guarantee if you work through this chapter you won't just write a better book, you'll build a better business. You'll serve your clients better. You'll help people more effectively. And you will make more money.

I want to make this as pain-free as possible for you, so here are the questions I ask my clients and readers when I want to find out as much as possible about the inner workings of their minds.

Some questions may seem odd, and you may not understand how they relate to your business—especially if you sell a physical product or a luxury item. Ask them anyway, because every human has hopes, dreams, and goals, whether they relate directly to what you sell or not. The more you know about people, the better you can serve them. Remember, it's not just the product you sell, it's how you sell it and the experience you deliver.

Take these questions and use them when you begin to write your book. Start by asking your current clients and customers. Take them out to lunch, one by one, and have a conversation. Or, rather, you ask questions and then shut up and listen. Record the conversations if you can. When you run out of clients to ask, look further afield for people who seem to fit your Weirdo Profile and ask if they'd be willing to help you. Most will. We all love nothing more than talking about ourselves.

Start with the painful stuff. I'll stick with the photographer example, but you can adapt these questions to your own industry:

- What stresses you out regularly about your business and brand?
- What worries keep you up at night?
- What in your business are you so afraid of that you avoid facing it?
- What do you secretly fear may be true about you and your business? (For example, the photographer's client may secretly fear she's not good enough to be successful, she has a glorified hobby, and everyone's laughing at her.)
- How do you think your friends, family, spouse, clients would react if they found out about your fears?
- Where will you lose power, influence, and control if things don't change or get worse?
- How do you feel when things go badly—when you realise your branding and website don't reflect who you are?

- If money were no object, what brand or product or service would you buy to solve your problem?
- What do you wish businesses in this industry understood about you?

Then move onto the aspirational stuff:

- What do you secretly wish was true about your life or business?
- If you woke up tomorrow and your business was perfect, what would it look like?
- What's your dream solution to your problem—the "OMG, this is it!" thing you'd pay almost anything for?
- If this dream product or service could drop into your lap right now and go perfectly, what would happen?
- What impact will fixing your problem have on your business and your life?
- How will your family, friends, spouse, and clients react if you fix your problem like a boss?
- What will you be able to be, do, have, and achieve if you solve your problem and create your perfect life?
- How and where will you be more powerful and influential if your dream comes true?
- How will you feel when you've fixed your problem?

If you don't do this exercise and go through these questions with real people, I know from experience you will do what most business owners do and simply guess at surface-level stuff. If you do this exercise and dig deep, you'll get the most incredible information and stories that will help you write the kind of book that can make a real difference in people's lives.

If you're too shy to do this yourself, get a trusted and independent third-party to do it for you and record it. However you decide to get it done, you must do it.

It sounds like a lot of work—and it is a substantial task, but you won't regret doing this. And I know you'll enjoy it, too, when you do it.

## Eavesdropping For Victory

Don't underestimate the power of listening to other people's conversations—either online or in real life. Please note, though: this is not a substitute for doing the interviews and asking the questions of your current clients and other people who fit your Weirdo Profile. This is something you can do all the time.

If your customers and clients get together in groups, listen to them. Pay attention to their stories, complaints, victories, and frustrations and fears. Hang out where they hang out: in coffee shops, gyms, the pub, Facebook groups, Mumsnet, specialist forums.

Here's what my lovely client Jill said about eavesdropping: "I love nothing more than sitting across from ladies discussing diets! I've got gold from my clandestine activities!"

As long as you're not creeping around in the bushes with a mic and a telephoto lens, listening in on people's conversations in public places is perfectly fine.

## How To Use Your Weirdo Profile

Another of my lovely clients, Kelly, said something interesting to me: "I still don't really know how this then translates into what I write. I get it in theory, but practically I'm not sure how I would allow it to influence what/how I write."

This is an excellent question, and I suspect it's an obstacle that prevents many business owners from creating a detailed customer or ideal reader avatar. Here's how you'll use your Weirdo Profile:

1. **To discover the real reasons people will buy and read your book.** The reasons people give you often aren't the real ones. Digging in and asking questions, pulling people's stories out of them, will help you uncover their true feelings and motivations so you can write about what they care about—which may not be the same thing you care about.

2. **You'll gather some colourful and detailed stories**

you can weave into your book, helping your readers understand they're not alone and you can help them.

3. **The language your weirdos use is important.** The words and phrases they use may be different from your words and phrases. You can bring their style into your book and use it to build a connection. If you talk about their problems in the same way they do, they'll trust you to help them find a solution.

4. **The information you unearth from your conversations may give you new material to include in your book.** You've probably got some great ideas about what to write about—but you may have missed a crucial point.

5. **These interviews can be turned into fantastic bonus material** if your interviewees allow you to use them. Everyone loves a peek behind the scenes.

6. **You can use these stories and insights elsewhere in your business:** in your emails, articles, on your website, in podcasts—everywhere your target audience hangs out.

Right now, you might feel like there's an awful lot of work to do before you even begin to write your first draft, but trust me when I tell you it's work well done and time well spent. It'll help you nail down your Big Idea and give you something focused to write about.

This step—finding your weirdos—is hard. Everybody struggles with it, including me—but those who persevere are the ones who find success. Do not skip this step; your book will be weak if you do.

Don't just imitate a chicken. Anyone can do that, and most people do. *Be* the chicken, and you will stand out as someone who genuinely cares about your clients and readers and is qualified to help. You'll find it easier to refine your Big Idea if you surrender yourself to the inner workings of your ideal reader's weirdo mind.

Take these Tiny Beetle Steps, then pick up your rod and staff and move onto Chapter 7.

## Tiny Beetle Steps

1.  Interview a select few of your clients or potential clients using the questions I suggested above.

2.  Go to the resources area on the website, and download and complete the Weirdo Profile exercise. I've broken it down into Tiny Beetle Steps, so it's not too daunting (I hope). It can be challenging to visualise what a "good" Weirdo Profile or ideal reader avatar looks like, so I've shared mine with you: www.moxiebooks.co.uk/moxie-book-resources.

# CHAPTER 7

# There's More Than One Way To Write A Book

*"Nothing ever comes to one, that is worth having,*
*except as a result of hard work."*

Booker T. Washington

Now you know whom you're writing for, I'm afraid I have bad news for you. Writing a book is hard work. It will take a lot of time, effort, and tears. There will be moments when you loathe your manuscript, your computer, and yourself—and want to set fire to the lot of it.

This is all normal.

Here's what's not normal for most of us: writing an entire book in a weekend. You are almost certainly not going to do so. Not if you're a regular human writing a book from scratch, and not if you have something substantial to share with the world.

Despite what certain internet marketing gurus will tell you, it's not possible for most of us to write a valuable book in two days. Even if it *is* "just a lead generator". I want to write something better than that; and I think you do, too.

Here's the good news: I know how to make writing your book much, much easier and much, much less painful—which is what this section is all about.

I'll share three basic ways to write a book. There's no right or wrong way, and none of them is necessarily better than the others. Which you choose will depend on your nature, the type of book you want to write, and what material you already have lying around.

## 1. Collect What You Already Have

The first way—some may call it the easy way, but don't believe them—is to create an anthology. If you have reams of writing lying around all over the internet and stuffed into the crevices of your hard drive, you may want to approach writing your book as if you were a curator at a museum.

This is perfectly valid, and I know many published authors who've written their books this way. I've got plans to do similar myself in the future. Take my friend, Kat, for example. Her first book, *101 Naked Confessions of a Gay Hairdresser*, was simply a collection of her daily emails.

Kat was part-owner of a hair salon in London. When she bought it, it wasn't doing so well; when she sold her share, she made a bulging wad of cash. Part of her strategy was to publish a lot of words. She, like me, wrote an email every single day to her list. She had thousands of emails lying around, waiting to be useful again. Rather than start from scratch, Kat gathered up all those emails, categorised them, edited them, topped and tailed them, and turned them into a book. She did some other stuff, too—added introductions, conclusions, calls to action, and the like—but mostly, she stitched her book together from material she already had.

If you're familiar with Robin Sharma, you may know he did something similar. He's written several books, one of which is called *Daily Inspiration from The Monk Who Sold His Ferrari*. It's a collection of his motivational thoughts and quotes, and I have a copy on my desk. It's lovely to dip into every day.

If your marketing strategy includes publishing articles, blogs, daily emails, short social media posts, videos, podcasts, newsletters, magazines, and the like, you may be able to do something similar. If not, take a look behind door number two…

## 2. Start From Scratch

I'm writing this book from scratch. Some folks call this the "hard" way. I suppose they're right, as far as it goes; writing a book is hard. But this method does have a few advantages over the "easy" way I've described. If you write your book using the framework I share with you in these pages, you'll have a strong structure and narrative, and your message will flow.

The danger in compiling a book from articles, blogs, and emails is it can feel a little tumbled together. There's nothing wrong with that if it's what you want, and such books are great to dip in and out of—as I mentioned with Robin Sharma's *Daily Inspiration*—but if you want to write a how-to book or cement your expert positioning, starting from scratch can be more effective.

I'll share a little-known secret with you: it's more difficult to edit than it is to write. At least, it is for me. You'll see what I mean when you get to the editing part of your book (unless you pay someone to do it for you, in which case sit back in bliss while your editor does the hard work).

This method is my method. There is a third option, though…

## 3. The Hybrid Method

The third way to write a book is a mixture of methods 1 and 2. In fact, this is how I wrote my first book *Business For Superheroes*, and I'm sure I'll write other books this way, too.

I'm a writer; I write words for a living. I have literally millions of words on the subject of writing.[1] I have hundreds of articles about writing, running a business, and marketing. There's no sense in reinventing the wheel. There's no honour or glory in dressing yourself in a hair shirt and indulging in unnecessary self-flagellation. If you've got material there already—for goodness' sake, use it!

Before you go any further on this book-writing journey, do this

---

1   Joe and I worked this out a while ago, and our conservative estimate was well over a million words. No wonder I'm knackered.

for me: gather all the material you've already written (or spoken or filmed) on the subject. Put it in your book research folder in Scrivener or on Evernote, or simply on your computer. You'll need it. Then, when you've written your outline (which I'll show you how to do in Chapter 9), you'll know what you need to write from scratch and what to pull in and reuse from elsewhere.

## Your Genre

Now it's time to choose your genre. Your non-fiction genre, I mean; we're probably not talking thrillers, or comedies, or horrors here (although if you have horror or comedy stories that illustrate a point you might want to make, throw them in there because stories are the heart of teaching, learning, and marketing).

You might not be sure about your genre, so let me give you an idea of what's available to you.

We've already talked about writing an anthology: simply gather up previous articles you've written. Or, write a book made up of chapters contributed by different authors. I recently edited a book for one of my clients in which he did the bulk of the first draft, then added in chapters from contributors to add depth to the subject.

If you want to position yourself as an expert, you'll want to write a particular type of book; one that weaves your narrative as the go-to expert in your industry throughout. Simon Sinek does this with his book, *Start With Why*. It positions him as a leadership expert (which he is) as well as giving you a philosophy to work with. Direct marketing godfather Dan Kennedy threads his expert status narrative through every book he writes.

*Walk Yourself Wealthy* by my good friend and Moxie Author Dom Hodgson is a super example of an expert positioning book: Dom is the UK's leading pet business expert, and this is only one of the books he's published on the subject.

You might want to write a straightforward how-to book, which walks you through, well, how to do something. Like *Decisive* by Chip and Dan Heath: how to make better choices in life and work. Or *Deep Work* by Cal Newport, all about how to focus and do higher-quality work.

You might want to write a memoir that helps solidify your expert status, like Elizabeth Gilbert did with *Eat, Pray, Love*—or Richard Branson's *Losing My Virginity*.

Motivational books are popular, like Steven Covey's *The 7 Habits of Highly Effective People* (a great book, if you ignore the preachy bits) or *The Go-Giver* by Bob Burg (a brilliant little parable, which you should definitely read—if for no other reason than it'll show you a different way to write a book).

You could write a book of quotes, like *The Founding Fathers: Quotes, Quips, and Speeches* by Gordon Leidner. He gathered more than 200 utterances from the Founding Fathers of the United States of America and bound them in a book. Simple and effective.

And, of course, there's the ever-popular self-help book, such as *The Chimp Paradox* by Professor Steve Peters or *The Miracle Morning* by Hal Elrod, to name two books that never fall out of favour.

Or, you could write a workbook, like *The 12-Week Year Field Guide* by Brian Moran or *The Little CBT Workbook* by Dr Michael Sinclair and Dr Belinda Hollingsworth.

You'll likely find yourself writing a book that combines more than one genre, like how-to and expert positioning. Your book may not fit into any one single style, and that's okay. This exercise is all about figuring out the type of book you want to write and making sure you get all the ingredients correct.

## Your Book's Purpose

Your book's purpose will influence the type of book it is. I wrote both my books—this one and *Business For Superheroes*—because they're the books I wish I'd had when I was at a certain stage in my business.

When I wrote *Business For Superheroes*, I didn't really know what I was doing. I read blog posts, articles, and various books on writing—but there wasn't a course (that I could find) or a book (that appealed to me) on how to write the type of book I wanted to write. To write it, I cobbled together useful information from all over the place. I gathered everything I'd learned from my mentors and noted how I'd used it, putting my own spin on things. I collated all the relevant email sequences, articles, and newsletters I'd written.

I already knew what I wanted my book to do for my reader: be a crash course in how to start and run a business more successfully than most small businesses manage. I knew who I was writing for. So my next task was to construct an outline. Then I started writing, and when I got going, it only took me 90 days.

From that experience, I created my course—*Published in 90 Days*. And a few years later, I wrote this book.

*How The Hell Do You Write A Book?* came from a desire to share everything I've learned and everything I've done over the past few years writing my own books, ghostwriting and editing clients' books, and teaching other business owners how to write books. I want it to help you write your book and avoid some of the mistakes I made at the beginning of my author adventures.

If you have a business already, you probably want your book to show your authority and help you find new opportunities. It's the hook that'll bring people into the rest of your business. Some call it the "ultimate business card" model, but it's much more than that. It's an introduction to you and your expertise, and it'll build a strong relationship with your readers. It's an entry point for your other, related, products and services. You might have an existing audience, and you want to write a book that will help them do something or achieve something.

Whatever your reasons for writing your book, it should give you an idea of the type of book you want to write. Once you've decided on your genre, you can start thinking about how your reader will use your book—what its structure is. Chapter 8 will walk you through the bones that make up the structure of your book.

But first, take these Tiny Beetle Steps.

## Tiny Beetle Steps

1. Gather your material. If you have blogs, articles, newsletters, podcasts, videos, and emails lazing around doing nothing, corral them together and get them working for you as the basis for (at least part of) your book. Start categorising and organising this material. Trello and Evernote will be extremely helpful here.

2. Choose your genre (or crossover genre, if you don't fit neatly into one box. Which is fine, by the way; I consider this book to be a mix of how-to, inspiration, and positioning).

## CHAPTER 8

# Your Book's Skeleton

*"Today's scientists have substituted mathematics for experiments, and they wander off through equation after equation, and eventually build a structure which has no relation to reality."*

*Nikola Tesla*

My husband and I are renovating a cottage that dates from the late 1600s. It's a massive project, involving demolition of ugly newer lean-tos, replacing unsuitable materials that are damaging the fabric of the building, and generally restoring it and making it beautiful.

One of the tasks is to pull out the concrete lumps around the timber frame because concrete rots timber… and replace it with new, breathable, lime-plastered panels. There's a lot of this to do, and when you look at how much work it is, you tend to want to hide under a blanket until it goes away.

We could just look at the task and gibber (and, to be fair, we did do that for a year) or we could make a plan and figure out what to do. We figured out the structure, then built the new wall panels around it.

The old, wet, brick and concrete came out to leave the timber frame. We built a wooden "picture frame" to hold the cork panels, then layered the cork using lime adhesive, and finally coated the cork with lime plaster.

We planned the structure, then filled it. Working from such a framework takes the job from, "Where on earth do I start?" to "We start from here."

If you're going to write a book, you need a structure and some understanding of how everything fits together. This isn't the same as your outline—we'll come to your outline in Chapter 9—because there's some structural work to do even before then. Let's look at your book's skeleton; the bones holding it up.

The reason this chapter comes before the one on outlining is because I want to ease you into writing. When you decide on your skeleton, you'll have more of an idea of what your book will look like, and writing it will seem a little less daunting.

Plus, you can create a few of the more straightforward elements straight away to get you started. Motivation comes from action and small wins, so if you struggle to get writing, try working on one of these structural elements, so you make progress.

If you take a couple of non-fiction books from your bookshelf, you'll notice similarities and conventions. Some content common to each of them. Different books contain different bones, but they all add up to a skeleton holding up the main body of the work. I've included some examples so you can see what other authors have done. These structural elements are essential because, like a picture frame, they give the main book some context and extra information, so it hangs together neatly and makes more sense. Your reader will expect certain details from your book.

This chapter is all about the structural elements you can include in your book. You don't have to include all these elements, but some of them are compulsory. Remember, it's your book, and you make the rules: if you don't want to include an optional element, don't! You don't have to. Look at what other authors have done and decide if something similar might work for you.

I've split this chapter into three sections:

1. Front matter (all the gubbins at the start of a book, which doesn't have page numbers).

2. Main body (the book proper—your main message).

3. Back matter (the finishing touches and factual references).

## Front Matter

This is the stuff that sits at the front before the book really gets going. Some of it is compulsory, some isn't. Look at the front of this book for some ideas—and check out other non-fiction books on your bookshelf, too.

These structural elements are listed in the order they usually appear in (if they're used at all).

- **Praise for the book** (optional): If you're fortunate enough to get people to read your book before you've published it, ask them for feedback. If it's good feedback, include it here. If it's bad feedback and it's funny, you could also consider adding it here! This element is optional.

- **Other books by the author** (optional or could go at the end): (Ooh look—you could write more than one book!) If you've written more than one book, list the others here.

- **Book Half Title:** The very first page of your book containing the title only—no byline[1] or subtitle.

- **Frontispiece** (optional): A decorative or informative illustration on the verso[2] page facing the title page. The frontispiece is different from decorated endpapers or an illustration on the title page. It's a little advert for your book, dating from the days before blurbs on the back cover or online advertising pages for books. It's like an intelligent version of a #mybookisbrilliant tweet, and I'd love to bring the frontispiece back…

- **Title Page:** This page shows your full book title and subtitle, your name, and any co-writer or translator's names.

- **Copyright Page:** This page contains the copyright notice, including the year of publication and the name of the copyright owner (usually the author, but sometimes

---

1 A byline is a line at the start of a book (or beginning of a news story) giving the writer's name.

2 In publishing jargon, a "verso" page is a left-hand page; a "recto" page is a right-hand page.

an organisation or company). It may also list the book's publishing history, permissions, acknowledgements, a biographical note on the author, publisher's address, country of printing, impression line, ISBN[3], ISSN[4], original language information, paper durability statement, and disclaimers.

- **Dedication** (optional): a short shout out to someone you want to dedicate your book to.

- **Epigraph** (optional): a phrase or quotation that sums up the feeling of your book. The epigraph may appear facing the Table of Contents or facing the first page of text. Include the author's name if you didn't write the quote or phrase.

- **Table of Contents:** This is where your section and chapter titles will sit, plus page numbers for your printed book. If you're publishing an ebook too, you won't need page numbers, but you will need a linked Table of Contents so your reader can click and go straight to that chapter. Your Table of Contents ought to read like a series of intriguing little headlines... but I'll come back to that.

- **Foreword** (optional): This is a short piece written by someone else, often an industry expert, to introduce your book and give extra credibility to you or your subject.

- **Preface** (optional): this is your chance to talk to your reader outside the framework of the book. You might want to talk about why you wrote the book, what your experience of writing has been, and how you've written the book. You can mention any research methods you used or people who helped you.

- **Acknowledgements** (optional): This is where you thank

3   International Standard Book Number, a unique commercial book identifier, assigned to each separate edition and variation of a book. I buy mine via my printer, Bill Goss—but you can buy them from www.nielsenisbnstore.com.

4   International Standard Serial Number. Same as the ISBN, but for journals and periodical magazines.

everyone who's helped you write your book. You don't have to include acknowledgements, but it's a good idea. If you put them at the front, they go after your Preface. Or you can choose to put them at the end, like me. Oh—and make them interesting, so people want to read them!

You're probably wondering how to deal with some of these elements—don't panic. In Chapter 9, I'll go through options for creating your Table of Contents, then in Chapter 10, I'll walk you through how to get a foreword (if you want one) and how to write your preface and acknowledgements (if applicable).

## Main Body

This is the cheese and potatoes of your book: it's where your main message goes. Here's what you need to include...

1. **Introduction:** This is where you set up what the book's about, what your reader can expect, and what you want your reader to be able to be, do, have, and know by the time they've finished reading. You make your promise in your introduction and explain how you'll fulfil it. We'll cover how to write your introduction in Chapter 11.

2. **Section Opening Page** (optional): if you've divided your book into sections, as I have here, your section pages sit within the main body.

3. **Chapters:** the main "chunks" of your book, each dealing with a distinct idea. In Chapter 12, I'll show you how to write chapters people want to read.

4. **Conclusion:** Here's where you'll sum up the book and recap your core ideas. You need a conclusion, so your book doesn't simply fall off a cliff and leave your reader wondering what happened. (See Chapter 13.)

5. **Call to Action/Next Steps** (optional): Although this section is optional, you'd be foolish to waste this opportunity to lead your reader onto the next steps to working with you.

In Section II of this book, you'll find everything you need to know about how to write the main body of your book.

## Back Matter

Here's where all the final bits and bobs go. If you put your acknowledgements at the back of your book, they should be the first element of the Back Matter.

- **Appendices** (optional): If you have information or examples which don't fit in the narrative, but add to the book and the reader's experience, include it in appendices. For instance, in my appendices, I've included my Writer's Toolbox and other information I thought you'd find helpful. Include appendices online instead, if you want.

- **Glossary** (optional): If you use lots of technical terms or jargon, include a glossary. One of my ghostwriting clients is a lawyer, and we put a glossary in each of her books.

- **Bibliography or References:** This is where your reference material goes—vital if you've quoted other work.

- **Index** (optional): an index is useful if you want to help readers find lots of specific information fast.

- **About the Author:** This can go in the front or back. I choose to put mine at the end, but it's a personal choice. It can be as long or short as you like; it's your bio and gives your reader a chance to get to know a little more about who you are and what you do.

- **Colophon** (optional): A brief note at the end of a book describing the text typography and naming the typeface, together with a brief history of it if you're a nerd like me. It may credit the book designer and others involved in the book's physical production. A colophon is usually only used for a specially designed or produced book, but I find them useful and interesting. Bring back the colophon!

## Your Book Structure

Don't worry about all the technical bits and bobs at this stage. I want you to be aware of what you can include if you wish to, and what you should include, so you can start building a picture of what your book structure will look like.

There's plenty of information on my blog about front and back matter—plus you can noodle around in the resources area on my website for more details.

Remember, it's your book and your choice—you can include as much or as little of these elements as you like. The only ones that are compulsory are:

- Book half title
- Title page
- Copyright page
- Table of Contents[5]
- Introduction
- Chapters
- Conclusion
- Bibliography or References
- About the Author[6]

In Appendix II, I've shared a few examples of what other authors have chosen to include in their book structures.

Once you've thought about the structure of your book, you'll be able to start on the outline. Which is what we'll be doing next. Take these Tiny Beetle Steps, then press on to Part II, where we'll get all your ideas down on paper. You're going to learn how to outline like a *boss*—so writing your book will be easier than you ever thought possible.

---

5    Some authors choose to omit the Table of Contents—for example, Peggy Noonan's *On Speaking Well* does not include a ToC. I think this is a mistake because it's difficult to find information if you're just dipping into the book.

6    Some may say this is optional; for a business owner, it's compulsory. The whole point of writing a book is to help potential clients and other interested people get to know you, so you can grow your business.

## Tiny Beetle Steps

1.  Look through a few books on your bookshelves and in libraries to see what front and back matter they include. Make a note of any features you like. There are four examples in Appendix II.

2.  Make a note of what you want to include in your structure. (Remember: you can change your mind at any time.)

3.  Every time you reference a book or an article, make a note of it and include all the information you need to add. Start now. I recommend using the Harvard Reference System—but whatever system you use, be consistent. Don't leave this until the end because it'll be a nightmare trying to remember what you referenced and where it was.

PART II

# Build Your Book Step
# By Tiny Beetle Step

*"Many painters are afraid of the blank canvas, but the
blank canvas is afraid of the painter who dares and who
has broken the spell of "you can't" once and for all."*

*Vincent Van Gogh*

## CHAPTER 9

# Outline Like A BOSS

*"If you don't know where you are going,
you'll end up someplace else."*

*Yogi Berra*

Do you do any kind of sport? Do you warm up before you get stuck in? I bloody hope you do, or you'll get injured. Writing an outline is like a warm-up session for your writing. It's critical.

Whenever I look at a sales page, or an article, or an email—or read a book—I can almost always tell whether or not the writer has taken the time to write an outline… or if they've just dived in and started pouring words out of their eyeballs onto the page.

If what I'm reading is chaotic, psychotic, or just plain confused I can pretty much bet my favourite pair of shoes the writer hasn't created an outline.

I read confusing copy all over the internet, in magazines, on blogs, and on websites. And I see confused text arrive in my critique box all the time.

Sometimes the writing starts out pretty well, then stops for a cider and wanders off track.

Other pieces of writing stumble right at the start, and never really get going.

Be honest: does that sound like what happens when you try

to write? There's no shame in it because if you're not a writer by trade, I bet you don't particularly enjoy writing… right?

I will help you change all that. I shall explain why writing an outline is so important, and give you a simple structure you can follow: the Moxie Book Blueprint.

## How To Enjoy Writing

"You there! Get up off your couch and run the London Marathon for me! Right now!"

What? What's that you say? You can't possibly do that, it's crazy, and you'll injure yourself? Quite right too.

So why would you sit down and attempt to write an entire book, from scratch, off the top of your head, risking injury to life, limb, and sanity? Answer: you wouldn't. Or, at least, I hope you wouldn't.

There are some writers out there who can sit down at their keyboard and let the pyroclastic flow of words smash through uncertainty. But those writers are few and far between. In fact *whispers* I think they're a myth.

Or, at least, they're the Stephen Kings of this world, who've been writing novels for 3,864 years and can write in their sleep.

For the rest of us mere mortals, I present this: how to outline your book *Like A BOSS*.

By the time you've finished working through this chapter, your book will have practically written itself. I am not kidding, nor exaggerating: you will have done the bulk of the initial hard work, and you will be amazed at how optimistic you feel. I promise.

Ready?

Okay. Let's start with your Big Idea, the one we looked at in Chapter 4. Your Big Idea will underpin your outline. It's your framework for success, which will become your Table of Contents. But let's not get ahead of ourselves.

Take out your Big Idea and look at it. Start by asking what your readers need and want to know most about the subject. In fact, if you have an email list, fire out a quick survey—much as I did before I created my *Published In 90 Days* book-writing course.

I asked my list three questions only (variations of the ones I suggested you ask in Chapter 4):

1. Have you ever considered writing a book?
2. If not, why not?
3. If you could sit down with me for half an hour and ask me anything about writing and publishing your own book, what would you ask?

I got some brilliant (in the sense they were illuminating) answers. Some of the answers confirmed that what I was doing was spot on; others gave me ideas to cover things I hadn't thought of—or at least, not in that amount of detail.

Survey your contacts. Even if you only get a few answers, they'll help you write your outline. Start broad. Start with what your readers most want to know about your topic.

I started with the idea that business owners—those who are my ideal clients—want to feel genuinely confident in their own expertise. I know that a great way to build confidence, stand out from the crowd, and position yourself as an expert is to write a book. I wanted to show people who want to write a book how to do it, and what success looks like.

## Your High-Level Moxie Book Blueprint

My Big Idea eventually crystallised into the horror most business owners express when I suggest that they could, in fact, write their own book. Where on Earth do they start? *How do they actually, physically, sit down and write a book*—much less finish it in ninety days? Within that Big Idea, it gave me these Chapter Ideas:

- Who you're writing for and why.
- How to come up with good ideas and a compelling hook.
- Preparing to write.
- Silencing your inner critic.

- What the structure of a book should look like.
- How to create a detailed outline.
- How to avoid boring people.
- The biggest mistakes most would-be authors make.
- The importance of shitty first drafts.
- How to write an introduction.
- How to structure a chapter.
- How to write a conclusion and call to action.
- How to keep going when you just want to cry into a bottle of gin.
- Editing for beginners.
- Storytelling.
- Publishing.
- The other details.

These topics may look familiar (hint: they're the basis for this very book). This isn't the order they started out in or finished in, and they're not the chapter titles I ended up with… but this is where it all started.

At this point, get your ideas down on paper. Paper and pen are suitable for this stage, I find, but whatever floats your boat. Don't worry about the order—you'll discover when you flesh out the details and start writing, you'll change your mind about what order works best.

I changed my mind several times; then again, after Joe (my husband) scribbled, "Why is this here?" in several places on my manuscript. Then I changed my mind *again* after a wonderfully enlightening conversation with my beta reader, John H.

I have seventeen subtopics here in my initial Moxie Book Blueprint. The final book, you'll notice, has 25 chapters. That's quite a lot, but these chapters are nice and short. There's a good reason: I'm writing a how-to book, and I don't want to overwhelm you with giant chapters and massive tasks. My whole aim is to get you to write your book as fast and as well as you can—without driving you into a bottle of 8 a.m. gin.

There's no real right or wrong about how many chapters you should have, but I suggest you aim for ten to start with, especially if you're writing more of a positioning book, a self-help book, or a memoir.

You might end up with seven chapters, or nine, or fourteen. It really doesn't matter. The most important thing is that you say everything you want to say, and that it makes sense.

## What Ideas Do You Want To Include?

It will be tempting to write down every single idea in your head at this point, so stay focused. I'll show you how to trim down your outline later in this chapter, but try not to let it get out of hand right now.

Start with your Big Idea and what you want your reader to get out of your book, then make sure each Chapter Idea you note down relates to it directly.

Let's take a look at *Made to Stick* by Chip and Dan Heath. Of course, I don't know how they wrote their book—but I can take a guess. I reckon they probably started out with a Big Idea—why some ideas are so persistent, and others sink without a trace—and went from there.

Looking at their table of contents, you can see what they wanted to include as their main chapter topics:

- Simple—why sticky stories must be simple.
- Unexpected—memorable ideas are also surprising.
- Concrete—why abstract ideas are forgettable.
- Credible—memorable stories must be believable.
- Emotional—and they must make you feel something.
- How to write sticky stories.

At the start, the Heaths write an introduction (What Sticks), and at the end, they add an epilogue and some sticky advice. Their Big Idea is all about sticky stories, and the chapters are all about understanding why some stories are successful, while others vanish.

## Chunking Your Chapters

Once you've listed your main Chapter Ideas, we drill down a little deeper. Take your top Chapter Idea, and consider what you could write about within the chapter.

Let's start with my first Chapter Idea: your book as the beating heart of your business. I drilled down and decided on these chapter chunks for Chapter 1:

- Why write your book?
- Excuses business owners make for not writing a book.
- I don't have anything new to say.
- Why would someone buy my book when they can just Google the information?
- I don't know enough.
- I'm not interesting enough.
- I don't have enough to say.
- I don't have time.
- My competitors will steal my secrets.
- I don't want to give away too much.
- I'm not a writer.
- Never a better time to write.
- Actions.

I've broken down "why a book can be the beating heart of your business" into chunks that make sense. They all feed back into my Big Idea of "how to write a business book people will want to read."

In *Made To Stick*, Chip and Dan Heath break their first chapter "Simple" down like this:

- Finding the core of an idea.
- Why you shouldn't bury your lead.

- Keep things simple (one idea at a time).
- How finding the core helps us make decisions.
- Sharing the core of your idea.
- Simple = Core + Compact.
- Why proverbs last.
- The Pomelo Schema.
- Complexity from simplicity.
- Pitching stories to Hollywood.
- Generative analogies.
- The power of simple.

If you can break your first main chapter idea down like this, your chapter starts to look promising. Certainly less blank-pagey and scary, right?

Once you've got your chapter chunks down, start to mess around with the order. The flesh of the book will become clearer to you as the bones move into the right place. Move the chapters around. Change the order of the chapter chunks. See which ideas follow on most naturally from the others. Get a feel for how your book will flow. Take it one chapter at a time.

If you're a touchy-feely person and you have plenty of room, you might find it useful to grab a load of coloured Post-It notes and a giant piece of paper. Move your ideas around and categorise them. If you don't have the space or inclination to faff around with bits of paper, use something like Trello or—better still—Scrivener. Scrivener allows you to pop all your chapters up onto a "cork board" as "index cards" and you can move them around. It's brilliant.

## The Tiny Points

Next, we'll dig even deeper because although you've now got your main chapter ideas and your chapter chunks, it's time to take your outline even further.

Take your first main chapter idea and start with the first bullet point—the first chapter chunk. Then break that down, too. Write down the tiny points you want to make about that chunk. Think of these as your paragraphs within the chunks in your chapter. Here's an example from this book:

Main Chapter Idea: *The beating heart of your business* | Chapter Chunk: *Why write your book* | Tiny Points:

- Core message.
- Shows everyone you're serious.
- Makes you sticky.
- Opens doors.
- Boosts credibility.
- 24/7 sales machine.
- Lets you charge more.
- Demonstrates your authority.
- Endows you with gravitas.
- Levels up your confidence.
- Builds connections.
- Takes your business in a new direction.
- Short-cuts relationship-building.
- Generates high-quality leads.
- Repurpose into new products.

Once I've listed out the tiny points for each of my chapter chunks, I'm starting to really get into the meat of this chapter.

Let's look at an example from *Made To Stick*. The first chapter chunk—finding the core of an idea—is called "Finding The Core At Southwest Airlines". The authors make the following tiny points within this chunk:

- The enormous performance gap between Southwest Airlines and its competition.
- Success through reducing costs.
- Southwest's "Commander's Intent"—their core idea.
- Southwest is a fun place to work.

- Elegance and prioritisation, not dumbing down.

Once you've split your chapters into chunks and your chunks into individual points, there's not much more to do to complete your Shitty First Draft except flesh it out into proper prose: pages, paragraphs, sentences, and words—and although that might still sound daunting, it's much easier with this framework in place.

## A Note On The Table Of Contents

When you create your high-level Moxie Book Blueprint, remember it'll eventually become your Table of Contents—and your Table of Contents is a persuasion tool. It's not enough to get people to look at your book and consider it; you want them to read it, too. What's the first thing you do when you're deciding whether to buy a new book (after you've read the front and back covers)? You open it up and read the contents.

If the Table of Contents puts you to sleep, you're probably not going to buy it. But if it tickles your pickle and intrigues you enough for you to want to read on, well… you'll probably buy the book. Your contents should read like a list of headlines. A headline has one job: to make you read the first line. Your contents headings have one job, too: to make you want to read the chapters they're pointing you towards.

There's no rule stating your contents must look a certain way. In *Expert Secrets*, Russell Brunson divides his contents into five sections, each containing the chapters—which he calls "Secrets".

In *The Bullet Journal Method*, Ryder Carroll divides his contents into five sections, too—then lists his chapters and sub-chapters underneath them. In *Made To Stick*, Chip and Dan Heath create intriguing little mini-stories under each chapter title. Take a look at the top of page 122, and you'll see what I mean.

The *Made To Stick* contents work well because they're intriguing mini-stories under each chapter title. The standard approach— merely listing the chapters and perhaps the sub-chapters—works well because it's easy to navigate and it's what you expect to see.

---

CHAPTER 1
SIMPLE
25
Commander's Intent. THE low-fare airline. Burying the lead and the inverted pyramid. It's the economy, stupid. Decision paralysis. Clinic: Sun exposure. Names, names, and names. Simple = core + compact. Proverbs. The Palm Pilot wood block. Using what's there. The pomelo schema. High concept: *Jaws* on a spaceship. Generative analogies: Disney's "cast members".

---

Other authors use other methods. Some books don't have a table of contents at all (see Peggy Noonan's *On Speaking Well*)— but I don't recommend you leave your contents out.

How you lay out your contents in your finished book is entirely up to you—but ensure it makes sense to your reader, entices them to read on, and makes it easy to navigate.

## Create A Scrapbook

As you're building your Moxie Book Blueprint, you'll probably have lots of random thoughts about what to include—stories, statistics, examples, evidence, and ideas for how to add value for your reader. Don't wait until you're working on the relevant part of your book outline—write them down now, in case you forget.

In Chapter 12, you'll find a Chapter Grid that gives you a little space to drop in your ideas. But I recommend you also create a Scrapbook to sit alongside your Moxie Book Blueprint: every time you think of a story, a case study, a quote, or another reference you might want to include in your book to illustrate your message, note it down in your Scrapbook.

Top tip: jot down precisely where you found it—the exact page number in the book, the URL, the podcast episode. I use Scrivener to do this because I can keep everything related to my book in one big book file. All the chapters sit within the manuscript part of the file, and then I have a Scrapbook where I dump everything else. I don't have to wonder where it is; I simply scroll down the navigation bar on the left-hand side and find what I'm looking for.

Make notes as and when you find ideas because it'll save you hours of pain and suffering later when you collate your references. All the extra stories, facts, quotes, and stats will bring life to your book. You don't have to do anything with them now except save them, so you know where to find them when you start writing. If you try to incorporate them into your outline or stuff them into your writing immediately, you'll get bogged down in the details and end up with an overstuffed book. At the moment, we're getting your ideas down on paper and organising them.

## The Lint Trap

Once your ideas are all down on paper, it's time to sort through them—and discard anything that doesn't relate to your Big Idea. You know how you need to empty the lint trap in tumble dryers every now and then? You'll do the same thing with your book when you've written the outline.

One of the biggest mistakes would-be authors make is adding too much padding. We want your book to be fluff-free. Outlining your book in the way I've shown you will help you do that. You need to get rid of the fluff that's clogging your book.

I know how hard it is to delete stuff you've painstakingly written, though, so I'm not going to make you do that. I'm asking you to put it somewhere else.

Open a file on your computer (or a document in Scrivener) and call it The Lint Trap: in it will go every idea that doesn't directly add value to your book or directly relate to your Big Idea—because although writing coaches (including me) will tell you to kill your darlings, you don't have to annihilate them.

If what you've noted down in your Moxie Book Blueprint doesn't fit easily into your Big Idea, take it out. You'll almost certainly use it somewhere else—in another time, another place, another book.

This book you're writing doesn't have to be titanic. It's not *War and Peace*. You do not have to include every tiny thing that pops into your head. The beautiful thing is, you get to decide what your reader needs to know—and what they don't. You get to share the fascinating and valuable ideas—and leave out the boring stuff.

## Start Your Moxie Book Blueprint

How do you feel about writing your book now? Hopefully, it doesn't feel like such an unattainable piece of wizardry... but if you still feel overwhelmed and a little bit scared, start outlining your book. Outlines have magical powers.

Take the Tiny Beetle Steps opposite and defeat the Blank Page of Doom. Getting your ideas down on paper will give you the confidence to carry on, I promise.

While you're doing it, try to let go of your need to be perfect (yes, I can see right into your brain, sunshine). We're just throwing ideas around here. Remember, at the moment we're in Shitty First Draft stage. What you write doesn't have to be great. It doesn't even have to be good. You just need to start.

Are you ready to move on? After you've taken these Tiny Beetle Steps, your Moxie Book Blueprint will be ready. The bones of your book will be there waiting for you to put flesh on them. When you've finished outlining, you'll have your book right there on paper.

## Tiny Beetle Steps

1.  Download my Moxie Book Blueprint Grid from www. moxiebooks.co.uk/moxie-book-resources and use it to create your own outline. You'll find a couple of examples from when I wrote this book to help you.

2.  Identify the topics people most want to know about relating to your Big Idea. Write them into your Moxie Book Blueprint Grid.

3.  Drill down into each Main Chapter Idea, and decide which smaller ideas you want to cover. These are your Chapter Chunks. Don't worry too much at this stage, and don't go into too much detail—get the bullet points down so you can see the shape of your chapters.

4.  Dig down further into your Chapter Chunks and note all the Tiny Points you want to make or talk about. This is probably where you'll want to start noting down stories, case studies, or references.

# CHAPTER 10

# What Goes First?

*"The fun thing about doing origin stories is you
are introducing the audience to characters."*

*Damon Lindelof*

Imagine you're a superhero. The superhero of your industry, the one who helps your clients change their worlds. What's your origin story?

You get to tell that story, if you want to, in your preface. But wait! What's a preface? I hear you ask. Do I need one? Is it more work? Waaaaaa!

The good news is, you don't need one. Not at all.

There are loads of strong opinions about what you *should* do. You might see people say all non-fiction books should have an introduction. They may say prefaces are only appropriate for memoirs or academic and technical publications. Or forewords are absolutely required if you ever want to be taken seriously. Or you can't have a preface and a foreword in the same book.

I say: tosh.

It's your book; your choice.

Unless you're handing over your book, your rights, and your first-born child to a traditional publishing house (more on that later), you can do whatever the hell you like.

Got it? Good.

That said, I do love a good origin story. Like Damon Lindelof said in the quote at the start of this chapter, it's your opportunity to introduce your readers to your character. In this case—you.

So this chapter is all about how to introduce your book before you get to the introduction. It's about how to write your preface, how to get someone else to write a foreword, and how to write an About the Author page that doesn't read like your first ever CV.

Let's start with your preface.

## What's A Preface?

If you do decide to write a preface, let's call it something else—because "preface" is kind of a stuffy word and it sounds a little like it might be a warning about a boring textbook. You're not writing a boring textbook (I hope). My preface is called On Not Writing because I am a World Champion Procrastinator and it's frankly a miracle this book exists at all.

Go through the books on your bookshelf and see what other authors have called their prefaces—if they've written one at all.

Jenny Lawson called her prefaces (yes, you can have more than one—it's your book, remember!) to *Furiously Happy* "A series of unfortunate disclaimers" and "Note from the author".

Charles Duhigg calls his prologue (another word for preface) to *The Power Of Habit* "The Habit Cure".

And Steven Pressfield splits his preface to *The War Of Art* into three, naming them "What I Do", "What I Know", and "The Unlived Life".

All these notes from the author set the scene for each book beautifully, and give me a glimpse into the author's world, which makes me love each of them a little bit more. Human connection is everything, and this sliver of you at the start of your book helps to create sparks with your reader.

Your preface can be anything you like, really. Do you have a story to tell about why you wrote your book? Or how you wrote it? If so, the preface is the place to do it. Your preface is your opportunity to speak directly to your reader, outside the confines of your core message. If you have something to say that doesn't quite fit anywhere else in your book, now's your chance.

You may think your introduction is enough—and it may well be. A preface is optional. Having said that, I recommend you write one. Your readers want to know more about you, so be an open book. So to speak.

I always include a preface in my books because I always have something to say about why I sat down to write it, what I did, how I changed as a human and all that jazz. It's my chance to tell a story, draw my reader in and give them a little taste of me, the real person—which is crucial if I want to build a relationship with you, my reader.

I mean, you feel like you know me a little now, right? What my motivations are in writing this book, what I care about, what I've struggled with, what my life looks like when I'm writing, and when I'm not.

Remember, your book is your big chance to start and develop a relationship with your reader.

So, let's say you decide you'd like to write a preface. Excellent. Here are a few topics you may want to include—remember, these are suggestions. You don't have to include them all, and you might not want any of them.

Again: it's your book, and it's your choice.

## What Goes Into A Preface?

Writing a book is bloody hard work. Your preface is the place to talk about how hard it was. What was your inspiration for writing this book? Why are you putting yourself through this exquisite hell? Was your message hammering on the inside of your skull trying to escape, only giving you respite when you allowed it to pour out through your fingertips? Tell that story.

Show the reader why they ought to read the book.

How your book came to life is a story all of its own, so tell it. People are interested. Did a special client ask you a question that kindled a fire in your belly? Do you get bundles of questions all on the same topic, and you figured the best way to answer them all was with a book? Tell us that in the preface.

Write about your writing journey in gory detail: what did you struggle with? How did you overcome it? When did you hit the Great Wall of Pain, and how did it make you feel? How have you changed as a person as you've written your book? (Because you *will* change, that I promise you.)

What was your research process—and where did your big breakthroughs land? How long did the book take you to write? If it took you two weeks in Lanzarote, tell us. If it took you ten years in a bedsit, tell us that.

The only rule is: don't repeat yourself. If you're talking about some of this stuff in your introduction, you don't need to repeat it. The introduction is your sales letter for the book, where you set the scene for your reader and persuade them to read on. Your preface is your chance to tell a little of your backstory. Your superhero origin story. And crucially: the preface gives the reader more reasons to read on. My preface might be about me and my origin story, but only in the context of how this book will help you, my reader. I had you in mind with every word I wrote in this book. And you must do the same with yours.

But what about a foreword? Where does that fit in? Aha. I'm glad you asked. Come with me.

## The $1 Million Book Deal

Once upon a time, there was a man named John Romaniello who got a seven-figure book advance for his first book *Man 2.0: Engineering the Alpha* (which he wrote with a co-author). He received a cheque for one million dollars. Not such big news if you're Stephen King or JK Rowling or Steven Pressfield or Oprah Winfrey... but for a first-time author? Totally unheard of, unless you're a US president or something.

A few stats:[1]

- Less than six per cent of all reported book deals get an advance of more than $100,000 (as of 2011, and it's decreased since then).

- Seven out of ten titles do not earn back their advance.

- On average, fewer than 100 Hardcover Nonfiction Bestsellers sell more than 100,000 copies in any one year, and only one or two titles usually sell more than one million copies.

John Romaniello decided he wasn't going to suffer the same fate. He built a company that makes him six figures in profit per month and writing a book was part of his strategy.

He did a bunch of stuff you can read about online, but Romaniello says part of winning this whopping advance was down to credibility: he persuaded Arnold Schwarzenegger to write the foreword. Almost everyone on the planet must have heard of Arnie; when you have the Terminator introducing your book, it gets publishers' attention. The story of how he got to know Arnold Schwarzenegger is fascinating and instructive (if you want to hear the whole thing, head over to Tim Ferriss's blog and read the full story).[2]

You've probably figured out that a foreword is written by someone else—but do you need one? Again, it's entirely up to you. The person you ask to write your foreword should be well-known in your industry because their job is to lend credibility to you and your book. The better known and well-regarded your foreword writer is, the better the reflection on you—especially if you're not particularly well known in your industry (yet).

A foreword introduces you to the reader and usually talks a little about your book, or at least about your work and business.

The person who writes the foreword may write about how you've affected their life, or the impact you've had on your industry, establishing your credibility for you. Think of your

---

1  Ferriss, T. 2013 https://tim.blog/2013/04/15/how-to-get-a-book-deal/

2  Ferriss, T. 2013 https://tim.blog/2013/04/15/how-to-get-a-book-deal/

foreword as a letter of recommendation; a little like a reference for a new job.

It's a recommendation not just for the reader, but for the publisher if you're not self-publishing. If you hope to be traditionally published, a foreword from a well-known person may help you get an agent and a publishing deal. Even if you're not planning to go the traditional publishing route, you may decide you want to include a foreword.

## Asking For A Foreword

Do you have someone in mind? Someone in your industry—or related to it—whom you'd love to endorse your book? Maybe you know of a celebrity who'd be a great credibility booster?

The first thing to do is to make sure your chosen foreworder is a logical choice. You wouldn't approach Helen Mirren to write your foreword if you're writing a book about web design, for example; but you might well contact her if you were writing about breaking into the film industry as a woman.

You might be thinking you couldn't possibly approach someone like Arnold Schwarzenegger or Helen Mirren to write the foreword to your book... but I say: why not? The absolute worst that can happen is they'll say "no" or totally ignore you.

The trick is to find the connection first. John Romaniello didn't have any connection with The Terminator at first—so he made one. He worked long and hard at creating and building enough of a relationship so he could reasonably ask for that favour.

Perhaps you already have a connection with someone famous in your industry—maybe a mentor or a teacher. If that's the case, consider asking them to write your foreword. It's flattering to be asked, so don't freak out.

When you do ask, approach it in a similar way as you would a sales letter: what's in it for them? Why might they be interested in writing an introduction for your book? In Romaniello's case, Arnie wanted to get back into fitness after he'd finished his term as Governor of California, and it made perfect sense for him to write a foreword to a book for a guy at the top of the fitness industry at the time. Romaniello was also writing a lot of the content for Arnie's website. It was win-win for both of them.

Make it as easy as possible for your chosen foreworder to say "yes". Give them a framework to work from if they want (but don't insist on it!) and make sure you send them at least a couple of chapters to read so they know what they're introducing.

Persuading someone to write a foreword for you is no different from convincing anyone to do anything else: build a relationship, find out as much as you can about them, and show them what's in it for them as well as what it'll do for you.

The whole point of a foreword is for someone else, someone who knows you well, to tell part of your story. It's your reader's chance to get to know you from someone else's perspective.

## About You

Unlike your preface and foreword, which are optional, your "about the author" page is compulsory. Even if it's only a couple of paragraphs, write one. It's a horrible, challenging job, I know, but it's worth doing. It's yet another chance for your reader to get to know you a little better.

One of my clients observed that most "about the author" sections are rather dull and often read like a tedious CV or resumé. Nobody is interested in a year-by-year account of the jobs you've done or the qualifications you have. Build your expertise and any qualifications into the story of you—and make it colourful.

You can include it as a few simple lines at the back of your book, as Ryder Carroll did in *The Bullet Journal Method*. Or you can do something longer, as I did.

Ryder Carroll's short bio name-drops some of the big companies he's worked with and some of the famous publications he's featured in, and it mentions the inspiration for the book (his TEDx talk on intentionality at Yale University).

Mine is a little bit silly, like me. I wanted to give you an insight into my life and brain outside writing because writing is most definitely not all I do. So I made a list of 24 Things About Me in case you're interested.

Think of what else people may want to know about you. What do you do outside of your business? What can you tell me to show me you're a three-dimensional human?

Read the "about the author" blurbs in some of your favourite books and note down what you like about their bios, what you don't like, and why. How can you model the good stuff and avoid the bad?

## Tell Your Story

If your title, cover design, and the blurb on the back are your book's shop window then your preface, foreword, and about me sections are your book's welcome mat. Your reader will look at the cover, decide they like what they see, and open it up. If your welcome mat—the preface, foreword, and/or about me sections grab their interest, they'll read on.

I've put some examples of different forewords and prefaces in the resources area of the website to give you some ideas about what you might want to include in your book.

Take the Tiny Beetle Steps on the next page, then push on. It's time to write your introduction.

## Tiny Beetle Steps

1. Decide if you want to include a preface or foreword, or both.

2. Start sketching out your origin story even if you don't want to write a preface—you may change your mind later, or you may want to use it in your introduction or "about the author" section. You'll definitely want to use it to market your book.

3. If you want to include a foreword, make a shortlist of people you'd love to write it, and think about how to make a connection and build a relationship with them.

4. Note down some ideas for your "about the author" section and gather ideas from other books.

CHAPTER 11

# My Name Is Inigo Montoya

*"Hello. My name is Inigo Montoya. You
killed my father. Prepare to die."*

*Inigo Montoya*

If you've seen the classic movie *The Princess Bride*, you'll be
familiar with the quote at the top of this page. But you may
not have considered it as the perfect introduction[1] when meeting
new people.

It's polite.

It gives your name.

It establishes a connection with the person you're meeting.

And it sets expectations.

Which is more or less what your introduction needs to do—
with a few additions and refinements, naturally. At this stage, most
people care more about how your book can help them than about
why you wrote it. Think of your introduction as a sales letter for
the rest of your book. Your reader is thinking, subconsciously,
"What's in it for me? Why should I give up my valuable time
to read this book?" These are splendid questions and you must
answer them in the introduction. Convince your reader not only
to read your book, but to take action on it. Set expectations for

---

1   I saw this on a meme, and it made me laugh, so I've used it here.

what your reader will find when they get going. And allow your reader to get comfortable with you.

Your introduction is not the place for you to "find your voice". I'm sick of hearing writing coaches telling people they need to find their voices. You already have a voice—all you need is the confidence to use it fully.

Your introduction doesn't need to be long, either. Keep it relatively short, so people want to read it, and so it doesn't get in the way of the main body of the book.

## Hook Their Attention

Call your introduction something interesting. Give it a subtitle that makes sense. Capture your reader's attention because you want them to read this part.

Then start with where your reader is now. Too many writers and business owners make the mistake of jumping into their fabulous solution—forgetting their client, their reader, isn't there yet. Think about the last time you were in pain: it takes over your whole world.

When I broke my leg and tore my anterior cruciate ligament leaping dramatically from a galloping horse like Zorro, I remember the pain like a white-hot ball of fire in my knee and in my brain. I remember writhing on the sofa when the painkillers wore off, screaming into my pillow. I remember my world shrinking until there was nothing left but freezing-hot agony.

I couldn't remember life without pain, and I couldn't imagine a future without torment. If someone had arrived then and said, "Hello! You'll be pain-free in a few days, it won't last forever! I have a load of exercises you can do to ease the pain." I would have scowled at them, burrowed further into my pillow, and muttered something that ended in "off".

If someone is mired in their own pain, they won't be able to connect with you if you pile in shouting, "I have the answer! I haven't heard you tell me your problem yet, but that doesn't matter—I have what you need!"

Your reader won't be able to see a pain-free future at the start of your book. Your job is to take them there as they read. It's the same even if your book isn't designed to take away pain. Perhaps you're writing a book to help people achieve a goal, but not necessarily escape from torment. The same principle applies: meet them where they are.

Start by listening. We do that in a book by writing about your reader's current state of affairs. What's their big problem, and what pain is it causing them? What are they dissatisfied with? How are they feeling right now?

If you completed your Weirdo Profile from Chapter 6, this shouldn't be too difficult to do now. You know your ideal reader better than you think. Don't jump ahead. Walk up to your reader, take their hand, and start the journey with them.

## Make A Connection

By doing this, you'll make a connection. Tell a story from your own experience, or from a client's experience. Don't just tell your reader you understand; show them you empathise and demonstrate that you feel what they feel.

Your introduction is your chance to start a relationship with your reader. Don't underestimate how powerful this can be—think about where you read books: in bed, in the bath, on the toilet… it doesn't get much more intimate than that, so don't waste the opportunity.

Once you've made a connection, make your promise. What will your reader be able to have, do, and be by the time they've finished reading your book?

Look back at my introduction in this book: what did I promise you? I promised you by the time you finish this book—if you complete your tasks—you'll have your own book in your hands faster than you ever thought possible.

You'll have a fantastic positioning tool to establish you as the go-to expert in your industry. And, most importantly of all, you'll have the confidence worthy of your skills and experience—confidence enabling you to go out and help more people, more often, more easily. You will be a published author, with all the kudos that goes along with it.

That's a pinpoint specific promise, and I am comfortable making it. I have been there, and so have my students, so I know if you do the work, you'll be grinning at a copy of your own book in a few short months. What's *your* promise to your reader?

## Overcome Their Objections

When you've made your promise, overcome any objections—because your reader will have objections. After all, you're making a bold promise about something they may feel unconfident about. Your reader is in pain, remember? And right now, that pain is swallowing their world.

Even if your reader isn't in pain, they'll still have objections because humans are contrary and cautious. Bring those objections front and centre, then get your cricket bat of truth out and smash them away one by one. What could your reader be sceptical about? What aspect of your promise may make them feel uncertain or insecure? In my introduction, I simply list out all the excuses people give me for why they "can't" write a book of their own, then dismantle them gently. Do the same with your reader's objections.

A disclaimer may help: make it clear not everyone will get the same results. Your method may not be the right method for everyone, so it may not work for some people—and that's okay. Definitely point out your book won't work for them if they don't act on it. Reading on its own is not enough.

## Set Expectations

Humans don't like surprises; not really. Set expectations in your introduction.

What's your book all about? What will your reader discover as they read through it? What's the best way for someone to use your book: dive in and read it all at once? Dip in and out of it, like a motivational book or an instruction manual?

Are there action points and exercises throughout? Tell your reader about them and explain how they work in the introduction, so they know what to expect.

Invite your reader to go on a journey with you, rather than preening on a throne and shouting instructions. If you're honest and real in your introduction, if you do a fantastic job of being yourself and building a relationship, you won't only get happy readers; you'll win loyal fans who rave about your book and recommend it to everyone they know.

## Create A Neat Little Package

Finish your introduction by inviting your reader to take the next step: read the first chapter. Do this with a gentle segue; you don't need to beat anyone over the head with glaringly obvious instructions.

If you're not sure what might work, take a look at the introductions to other books in your industry. You don't have to buy them all; on Amazon, you can "look inside" most books, which usually includes the introduction. Remember, the introduction acts as a sales letter so if you make it available for free and write it well, chances are the reader will buy the book.

Pay attention to the introductions you read: which ones did you find engaging, useful, and entertaining? Which ones made you want to learn more?

Which introductions lost you or actively put you off reading the book? Why?

You could get your reader to make a commitment if you're writing a how-to book or a self-help book, as I've done at the start of this one. I like to extract a promise at the beginning of every book I write and every course I create because if my client makes a declaration or a promise, especially in public, they're more likely to follow through and do the work—and get the results they want.

Here are the elements of a good introduction:

- Hook: what's the hairy problem your reader faces, and what pain is it causing her? Start with a story, if you can.

- Create a connection: introduce yourself, tell your story, and share your experiences.

- Make a promise.

- Overcome your reader's objections.

- Tell your reader how to use the book and set expectations.

- Get your reader to make a commitment to take action on what you've written.

Russell Brunson's introduction to *Expert Secrets* does a beautiful job of hitting all these elements. He uses his introduction to tell the story of how he became a potato gun expert one Spring Break in college, and how his experience led him to create Clickfunnels, and the enormously successful business he's since built teaching others how to become experts and make money.

In *The Bullet Journal Method*, Ryder Carroll tells his story of all his childhood notebooks and the system he built to manage his ADD[2]. He introduces a friend, whom he helped with his system—and how she encouraged him to teach others how to do what he does. He shared how his Bullet Journal has helped people who thought they were unhelpable and promised it'll do the same for the reader. And it tells us how to use his book and what results we might expect.

## Introduce Yourself To Your Reader

Do you feel ready to have a go at writing the first draft of your introduction? Yeah, you do. Don't worry about making it perfect, there's no such thing. Get some notes down on paper.

---

2   Attention Deficit Disorder.

Remember this is your Shitty First Draft. You will definitely want to come back and make some changes to your introduction during the final edit. I changed my Introduction substantially after this book came back from my beta readers because I got feedback telling me it would be helpful to explain why I'd structured things this book as I have. Your book will change as you write it, so your introduction will need to change, too.

You could leave writing your introduction to the very end if you want to, but I'd like you to get your first draft done now to ease you into writing the rest of the book.

Take these Tiny Beetle Steps before you do anything else.

## Tiny Beetle Steps

1. Read a few introductions to popular books, and note down what you like and don't like. Do any ideas come to mind? What format appeals to you? Which introductions were most useful to you as a reader?

2. Outline your introduction using the Moxie Introduction Grid I've provided at www.moxiebooks.co.uk/moxie-book-resources.

3. Write the Shitty First Draft of your Introduction!

# How To Write Chapters People Want To Read

*"What really knocks me out is a book that, when you're all done reading it, you wish the author that wrote it was a terrific friend of yours and you could call him up on the phone whenever you felt like it. That doesn't happen much, though."*

*J.D. Salinger*

Do you want people to read your book? From cover to cover, avidly, and be sad when they've finished it?

Good; because if they do, they'll become the best sales team you could ever hope for. But that's not all. I mean, sales are essential. You're writing this book to boost your business and your credibility; I know that. But that's not the only reason you're writing it, is it?

I've heard experts say it doesn't matter if nobody reads your book; reading your book isn't the point. They say your book is simply a lead generation tool to introduce potential clients to your world. I understand their point of view, and if a business owner just wants a glorified business card, that's up to them. I'd rather the world was filled with wonderful books, not filler books, but I don't always get what I want. A glorified business card is not good enough for me, and I hope it's not good enough for you, either.

I think you, like me, want to write a fabulous book that speaks to people. A book that rocks your reader's world in some small way (or in a titanic way). I think you want to write a book you'll be proud of. Yes, a book that acts as the ultimate sales letter—but it's so much more than just that. To write a better book, you must do something most authors won't do. You must write in such a way that people are compelled to read it, to engage with it, and to act on it.

Most books contain too much tell and not enough story. Too much dry, factual, boring information... but what we want when we're reading is *entertainment*. When we read books, we're in Enjoyment Mode. Unless we're at school or college and working through our required reading list, we read books we choose to bury ourselves in. If those books aren't entertaining or enjoyable, we stop. We put them back on the shelf and forget them.

If you can show your reader a wonderful time, and engage them, they'll read every word you write—all the way to the end, until they've finished. After which they'll hop online and stalk you, so they can find out as much about you as possible. Your reader will join your email list, read your articles, watch your videos, and listen to your podcasts. Then, if you've done your job well, they might buy from you.

If your reader doesn't read right to the end with relish, they almost certainly won't get as far as buying from you. Instead, they'll go in search of a writer who understands how to hit their reading G-spot. Now comes the scary part: you must do this in *every* chapter; not just the first one.

## Asking The Pertinent Question

Let me ask you a question that may raise your hackles: do you think what you're writing about is earth-shatteringly new? Do you think you're the first person to know it, do it, or share it? Do you think, if you're honest with yourself, that your reader can't find everything in your book for free if only they explore the vast vistas of the internet?

I can tell you now: the facts you want to share are almost certainly not new. On their own, they're not interesting. They're probably not groundbreaking.

Your reader can find all those facts, gratis, if they hop onto

Google and search for them. But before you get the hump, let me reassure you: it's the same for me. There are no facts in this book you cannot find somewhere else.

Here's what you *can't* get anywhere else, though: me.

As a reader, I'm not interested in the dry, boring facts of your message. I'm interested in your opinion of the facts. Your experiences, your take on the world—and how it relates to the problem I have. I want to learn from someone I know, like, and trust, and so do you. So do your readers.

Start your chapter with your hook—the big question this chapter is answering. What's the problem your reader expects you to solve? Ask a question, like: "How do you write a chapter people want to read?" Or: "Do you need to wear makeup to look good in photos?" Or: "What makes a story sticky?"

Tell a story to illustrate the problem. If you start one chapter with a question, start your next chapter with a story; mix it up. Then tell me why I should read the chapter. What's in it for me? What are the benefits? Give me a reason to read on, and I'll read on with delight.

Don't start your chapter with instructions. Don't tell me stuff. It's flat and dull, and nobody will want to read it. Your outline is the place for dry facts and notes. When you write your chapter, breathe life into it.

In *The Power of Habit*, Charles Duhigg starts Chapter 3—The Golden Rule of Habit Change—with this story:

"The game clock at the far end of the field says there are eight minutes and nineteen seconds left when Tony Dungy, the new head coach of the Tampa Bay Buccaneers—one of the worst teams in the history of professional football—starts to feel a tiny glimmer of hope."[1]

We know what the chapter is called, but Duhigg doesn't start with facts about how to change habits. He begins with a story, and he makes it emotional. Even if we have no interest in American football (I couldn't be less fascinated by it) he creates tension we

---

1    Duhigg, C. 2012, *The Power Of Habit*, p. 60.

can all understand: the game has a few minutes to go, and our hero's team is the worst team ever. They lose every game they play.

But wait! All may not be lost, because the coach suddenly feels like things are looking up… And we're hooked. Duhigg goes on to tell us more about the game and the stakes involved. Then he talks about Tony Dungy. Then he starts to tell us the story of how Dungy took the worst team in America from losers to winners—and it's all to do with habits.

## Sharing Your Big Idea

This is where things get hot and steamy because I want you to strip yourself bare, steel yourself, and be brave. I want to know what your opinion is—especially if it's contrary or, better still, controversial.

What do you think about the problem you address in this chapter? What do you think about the possible solutions? Keep all that in mind when you structure your chapter because your take on things will keep your reader fascinated.

The middle of your chapter is where you answer your reader's question or solve this particular aspect of their problem. Be specific when you do this and don't wander off on a tangent. Take this chapter as an example: I haven't drifted off-topic to talk about typeface, publishing, or writing the introduction to your book. This chapter is purely about how to write chapters people want to read.

Use case studies and stories relating to your topic, if you have them. If they're stories from your own clients and your own business, all the better; if you don't have any suitable stories, find stories from elsewhere. Haunt Facebook groups and internet forums. Talk to people in real life who have the problem you're solving—then show your reader how you'd solve it for them.

Add compelling statistics and evidence to back up what you're saying. This is where I add my caveat to what I said at the start of this chapter chunk: we want your opinion—but make sure it's based on substantial evidence. Without data, your reader has no reason to believe you. When you gather your information, make a note of it immediately, so you don't waste hours later trying to find out where it came from.

Consider supporting your assertions with quotes and stories from other experts. Their work lends credibility to your own ideas. And if you disagree with them on some aspects of what they do, say so—and explain why!

In the middle of Charles Duhigg's chapter on The Golden Rule of Habit Change, the author brings in his evidence. He talks about the habit loop, and what neuroscientists have found out about how our brains work.[2]

He brings in a variety of case studies and stories about people who've changed damaging habits for healthy ones. But he focuses on the story he started with: Tony Dungy's football team, and the work he did with them to improve their performance by improving their habits.

The middle of Duhigg's chapter 3 follows on perfectly from the start of the chapter. It carries on with the original story, satisfying our human need for a good story—and it backs up that story with many other examples. The whole thing is underpinned by scientific studies, giving us a reason to believe him.

## Wrapping It Up

When you've answered the big question, what's the best way to wrap your chapter up? This is a tough aspect of writing. It's all too easy to tail off into a mumbling ramble—which will leave your chapter stuck in the mud. Get your reader fired up and raring to take action. Get them eager to read the next chapter.

Finish your chapter by summing up your reader's problem, your solution, and your feelings on the matter. Then ask yourself: what now? What do you want your reader to do next? Do you have actions for them to take? Or is the next step moving onto the

---

2   Duhigg, C. 2012, *The Power Of Habit*, p. 72.

next chapter? Whatever you want your reader to do—tell them.

In *The Power of Habit* Chapter 3, Duhigg ends his chapter on a threefold high. He starts with Dungy's football team triumph, finishing the story he began at the top of Chapter 3. He closed the story loop for us, leaving us satisfied.

Next, he summed up everything he covered in the chapter about how we can't break habits, but we can change them.

Finally, and best of all, he left us with hope: we can change our destructive habits, too. If your book is solving people's problems or helping them live better lives, this is crucial. Here's Duhigg's last paragraph:

"We know that change can happen. Alcoholics can stop drinking. Smokers can quit puffing. Perennial losers can become champions. You can stop biting your nails or snacking at work, yelling at your kids, staying up all night, or worrying over small concerns. And as scientists have discovered, it's not only individual lives that can shift when habits are tended to. It's also companies, organisations, and communities, as the next chapters explain."[3]

You'll also notice he gently signposts what's coming next, to keep us interested. Duhigg does this beautifully and seamlessly in one paragraph—and believe me, you are fully capable of doing the same for your book.

## Start Writing

You know enough now to start writing the first draft of your chapters. You have your outline, and you can download the Moxie Chapter Grid to help you sketch out each of your chapters. It may seem scary right now, but I promise you this: if you fill in the grid the way I suggest for each chapter, you'll be well on your way to writing the first draft of your book.

If you know your subject and have plenty of stories and successes to share, your book will be fabulous. After that, it's a matter of learning writing techniques to tie it all together.

---

3   Duhigg, C. 2012, *The Power Of Habit*, p. 93.

When you're feeling nervous about this, remember: readers don't really want your writing. They want your mind. Your writing shouldn't get in the way of your message. Your readers won't get any insight into who you are or what your message is if you don't share your opinions and feelings with them.

And anyway, we're still at Shitty First Draft stage. All you need to do right now is shovel words onto paper, so later you can create a book you'll be proud of. Write your chapters, word by word, section by section, chapter by chapter. Steady and consistent.

Then, when you've built your book piece by piece, you'll be wondering how to end it. Which is what we're covering in the next chapter.

## Tiny Beetle Steps

1.  Download my Moxie Chapter Grid from www. moxiebooks.co.uk/moxie-book-resources.

2.  Note down the big question you're answering or the idea you're introducing.

3.  Write down your opinion—even if it's controversial. Especially if it's controversial. And note down how you feel about it.

4.  Collect evidence—stories, case studies, quotes, and statistics—to back up your opinions and solutions.

5.  Note down the feelings your reader might be having about this topic—the pain they might be feeling, and the features and benefits of reading this chapter.

# CHAPTER 13

# How To End On A High

*"She wanted none of those days to end, and it was always with*
*disappointment that she watched the darkness stride forward."*

*Markus Zusak*

Isn't it the worst? When you've been reading a captivating book,
you've invested time and effort and emotion, and it just…
fizzles out, like a sad birthday candle.

I don't want your book to end that way. You don't want your
book to end that way. And your readers definitely don't want your
book to end that way.

In this chapter, I'll show you how to avoid a sad fizzle—
and instead create an ending that leaves your readers feeling
simultaneously bereft because your book has finished *and*
energised and wanting more.

Your book's conclusion is at least as important as its central
message, and it deserves the same care and thought. We
remember most clearly the beginning of a thing and the end of
it. The conclusion of your book is the lasting impression you'll
leave your reader with.

If you're at all like me, however, you'll get overexcited as the
end draws near; after all the time, pain, and bittersweet tears of
writing a book, we finally glimpse the finish line.

We accelerate as we hurtle downhill. Our chapters and

our tempers get shorter, and relief and resistance bully us into scribbling a few perfunctory lines—and we hope they'll do. They won't do. You may feel like you've nothing of substance left to say, which might be the case—but that doesn't mean your conclusion must leave your reader cold.

The end of your book is more than a simple summing-up. Your conclusion, written well, makes your reader think, feel, and act in a way that'll bring them closer to the results they wanted when they picked up your book in the first place.

If you're genuinely stuck for how to start your conclusion, start it with grace and gratitude. Thank your reader for coming on this journey with you. For trusting you with their hopes and dreams. For believing you can help them reach their goals, whatever they are. Then decide what type of conclusion you want to write.

Most writers won't spend enough time on their conclusion, because they get caught up in the excitement of finishing— or because they're so close to their subject, they can't see the clownfish for the anemones. Don't you be one of them. Think bigger, wider, freer.

And remember this is a marvellous opportunity to advertise your products and services. How else can you help your reader reach their goals? If you've written a fantastic book and your readers love it, they will want more from you. Don't feel uncomfortable about this. Open up old fiction books, and you'll see not just adverts and snippets from other titles at the back, but actual order forms you can cut out and send off. Publishers have always been selling more books to their readers. You can, too.

It's your book, and you can end it any way you like—but if you're stuck, let me give you a hand. For a non-fiction book, you have five main options.

## 1. The "Why Should We Care?" Ending

The most common—and arguably the most effective—way to finish a non-fiction book is the "why should we care" route. You may have addressed this throughout the book—and, in fact, I hope you talked about what's in it for your reader in the introduction—but you can refer to it again in the conclusion.

To avoid repeating yourself like the pub bore, step out from the main focus of your book and look at how your message fits into the bigger picture of your reader's life (and/or business).

What are the implications of your Big Idea—the one you're writing your book about? What does it mean for your reader? What does it mean for your industry? What did your Big Idea mean for you when you first discovered it or started on the process you've been writing about?

Professor Steve Peters uses this ending as a kind of summing up in his book *The Chimp Paradox*. He calls his conclusion "Looking Forward" and notes what kind of changes you might see if you put his book into practice. He talks about change and asks the reader what they'll do to make change happen. Finally, he thanks us and wishes us luck.[1]

He doesn't include any call to action or encourage us to buy from him or read further books, however. I'm sure he's doing brilliantly because he's the leader in his field—a quick look at his website and his work shows us that.

However, he's missing an opportunity. At the end of his book, I was left wondering where to go next. Sure, I can Google—but it's much better if you tell me precisely what my logical next step should be.

## 2. The "What's Next?" Ending

The "what's next" ending is ideal for how-to or self-help books. If you go for this option, you have several choices.

- You can leave the final step of your "how to" process until the conclusion, to wrap everything up neatly and give your reader the last piece of the puzzle.

- You can give your reader the next step: show them how to put your book into action, so it gets tangible results.

1   Peters, S, 2012, *The Chimp Paradox*, Vermillion

- You can explain how to get started all over again. If what you're teaching your reader isn't a one-off skill, or it requires regular practice (like writing or drawing cartoons), use the conclusion to explain how your reader can keep improving.

In *Living Forward*, the authors write a conclusion subtitled "The choice is yours". They don't recap what we've read so far; they give us a choice and encourage us to act. And they tell a final story; a parable about how the power to choose is ours.[2]

Then, in the following pages, they give us the tools to do so: a series of quick guides and life planner examples so we can get started. In the final pages of the book, right at the back, there's a series of adverts for toolkits, online advice, coaching, and productivity tools with clear instructions for how to access them.

In *Expert Secrets*, Russell Brunson does a brilliant job of moving the reader onto the next stage. He sums up his book, then says: "But no matter how good you make a book, it can never be as good as having me or my team work with you personally on your funnel, stories, and presentation. If you'd like to work more closely with us to develop your expert business, I invite you to attend one of our Funnel Hack-a-Thon events."[3] Then he explains how to do so, and tells us how to find him elsewhere online and offline.

## 3. The "Where Are They Now?" Ending

In this ending, you can explore how your reader has changed since they started reading your book—or how you changed as you went through the learning process yourself.

How do the ideas in your book relate to your reader's real-life experience? How will your reader change when they put into practice everything they've learned from you? This can be powerful because we all want to improve ourselves. If you can paint a picture of how your reader's life will be better, or how

2   Harkavy, D & Hyatt, M, 2016, *Living Forward: A Proven Plan To Stop Drifting And Get The Life You Want*, Baker Books, p158.

3   Brunson, R, 2017, *Expert Secrets*, Morgan James Publishing, p263.

their business will be better, or their relationships or their mental health, it will help them take action on what you've written.

*The Bullet Journal Method* is a good, albeit brief, example of a "where are they now?" ending. In it, Ryder Carroll sums up the journey we've been on throughout the book and highlights our increased self-awareness and self-improvement if we do what he suggests.[4]

The book *Write. Publish. Repeat.* is structured slightly differently, but ends with an appendix called "Interviews with successful indie authors"—the perfect "where are they now" ending.[5] The authors show you what you could achieve if you follow the methods in the book.

## 4. The "Cliffhanger" Ending

The cliffhanger ending isn't just for fiction; what if the book you're writing is only one in a series of books? If that's the case, use your conclusion to drop a hint about what's coming up in the next book. This has the added bonus of encouraging people to keep buying and reading your work.

One of my clients is writing a series of four books—at the end of each one, he talks about what's coming up in the next one. When they're all finished, we'll put them together in one chunky volume—and there'll be more to come after that, too.

Another client is writing a series of dog training books, and she's doing the same: at the end of each book, there's a signpost for the next one.

## 5. The "Mix Tape" Ending

Finally, your conclusion can be a combination of endings. In fact, it probably will be. Most of my endings don't fit neatly into any single category.

---

4   Carroll, R, 2018, *The Bullet Journal Method*, Penguin Random House.

5   Platt, S, Truant, J, & Wright, D, 2013, *Write. Publish. Repeat.*, p383.

"Why should we care" and "what's next" go together like cheese and beans. "What's next" and "cliffhangers" are comfortable bedfellows. And everything goes well with "where are they now".

The conclusion you ultimately write will depend on why you're writing the book in the first place. Go back to your why: what do you want your reader to get from reading your book? And what do you want your book to do for you and your business?

In *The Brain Audit*, Sean D'Souza finishes with an epilogue which is kind of a "why I wrote this book". He talks about how the book evolved over the years and editions and the journey he went through writing it. His epilogue ends with a thank you and a gentle invitation to find Psychotactics online.[6] Then he gives us the next step—a system you can easily follow, which leads on perfectly from the book. There's a URL and step-by-step instructions on what to do next.

And finally, Sean gifts us a couple of pages of his brilliant cartoons.

## The Art of Asking

Your why may have changed a little or a lot as you've written your book. That's okay. The important thing is to be clear about your why as you write your conclusion—and as you ask for action.

Knowledge without action is no use to anyone, so what do you want your reader to do now? Do you want them to teach their dog good manners? Do you want them to learn to play the guitar? Do you want them to finally feel comfortable having their photograph taken?

And what do you want them to do next about you? You're reading this book because you want to write a book. You want a way to stand out from the crowd, establish yourself as an expert, and create opportunities you wouldn't otherwise have. You want your book to bring you the right kind of clients and more money.

---

6   D'Souza, S, 2009, *The Brain Audit*, Psychotactics Ltd, p150.

Right? So you need to offer your reader something more before you leave them.

This call to action can go within your conclusion—or you can create a separate chapter afterwards. There's no hard and fast rule; it's up to you. But you must have a call to action, or you're wasting an opportunity.

If your reader loves your book, gets tremendous value from it, and sees results, I guarantee they'll want more on the topic—hopefully from you. If you don't offer them the chance to get more from you, you're missing a trick because they may go to someone else. What can you offer? What's the logical next step? Is it an online course? A discovery call? Coaching?

If you're a photographer who's written a book about how to get the best personal branding photography ever, the logical next step is to invite your reader to book a call with you so you can see if you're a good fit.

In a book on divorce I wrote for my lawyer client, the call to action was always to book a free thirty-minute consultation to see if they could help. They've already pre-qualified the potential client: anyone who reads the whole of your book is likely to be a good fit, and the meeting is a great way to check that—and to find out if they want to work with you.

There's no reason why you can't have more than one call to action. Don't assume your reader will only want the next step, say an inexpensive online course. They may have the will and the money to invest in a higher-ticket coaching programme with you—don't deny them that opportunity.

Present your reader's options in a logical order and explain each option thoroughly. Make it very easy to contact you or take you up on your offer. Make it easy for them to find out as much as they can about you, and get their hands on as much of your content as possible.

You may want to offer free resources, as I've done throughout this book. This is a great way to get people from your printed book or your ebook onto your website, so you can capture their contact details and continue the relationship online. It's particularly important to get readers onto your website if you sell your book through Amazon because Amazon doesn't give you access to your readers' contact details.

In Chapter 24, you'll find out much more about marketing your book and capturing your readers' contact details.

## Tie Everything Together

When your reader finishes reading your book, you want everything to make sense for them. If you have loose ends, tie them up in the conclusion. If you wish to signpost what's to come in future books, hint at it here.

Leave your reader on a high. When you've finished reading this book, I want you to believe you can you write your own book too—not only that, I want you raring to go. I want you to grab a piece of paper and start writing down your Big Idea, noting everything you want to cover, and setting out what you want your reader to do, be, have, and feel.

You're now ready to write the Shitty First Draft of your book. You know what groundwork you need to do, how to create an outline, how to write the introduction and your main chapters—and now you have everything you need to write your ending.

Make sure your ending leaves your reader feeling satisfied, full of confidence, and able to do what you want them to do. Does it empower them and inspire them? Does it make people believe they can change their world, despite all the obstacles in their way?

It's your job to dismantle those obstacles for your reader—just as I will do for you in the next chapter. Because as you're writing your book, you'll hit the Great Wall of Pain and it will seem insurmountable. It isn't. I will help you smash through it.

Then, after we've sorted out The Wall, we'll look at how to take your Shitty First Draft and make it wonderful.

## Tiny Beetle Steps

1. Go back to your why, which you looked at in Chapter 1 and Chapter 6. Is it still your why? Has anything changed? If so, redefine it now.

2. Choose the type of conclusion you want to write—or scribble down ideas for combination endings.

3. What do you want your reader to do next? List out their options.

4. Outline your conclusion using the Moxie Conclusion Grid from www.moxiebooks.co.uk/moxie-book-resources.

5. Write the Shitty First Draft of your conclusion!

## CHAPTER 14

# The Great Wall Of Pain

*"There is nothing to writing. All you do is sit
down at a typewriter and bleed."*

*Ernest Hemingway*

You will want to cry. In fact, you will cry. You will want to
break things. You will want to just stop. And you will want
to fling your book into the great trash compactor of the universe,
never to look at it again. Please don't. This, too, shall pass.

This chapter is all about the Great Wall of Pain—and if
you've ever written a book before, you'll know full-well to what
I'm referring. There will be pain. You will hit the wall. And you
will, for at least a little while, feel despair so deep it's eternal.
Which is why, in this chapter, I shall prepare you to accept the
Great Wall of Pain, then take the sledgehammer of your will to
it, smash it into trifling fragments, and keep going.

If you haven't written a book before, and this is your first bash
at it, let me find an example you may be able to relate to.

Are you a runner, perchance? Or a rower, or a cyclist, or a
climber—or in fact anyone with an active hobby? I'm a runner
and a pole dancer and a trapeze artist, and I am exceptionally
well-acquainted with the Great Wall of Pain. It's that moment,
perhaps two-thirds into your run (or your row or your climb
or your trapeze training session) when your body—or, more

accurately, your mind—betrays you. It sits down, folds its arms, hunches its shoulders, sticks its bottom lip out, and refuses to budge. "We can't!" it says. "We're done. If you make us do any more, we will surely die." Your legs are suddenly carrying sacks of potatoes, there's a bear squeezing your lungs, your last meal is waving at you, and someone seems to have filled the air before you with fog.

This is The Wall. It's enormous. So big, you can't see the top of it. You can't see around it, because it stretches forever. And you can't turn back, because it's encircling you like an oubliette.[1]

There's only one thing for it: we're going to take a sledgehammer to the bastard.

## Arm Yourself

Let's start by arming you, and recognising the false walls that may stall you needlessly. They're called resistance, and I'd like to send you to Steven Pressfield for a little masterclass in how to overcome them. Read *The War of Art*. Keep it on your desk and pick it up every time you feel like flaking out.

Learn to recognise the signs and put coping mechanisms in place. Here are a few of my coping mechanisms:

- My mobile phone lives in another room, on silent. If it's in the room I'm writing in, it saps my willpower[2].

- Freedom app runs on my laptop, so I can't access social media during my working hours. Similar productivity apps are available, which stop you from mindlessly surfing when you should be writing.

---

1 Oubliettes are a fairly horrifying form of medieval punishment. You find them in castles sometimes. They're deep holes reached only by a trapdoor, and prisoners were thrown into them to be forgotten ("oubliette" comes from the French meaning "little place of forgetting").

2 A study from the McCombs School of Business at the University of Texas, Austin, found cognitive capacity is significantly reduced when your smartphone is within reach—even if it's switched off. https://news.utexas.edu/2017/06/26/the-mere-presence-of-your-smartphone-reduces-brain-power/

- I plan my day the evening before, so I don't spend half an hour faffing around—because a half-hour turns into one hour, then two. When I sit down to work, I know precisely what I'll work on, where I'll start, and where I want to be when I'm done.

- My desk and tools are all set up and waiting for the same reason I plan my days: I can just sit down and write.

- Pay attention to your person, too: take good care of yourself physically and mentally. When I say don't allow resistance to stop you working, I don't mean torture yourself. When you can't feel your butt anymore, don't push on through: stand up, move around, and get the blood flowing.

- Drink plenty of water because your brain works more efficiently and more creatively when it's not gasping like a stranded fish.

- Eat well. I don't know about you, but whenever I get into any kind of workflow zone, I forget there's such a thing as food... and by the time I remember, I'm so hangry I will cut anyone who gets between me and the first thing I can cram into my face.

Obviously, I will recommend fruit and vegetables, but here's the sordid truth about my writing habits: at least one chapter of this book was powered by three-Euro fizzy blue wine (yes blue) and Oreo cookies. And an enormous bag of pretzels. You'll probably do similar at some point (although I strongly recommend avoiding fizzy blue wine) and the odd blowout is fine—but don't live on crap food. Your writing will suffer.

Now the obvious is out of the way, let's get down to business.

## Brain Tornados

As I write this, I'm in an Airbnb in a little town called Haría, on the beautiful island of Lanzarote. There's a black pumice garden outside filled with tiny lizards and fruit trees, and I can see palm trees in the distance. And there are three other writers, whom I love dearly, and without whom you wouldn't be reading this right now. They've kept me writing when I didn't want to. And I've helped them, too.

We've all had a brain tornado.[3] They're swirling thought vortexes that snatch up everything in their path, spinning faster and faster, sweeping away your day.

I think Kenda's three-hour paragraph is my favourite example. Head in hands, she wailed, "I've been at it for three hours, and I've written one fucking paragraph! *I can't do this!*"

This is the perfect example of a brain tornado mixing with Imposter Syndrome (oh yes, we all suffer from that) and smashing her into the Great Wall of Pain.

You, like Kenda, may feel you've wasted hours trying to write the first paragraph of a chapter. Or, like me, you may squander hours failing to write the final paragraphs of a chapter.

Or perhaps this will sound more familiar: "Oh god. I think this section would go better in the introduction chapter. But then it'll be a big chapter, and the preface and foreword aren't the same things. But they're all part of the introduction to the book. But actually, I think they could all have a chapter to themselves. But then there'll be 481 chapters, and that's silly. So maybe I should…"

And so the merry-go-round spins until the blue, fizzy, three-Euro wine creeps up behind us and smacks us on the head. (Yes, I'm judging myself for that choice of drink, so you don't have to.)

You'll walk miles pacing backwards and forwards. You'll chew your fingers, tear out your hair, and shred a million paper napkins in your frustration. You'll suddenly discover critical jobs that need doing right now or the world will explode. And you'll wish you'd never heard of a beautiful little game called *Hidden Folks*.

Then you'll throw your manuscript into a drawer in disgust, and walk away.

---

3   At least, that's what Suzi Hoare, another splendid writer I know, calls them. I like it.

## What Next?

DO NOT ABANDON YOUR MANUSCRIPT.

I cannot emphasise enough how tempting it will be to abandon your book and start another big project. Here's how I know: more than a year before this book was born, I started writing another one with a friend of mine. I got one chapter into it, and it languishes on my hard drive, waiting for me to pick it up again. I wondered at this because I'd written and published a book once; surely, I could do it again. What was going on here?

A year later, I took myself off to Fethiye on the sparkling Turkish coast, on my own, to write another book. I'd had this great idea that I thought would make people laugh. I still think it'll make people laugh. That book isn't written yet, either. I wrote, and I wrote, and I wrote, and I thought I'd written about half of it. In fact, I wrote 2,809 words, then went to the beach. I haven't looked at it since. Until I wrote this paragraph and checked, I had no idea how many words I hadn't written of that book. It's barely an article. Shame overload.

A few months later, I started yet another book—at home this time—and managed 53,802 words. Not bad at all… but I haven't picked it up again since.

You're reading the next effort right now. How did I manage to write this book, when my three previous books had failed so spectacularly?

This time, things were different.

For one thing, I had a Big Idea. I knew exactly how this book would fit into my bigger picture and how it slots into my business. I knew exactly whom I was writing it for, and why. And I knew what I wanted to do with it afterwards.

I made a plan, set my goals, and stuck to them. In fact, I did all the things you've been reading about in these pages.

And, crucially, I decided not to go it alone. I gathered three friends and dragged them to Lanzarote. Together, we solemnly pledged to Get Shit Done. And we did. Never, ever underestimate the power of a small group of motivated people to move mountains, my friend. You don't have to do this alone. You have me as your paper-based writing coach, and I want to hear from you. It's why I asked you to write me an email when you first started reading this book. It's why I've created an online community for writers like you.

Please find some writing buddies. If you can join a local group—fantastic. If you can find an online group like mine—splendid. And if you can go away with a handful of people for a week, somewhere lovely and quiet and away from your everyday drudge—even better (I run regular writing retreats, and they work like a charm).

Don't misunderstand me: I was still tempted to do Other Things. I made mistakes this time around: I should have set my out of office reply, and rescheduled all my coaching calls and group calls. I should have scheduled my daily emails in advance and pre-recorded my podcasts. But we live and learn, and next time I go away—to finish one of those abandoned books—I will know better.

Expect the Great Wall of Pain, my beautiful writer—then it won't take you by surprise when you hit it. You'll be ready for it. You'll understand its nature, and you'll be wary of its teeth. You have the tools to smash through the Great Wall of Pain and keep writing anyway. I know you can do it. I'm proud of you already.

You're on the final stretch now: your Shitty First Draft is done. Maybe you've even swept over it with a first edit and shown it to someone you trust. Next, we'll find out how to illustrate your Shitty First Draft with stories that will bring your chapters to life.

Take these Tiny Beetle Steps, then read on to find out what makes a compelling story, and how to write one…

## Tiny Beetle Steps

1. Eat well and drink plenty of water. Avoid three-Euro fizzy blue wine.

2. Move around regularly, particularly when you can't feel your butt anymore.

3. Re-read Chapter 3 on how to sort out your Inner Dickhead.

4. Be ready for pain—and have a plan to deal with it when it arrives. When it does arrive, share the pain with your writing buddies, with me, or in the Facebook Group here:

5. Do. Not. Abandon. Ship. Do not start another Big Project. Commit to finishing this one and *finish it*.

6. Email me again: 1000authors@vickyfraser.com. Tell me how you're getting on. Report on your progress and tell me where you struggled—and how you dealt with your struggles to carry on writing.

CHAPTER 15

# The Secret Of Story

*"No, no! The adventures first, explanations take such a dreadful time."*

*Lewis Carroll*

His torchlit face appeared suddenly at the window, pale— and I jumped. "Are you coming in?" He grinned and raised an eyebrow. "You got home fifteen minutes ago!" I smiled and turned off the radio, reluctantly. I'd just experienced The Driveway Effect... and I wonder if you have, too.

The Driveway Effect is when you're glued to your car seat, ice-cream melting in the shopping bags because the story you're listening to on the radio has you riveted in place. I was listening, spellbound, to commercial pilot Mark Vanhoenacker's tale on Radio 4. That was years ago, the first time I realised what The Driveway Effect was. Since then, since I started listening avidly to podcasts, I've been superglued in place many, many times by the power of story.

There's a good reason Lewis Carroll wants adventures first and explanations later: stories are fun and explanations are (usually) tedious.

If you want people to remember you and your message, don't give them facts and figures. Tell them a story. When I was at school, I had a history teacher who refused to bore us all with

171

endless names and dates and faceless moments in time. He was teaching us about World War I, and he brought it to life for us. Actually, to be truthful, he sat back in a stroke of genius and allowed *Blackadder* to bring the trenches into the classroom.

That lesson kicked off a lifelong interest in history—and in storytelling. If you want to teach something to anyone, do it with stories. Before you start, though, forget "brand storytelling". Forget the latest trend. Forget the marketing buzzwords. Anyone would think the online marketing world had recently made this magical discovery about storytelling, the way it's touted around as the next big shiny thing.

Storytelling is marvellous, of course... but not the way many businesses and brands are using it. Most "stories" are thinly disguised sales pitches and tedious corporate histories. We are drowning in a deluge of crap because everyone has jumped on the idea of content and story. This is both bad and good.

It's bad because people will be more suspicious about any messages we put out there in our books and general marketing. And because, frankly, I'd rather be drowning in stories that fill me up and make me explode with emotion.

It's good, though, because if you can learn to tell captivating stories, you'll stand out like a flamingo at a penguin party.

But wait: there's more—storytelling for the sake of it isn't going to help you sell books and persuade people to change their lives. In this book, you're getting the secrets of not only storytelling but (wait for the horrible cliché) storySELLing.

Storytelling is a gargantuan subject, and entire library shelves have been devoted to it. I'm giving you the basics, here.

By the time you finish this chapter, you'll be able to tell stories that keep people hooked from start to finish—then persuade them to take action on what you've written. I'll explain why story is so powerful and how successful stories are structured—including the four essential story elements. You'll discover why some stories stick, and others don't. And I'll explain how to kill the bloat and keep your story moving.

But first, some neuroscience. Because neuroscience is fascinating, important, and understanding why we respond to story will help you market your book and your business.

## Wired For Story

In her excellent book *Wired For Story*, Lisa Cron describes storytelling thusly and beautifully: "Opposable thumbs let us hang on. Story tells us what to hang on TO."[1]

Human beans are problem-solvers, and the way we solve problems is with stories. We can do something no other animal can (as far as we know). We can think stuff through. We can take a hypothetical problem and create a scenario to help us work through problems in the real world.

This nifty evolutionary trait allows us to plan rather than always reacting. Of course, we don't think about situations in that much detail on the surface, but storytelling goes on underneath, deep down. Our brains construct stories to explain what happens in the world around us.

If you don't believe me, ask neuroscience. Brain imaging shows that our brains don't seem to distinguish between actually doing an activity and experiencing it, and just reading about it. Which means our brains react in the same way to reading about something as they do when we actually physically take part in it.

I hope you realise why this is so important for you as a business owner, author, and marketer… If you can write a good enough story, you can elicit a reaction in your reader's brain that's the same as if they were truly experiencing what you're writing about. Which means if you're showing your reader how you can solve a problem they've got, so they live vicariously through your story, well…

Actually selling them your product shouldn't be too much of a stretch after that, should it?

Your book's primary purpose is to help people—and its

---

1  Cron, L. 2012, *Wired For Story*, p1.

secondary objective is to help you build your business. If your book is stuffed full of stories that hit people in the feels, they'll be primed to buy from you when they've finished reading.

When my beta reader Jamie got to this chapter, he emailed me this little anecdote which beautifully illustrates what I've just said: "An investor told me that they love 'stories and spreadsheets.' The story brings to life the pitch they are being asked to invest in. They look at the evidence/facts/numbers only after they've already been emotionally engaged. They use the spreadsheet only to justify their emotional response to invest…"

Tell your readers a story, then back it up with evidence. If you don't believe me, believe science. While we're on the subject of neuroscience, I'd like to talk to you about mirror neurons.

## Cringing in Vicarious Embarrassment

Have you ever watched someone on TV or up on stage at an event or even just in everyday life do something toe-curlingly cringeworthy—and curled your own toes in a sort of sympathetic horror? Or maybe you've seen someone get horribly injured and almost felt that pain yourself, huddling protectively over said body part in sympathy? You know what I'm talking about, don't you? That experience is caused by your mirror neurons firing.

How about when you've read a book that's scared the bejesus out of you because the main character's terrified? Or perhaps you've felt heartbroken when something awful happens to a character in a book and *they* feel sad?

That's your mirror neurons again. These brain tentacles are visuospatial neurons which respond to actions we observe in others. Fascinating… but what do they have to do telling stories?

## If They Don't Feel It, Nothing Will Happen

Bill Bernbach was one of the godfathers of modern marketing and advertising, and he understood how human brains work. He said: "You can say the right thing about a product and nobody will listen. You've got to say it in such a way that people will feel it in their gut. Because if they don't feel it, nothing will happen."

If your book—if your marketing—doesn't move people and make them feel something, they'll never buy from you. The easiest way to make people feel something is with stories.

Good stories are powerful because when we're fully engaged in them, our boundaries crumble, and we become the protagonist in our heads. The way your protagonist (the person the story is about) reacts and feels in your story is the way your reader should react and feel. The protagonist acts as a role model for the reader.

We're back to mirror neurons: if you can make people feel like the person in your story—make them feel your character's pain at the start, right through to joy and relief as their problem is solved at the end—you've got your reader right where you want them. Your story will intensify their pain... then show them what solving and salving that pain will feel like. Your reader will literally—if you've told your story well—feel better because of you and your book. Surely that's the end goal of any ethical business owner?

This type of storytelling isn't about using fear and pain to manipulate people into buying from you. It's about empathy. It's about genuinely understanding what your reader is going through and showing them how you can help. If what you're doing feels icky, you're not hitting the right notes. If it feels empathic, you're doing well.

What I'm really saying here is: *make* people feel something. Don't *tell* them what to feel. Do it with a story and make it sticky.

## The Aspects of a "Sticky" Story

In *Made To Stick*, Chip and Dan Heath set out on a voyage of discovery to find out what makes some stories stick while others disappear forever. They start with a story you may have heard;[2] I remember hearing a version of it when I was a teenager.

It's about a friend of a friend who went to a bar and met a

---

2   Heath, C & D, 2006, *Made To Stick*, Arrow.

stranger.

> The stranger bought the friend of a friend a drink, he took a sip
> —and that's the last he remembered. Until he woke up in a hotel
> bathtub, submerged in ice.
>
> He looked around in a panic—and spotted the note: DON'T
> MOVE. CALL 999.
>
> A mobile phone sat next to the note on a small table by the
> bathtub. He picked it up and called 999, and the operator seemed
> unsurprised by his story. She said, "Sir, I want you to reach behind
> you, slowly and carefully. Is there a tube protruding from your lower
> back?"
>
> He felt around and found a tube.
>
> The operator said, "Sir, don't panic. One of your kidneys has
> been harvested. There's a ring of organ thieves operating in this city,
> and they got to you. Paramedics are on their way. Don't move until
> they arrive."

Do you recognise one of the most successful urban legends
of recent times? There are many versions, but they all share the
same three basic elements:

1. Drugged drinks.
2. Ice-filled bathtubs.
3. The kidney-theft explanation.

It doesn't matter that it's not true. That it never happened
anywhere ever. This story is easy to understand, remember, and
repeat. And the moral of the story—don't accept drinks from
strangers—is clear.

Some ideas are fascinating, and some are not. A gang of kidney
thieves is fascinating; a sore head and a faint sense of regret are
not. If you want your readers to remember your book and your
message, understand what makes a message memorable. What
makes a story worth listening to and retelling.

A "sticky" story needs five elements, according to the Heaths:

**1. Simple.** The kidney story—and every other story you

remember well—is simple. By simple, I don't mean dumbing down; I mean, dig until you find the core of your idea. What's the most crucial goal of your story?

2.  **Unexpected.** If you want people's attention, you have to break the pattern with something unusual. Ever been on an aeroplane and actually listened to the safety briefing because the flight attendant broke script and made you laugh? I have. Pop something unexpected into your story and your readers will remember it.

3.  **Concrete.** Humans don't think in abstracts, we think in real, concrete, living ideas. Have you seen Jane Elliott's social studies experiment?[3] She was trying to teach her class about prejudice and how wrong and damaging it is. They struggled with the concept... until she divided them into blue-eyed kids and brown-eyed kids and gave them different rights and privileges. As soon as Elliott made a difficult abstract idea concrete, so the kids could live it, they understood it.

4.  **Credible.** Your story has to be believable, or it will fail. Tell your stories on a human scale and make them relatable. Back them up with details and real examples.

5.  **Emotional.** Your stories must be emotional if you want people to remember them and act on them. The anti-tobacco lobby spent millions on ads that didn't work, explaining facts and figures and showing horrible pictures of gammy lungs. It took them a long time to realise an interview with a real, dying person and their real, grieving family made far more of an impact than cold, hard facts.[4] If you want people to care, associate something they don't yet care about with something they do care about.

---

3  There are plenty of articles and videos about this, but if you want to watch it fast, go to: http://bit.ly/moxie-browneyes

4  A study published in the *American Journal of Public Health* concluded: "Emotionally evocative ads and ads that contain personalized stories about the effects of smoking and quitting hold promise for efforts to promote smoking cessation and reduce socioeconomic disparities in smoking." https://www.ncbi.nlm.nih.gov/pmc/articles/PMC2775761/

Let's apply these elements to the classic film *Die Hard*. It's the simple story of a man who's trying to win back his estranged wife. He turns up at her office Christmas party at Nakatomi Plaza, only to become embroiled in a terrorist attack. The main characters are John and Holly McClane, Joseph Takagi (who dies pretty early on), Argyle the limo driver, Sergeant Al Powell, and Hans Gruber[5]. They all react to this unexpected attack in different and very human ways. The story is credible because terrorist attacks and giant heists do happen.

And, believe it or not, there are a few emotional moments in this most noble action film (when John catches Holly, when Hans Gruber plummets off the top of the building, and when John and Al finally meet and have a big man-cuddle).

The film is memorable.

If your story is simple, unexpected, concrete, credible, and emotional, you're on the right track. But don't get too complacent: one of the biggest challenges we face as writers is staying on message.

## Kill The Bloat

Everything you write—every single word—should be there on a need-to-know basis only. Every word should do a job well.

You know how small children tell stories? Repetitively and with loooooong pauses? And with literally thousands of random tangents? In a terminally dull stream of consciousness?[6] That's not storytelling; it's droning on. There's a serious danger of doing the same thing in your book, too. It's easy to get bogged down in the details and drone on.

---

5    Hans Gruber was Alan Rickman's first ever big-screen acting role, fact fans—proving you're never too old to try something new.

6    Before you get out your pitchforks and screech at me that I'm a child-hating monster, one of my parent-friends reminded me how painful it is listening to their kids' tales. If the person you love most in the world is too painful to listen to, imagine how your readers will feel if you tell stories like a toddler…

If you're writing for the sake of filling space, people will not read your stuff. Alfred Hitchcock, one of film's greatest storytellers, said, "Drama is life with the dull bits cut out."

This is true! Keep it in mind whenever you write.

Have you ever seen the TV show *24* with Kiefer Sutherland? The entire series is twenty-four shows long, each show representing an hour of Jack Bauer's day. Minute by minute. It's a nifty concept.

If you're familiar with the show, you might have noticed you never see Jack Bauer doing a poo. Well, they probably wouldn't show that anyway, but my point is: you don't see characters doing the mundane, boring stuff we all do every day. They don't generally brush their teeth or do the washing up—unless the action furthers the story.

Why? Bloat.[7]

We take for granted the mundane stuff happens around the story. We don't need to see it because we know it's there in the background. Most of the time, it has nothing to do with the story.

Don't fill in mundane detail—and don't set the scene, either. Scene-setting is another form of bloat. Jump in with the action. Start in the middle if you like.

Keep the point of your story in mind. The story is not the plot; the story is how the plot affects your protagonist (usually your client). The plot should facilitate the story, rather than be the story. Stories start to get bloated and dull when they become all about what's happening, rather than whom it's happening to and why.

This is a good place to introduce the four essential story elements.

## The Four Essential Story Elements

Before we dive into the four elements, let's look at what a story actually is. According to Lisa Cron, "A story is how what happens

---

7    All credit to Sean D'Souza for the concept of bloat in stories.

affects someone who is trying to achieve what turns out to be a difficult goal, and how he or she changes as a result."[8]

There are four essential elements within that explanation, which every story needs if it's going to work. It doesn't matter how good the writing is; if any of these elements are missing, the story will fail:

1. What happens to a person.

2. A person—the protagonist or main character.

3. What the person wants to achieve—their difficult goal.

4. How the person changes as a result of what happens to them.

Keep these elements in mind when you're writing any story because, without them, your story will be dull. When you read a good case study or testimonial, look closely at it—you'll find these elements are all present and correct. When you read a tedious case study, on the other hand, you'll probably find it's stuffed full of dry facts and doesn't tell you about the client's journey at all.

A good story is all about people, not things and it's about specific people, not people in general. Listen to E. B. White: "Advice to young writers who want to get ahead without any annoying delays: don't write about Man, write about a man."

We care about individuals, not groups (more on that shortly).

A good story makes your reader feel what it's like to be the protagonist (that's those mirror neurons coming into play). And that's good for you because you want your reader to feel what it'd be like to reach their goal or solve their problem—with your help, of course.

Let me explain using the film *The Matrix*. On the face of it, *The Matrix* is about good versus evil, man versus machine, slavery versus freedom, right? That's the plot. The good guys are fighting Agent Smith and his cronies to free the human race. But that's not the story. The story is about Neo. It's about Neo's realisation that the world is not as it seems, nobody is who he thinks they are, and he has to somehow survive in this new world. And get the

---

8   Cron, L. 2012, *Wired For Story*, p11.

girl, obviously.

If *The Matrix* were just about man versus machine, it'd be rubbish. We wouldn't care because we wouldn't have a reason to care. But we do care because *The Matrix* is about a man who finds the world is not at all as he thought it was. Storytelling, at its heart, is all about specifics. A big seething mass of humanity grown like battery chickens to power the world of machines is horrific in an abstract way, but we don't really care. Focus on one person, though—Neo in this case—and we care very much.

## Focus On The Details

I can give you an example from the real world. You might not want to hear it, and it might put your back up. Good, because you need to understand why this works.

When we see or hear about massive, horrific events that happen halfway around the world, we struggle to care about them enough to stand up and do something.

On Boxing Day 2004, somewhere between 230,000 and 280,000 people were annihilated by a tsunami. That's a staggering number of deaths. Staggering. So big, our brains struggle to comprehend it, so we switch off. Partly because it's too awful to think about, but partly because it's just numbers.

That sounds callous but bear with me.

When we hear about famines in places like Ethiopia, with millions of people starving to death, it's awful. We switch off because it's too big. It's numbers.

When we read about the thousands of people living on our streets, homeless, we're horrified. We shake our heads, we say something must be done... and we switch off. We go back to our lives. Because these faceless people are nothing to do with us.

But when we dig into those world events and atrocities, when we burrow down into the humanity beneath it, when we pull out individual stories... then we act. We donate money. We give clothes. We do something.

We learn about June Abeyratne, who was forty-eight years old. June died in the tsunami on Boxing Day 2004. She moved to Sri Lanka from Surrey to open an orphanage and married a Sri Lankan man named Viraj. Viraj lived; his wife wasn't so lucky. June pushed her eleven-year-old daughter Alexandra through a bedroom window and saved her life before she was swept away and drowned.

A million people starved in Ethiopia in 1985. Eseye Tiruneh and her family got on a bus, fled their farm, and ran for safety. Her mother, grandmother, and two siblings died in a malaria epidemic. Only she and her father survived. I'm horrified by the million deaths, but I care about Eseye and her family.

Joe and I visited Oradour-Sur-Glane, the martyr village in France, in 2018. On June 10, 1944, 642 men, women, and children were massacred by a German Waffen-SS company. The village was wiped out, many of its buildings destroyed. I'd read about it before, and was shocked and fascinated… But walking around the town, seeing the homes they'd lived in, the church where the women and children were penned up and murdered was… I don't know. I fell apart completely when we left because you walk out past the names and photographs of all the people who died. They become real.

You can look at the numbers of deaths in a totally detached way. Yet I have tears running down my cheeks writing this because June was a real person and Eseye is a real person and all those people with photographs from Oradour were real people with families and lives and hopes and dreams.

I'm outraged about homelessness in this rich country in 2019, but it's the people I meet and talk to who make me care.

That's why charities, when they send their fundraising letters, tell you stories. You'll read about the homeless person called Simon you could help house, or the African orphan named Kofi you could help educate, or the baby elephant named Elsa you could save. You'll learn their names, hear their life stories, tear up at the horror and smile at the hope they now have.

Storytelling works. Charities wouldn't tell stories if it didn't work. If putting a bunch of facts and figures about how many are dying worked, that's all we'd get. But it doesn't work, so charities give us the facts and figures buried in real human stories. All we really care about are the human stories (or the elephant stories)[9] behind the events. We care because all good stories are emotional.

You might be wondering how to use this information if your business is all about making or selling widgets—tangible things—rather than services or charity donations. My answer is: you're not selling widgets. You're selling what the widget can do for your client. It's not about the product, it's about how the product changes your customer's life. As soon as you grasp that and start using it, your marketing will change—and you'll understand how you can write a book someone wants to read.

We're back to feelings again. Make your reader feel something, or there's no point in writing. This doesn't just go for your book; it applies to everything you write. And everything you write must have a point.

## What's Your Clear Goal?

It's easy to get swept away in emotions, though, and start rambling. Always keep your aim in mind. Your story must go somewhere. Think back to the pub bore: his rambling tirades never have any focus. They're random streams of consciousness containing every thought in his head.

When you write your story, keep your clear goal in mind: where is your tale going and *why*? What's your protagonist doing and *why*? Otherwise, you're just writing a sequence of stuff that happens—and that's dull.

For selling, this comes down to: what action do you want your reader to take? Do you want them to buy from you? Do you want them to sign up for something? Whatever it is, make it your focus.

Everything you say should lead your reader to take action. You might weave a story about a client, in the form of a case study,

---

9    I love elephants so much even thinking about them makes me cry. I've never even seen a real one. That's my life goal, to see elephants in the wild.

showing your reader how your client overcame his problem and won the day. You show your reader how they can achieve their goal, too. Then you can ask your reader to do the same thing.

You might tell a tale about how you helped a client solve a problem or achieve a goal, so your reader can follow the story and recognise it, and realise you can help them too. So when you ask for the sale, they're right there with you.

Keep the focus on your reader's objective because that will keep the story tight and interesting to your reader. But the goal isn't always obvious, and you need to keep that in mind, too. For example, in the most excellent Christmas film *Die Hard*, which I mentioned earlier, you might think John McClane's goal is to defeat Hans Gruber and save all the hostages at Nakatomi Plaza… but you'd be wrong.

McClane's goal is to win back his wife, Holly. All that other stuff going on—running around with bare feet and explosions and shooting terrorists—is incidental. The action is the plot that moves the protagonist—John McClane—closer to his goal, which is winning back his wife, Holly.

Go deeper. You'll find your clients' goals are rarely simply to make more money. Why do they want to make more money? Nobody[10] loves money for money's sake, it's all about what you can do with it. What do they want to do with their money?

That's the interesting part.

Everything the star of your story does should have a reason. "To avoid going broke" is just the start… what will happen if he goes broke? What will happen if he doesn't? There is always a reason for doing something. What will it mean to your prospect if XYZ happens? Tell the story.

## Kill Your Abstracts

And that brings me back to specifics again because we humans don't think in abstracts—not without an effort of will, anyway.

---

10   Except Scrooge McDuck.

We think in concrete, specific, real terms. We think about this woman, not a woman. That book, not a book. This problem, not a problem.

I mentioned earlier that real human stories about individuals touch us, whereas reports of huge numbers of people don't. It's the same when you write about anything.

When you tell stories—or write any marketing copy at all—avoid generalities. Avoid being vague. Generalities are boring.

The top three reasons you might be too vague in your writing are:

1. Too much knowledge about your subject.
2. Not enough knowledge about your topic.
3. You don't want to give too much away.

Let's tackle the first of those three problems. The "curse of knowledge". The easiest way to get around this is to assume your reader is utterly clueless about everything—because they probably are. When you know a lot about a subject, you tend to assume everyone else knows a lot about it, too. Usually, they don't. Explain everything. It may feel like you're over-explaining, but trust me, you're probably not. Every time you catch yourself making an assumption, check it: will my reader know what's going on here?

If in doubt, give your writing to someone else to read—someone who knows little or nothing about your business. If they don't understand something, they can tell you.

Being vague can also be a sign of not knowing your subject well enough, which is a surprisingly common problem—particularly in the marketing industry. If this is your challenge, get busy learning more—or scale back what you want to write about.

The only antidote to not enough knowledge is to get cracking learning the skills you need. And stop selling stuff to people until you know enough to do so!

The third reason for being vague is because you don't want to give too much away. I get it. But your fears are unfounded. I used to worry about this, too, thinking, "If I give away my good stuff, why would anyone buy my products? If I teach people how to write, why would they pay me to write for them?"

Let's flip this objection on its head. Your readers will look at your free stuff and think, "Gosh, if she's giving away this amazing information, her paid-for stuff must be stonkingly magnificent! I must buy it now." This happens all the time, and the most successful people in business understand how it works.

Giving people information doesn't mean they'll use it. Mostly, they won't. I've given away plenty of information about how to write books, and I still receive messages from people saying, "This is fantastic, how do I get started?" They already have what they need to get started… but not in the format that'll really help them. So they buy my course or sign up for my coaching programme, get the support and instruction they need—and write their books.

A tiny fraction of people will take your information and run with it, and love you for it because you've taught them a new skill. They'll shout your name from the rooftops and refer others to you. The vast majority who read your book, though, won't do that. I might read a book about how to build a website, but I don't want to do it myself. I don't have time! I want to pay someone else to do it—but I want to understand enough about it so I get what I need and don't get ripped off.

Write your book and give your best knowledge away. As Zig Ziglar, one of the world's most successful salesmen, said, "You will get all you want in life, if you help enough other people get what they want."

## Tools of the Trade

My final, most important piece of advice about storytelling is this: read lots and collect stories. Good writers are good readers. And don't just read novels either: here's a whole bunch of stuff you can do to study great stories and learn to tell good ones yourself…

Read lots of books—fiction and non-fiction. Start with *Telling True Stories: A Nonfiction Writers' Guide* by Mark Kramer and Wendy

Call. Watch lots of films: how are the ones that grip you put together? Do the same with TV series. Listen to podcasts and audiobooks.

Watch David Attenborough documentaries. I mean, you can watch whatever documentaries you like, but David Attenborough is a master storyteller. You learn tons from watching his films, but it doesn't feel like you're learning. He's a master of infotainment. Then watch a non-Attenborough documentary, and you'll see the difference.

Create a swipe file of stories and keep them handy—I find the easiest way to do this is using Evernote, as I mentioned in Chapter 4. You can upload images, emails, voice notes, and videos to Evernote.

In short: read. A lot. Then write stuff that people want to read.

Master the art of storytelling, and you'll never struggle for an audience. Fantastic storytelling isn't the only way to take a book from good to great, though. In the next chapter, we'll look at how to infuse your book with the essence of you.

## Tiny Beetle Steps

1. Watch the David Attenborough hermit crab video at www.bit.ly/Moxiecrabs.

2. Download my story grid from www.moxiebooks.co.uk/moxie-book-resources and use it to sketch out a story for each chapter—what's the Big Idea for your entire book, and what's the Idea for each chapter? Which stories will get your point across?

3. Go through your outline (or your Shitty First Draft) and make a note every time you say something you could illustrate with a story.

## CHAPTER 16

# Flamingo Your Writing

*"The opposite of courage is not cowardice, it is conformity. Even a dead fish can go with the flow."*

*Jim Hightower*

A re you willing to take the risk that half the people who read your book will hate you?

If you're not willing to take that risk, you won't be able to write a tremendous book. You won't move anyone to feel anything because you're too worried about offending everyone. When I talk about Flamingo-ing your writing, I mean giving yourself permission to be you.

Your book isn't only about giving people the right answer; they can Google that. It's about giving them your answer.

This chapter is all about how to do that. You don't need to worry about doing it right away on your first go; remember, your Shitty First Draft is for getting the facts down as fast and as comprehensively as possible. Do that first.

Only when you're onto your second or even third edit do you need to think about Flamingo-ing your writing and let your voice out.

You don't need to "find your voice"; you already have one. You just need to find the courage to let it out, loud and proud and with no fucks given if Trevor in Northampton has his panties in a twist about it. But that's easier said than done, right? Of course.

I still cower under my duvet at the thought of putting myself out there. As I'm editing this, I'm sharing snippets with my Launch Team Beta Readers. They've had my Not-A-Preface and my Introduction. But it took me two weeks longer than I planned to send it to them. Not because it wasn't ready. Not because I hadn't got organised. Because I was terrified.

Even though the people on my team are people who already like me, there was still a chance they might hate what they see. I was tempted to water down my opinions. Dampen my enthusiasm. Share a little less and throw up my shields.

The fear doesn't go away. We just learn to work around it, to use it. Then we remember: Some will love it. Some won't. So what?

## Be A Little Bit Extra

What do you care about? What makes you scream with rage or explode with joy? What's your opinion on the things that matter in your world? Get them down on paper. Put them in your book. Because if you don't, you'll produce a watered-down version of other people's books—and that would be a tragedy.

Everything in Chapter 18 will help you edit your book, so it's easier and more enjoyable to read. But none of that advice matters without this crucial ingredient: add outrageous flair to your content. Be a little bit "extra", as kids and drag queens say.

Too many books are boring. Too much writing is boring: regurgitated facts without personality, fear masquerading as professionalism. Too many books are collections of censored and emasculated thoughts, pulled from your own core and beaten down to wisps and ghosts; writing without substance.

We don't just want facts; we can get those anywhere on the internet for free, anytime. We need to know why you believe what you believe. What your message means to you, and why you think it's important enough to put in a book. We need to understand your honest opinion—the things you'd say if you thought nobody would ever disagree with you.

We need you to show us why you're passionate about what you do, and why we should be too.

"He's muffed it," said Simony. "He could have done anything with them. And he just told them a lot of facts. You can't inspire people with facts. They need a cause. They need a symbol."[1]

This quote is from Terry Pratchett's Discworld book, *Small Gods*. He was talking about inspiring a movement among people so they'd have a revolution... I'm talking about inspiring a movement among your readers, so they start a personal revolution to change their lives.

You might not be starting a religion with your book, or inspiring a world-changing rebellion, or petitioning a government—but you're writing with purpose. Your purpose is to change people's minds, to engage them, to move them to think, to help them do something, no matter how small. Maybe you want them to choose you instead of your competitor. Or consider something they hadn't considered before. Perhaps it's to buy a product or service. Possibly it's to take an action that'll improve their life.

Whatever it is, your reader will need more than facts if you want them to change in some way—because that's the ultimate goal of all writing, fiction or non-fiction. We want the reader to change somehow. To do that, they'll need more than dry, "professional" writing or videos or podcasts. They need you: your personality, your opinions, your passion. They need your vulnerability. They need to know you're human, too, and you've fucked up—and this is how. Own your mistakes, embrace them, and share them, because only then will your reader trust you enough to let you in.

Your reader needs plenty of "get out of my head" moments; you know the ones. We've all read something that's made us say, "Holy shit, that's so true! How did she know?"

Your reader needs your outrageous flair.

---

1    Pratchett, T. 1992, *Small Gods*, p297.

You don't have to put pants on your head or anything. You don't have to pretend to be something you're not. You just have to be you, but *a little bit more*.

Most of what we read has no staying power: it goes in through our eyeballs and then dissolves. It's not interesting enough to stick around. Think about the last thing you read or watched that buried itself indelibly in your brain, something you couldn't dislodge if you tried. Aim for that!

## Embrace Your Inner Drama Llama

Your writing needs conflict. Writing without conflict doesn't have a story, and a book without a story isn't worth reading. Every single book (or movie) ever written is all about the way someone has changed and responded to conflict. That's it.

*Buffy The Vampire Slayer* (one of my favourite TV shows *ever*) isn't about fighting monsters and vampires. That's just the plot. The story is about growing up, surviving high school, making friends, losing friends, working through grief, falling in love, coping with all the shit life throws at you—and how you change so you can deal with it.

*The Lord of the Rings* isn't about good versus evil. It's about how Frodo and Sam—and the rest of the Company of the Ring— changed as they moved along their quest.

And before you waggle your finger at me and shriek, "But I'm not writing fiction!" Hush. It doesn't matter. Non-fiction needs conflict, too. Your non-fiction book is all about your Big Idea— the big problem your reader is facing, and which you're solving for them—chapter by chapter, word by word. The elements of a story apply to non-fiction as much as to fiction. You're writing about life, and life is a story. Your book is about how you—and your reader—change as you travel through the book.

In this book, I'm taking you from your starting point: "How the hell do I write a book?" all the way through to publishing. I'm walking you through everything you need to know and do, including dealing with your critics (inner and outer) and showing you how you can change and become a writer. An author.

There's plenty of conflict in this book—in my story, in the struggles I've overcome on my journey to becoming an author back when I wrote my first book—and in your story, as you read this and realise what you're capable of achieving.

You're capable of moving me to tears. All you need is the courage to do so and the will to stand out.

## Visualising Stories

The best writing helps us visualise the story. Not on every page, necessarily—especially for non-fiction—but when you want to make your reader feel something or do something, help them step into the experience. To do that, we create images and write about concrete details.

Go back to Chapter 15 again, where I wrote about abstract ideas. We can't visualise abstracts... but give me a vivid description, and what you're writing about springs into my mind like a photograph.

Think about the words you use and the phrases you write and how they conjure images in your reader's mind (or fail to). Humans are visual creatures: if you want to move us, make us see and make us feel in glorious technicolour.

Instead of describing something literally, write something more interesting. If you want a masterclass in doing this, read Terry Pratchett's Discworld series. He was a genius word-painter. One of my favourite descriptive phrases from Sir Terry is, "the atmosphere inside the yurt was like a blacksmith's armpit".[2] We know exactly what he means: hot and sticky and smelly and gross. He doesn't need to say those words, though; he conjured up the image and the feeling in two simple words.

There's no reason why you can't do that, too—despite the fact you're writing non-fiction. In fact, do it *because* you're writing non-fiction: it's too easy to lapse into a monotone of "professionalism".

---

2   Pratchett, T. 1986, *The Light Fantastic*, p393.

## How To Write Pictures

These are my five top tips for writing pictures in your reader's mind:

1. **Imagine your book as a movie** playing in your head. Who's doing what? Where are they? How does it feel? Hot? Cold? Loud? Quiet?

2. **Get specific.** When you're outlining and writing your Shitty First Draft, generalities are fine. They're a starting point. When you're editing and polishing, though—get specific. Find a story to illustrate your ideas and colour your story in.

3. **Understand the physicality of what you're writing:** what does one hundred metres look like? A football field? A park? What does it feel like to be punched in the stomach? Do you know? Find out. How do you feel when you're afraid? What's the taste in your mouth? How sharp do things look? What do sounds sound like?

4. **Create symbols to describe abstract concepts.** Emily Brontë's character Catherine describes her love for Linton and Heathcliff using symbolism: "My love for Linton is like the foliage in the woods. Time will change it; I'm well aware, as winter changes the trees. My love for Heathcliff resembles the eternal rocks beneath; a source of little visible delight, but necessary."[3]

5. **Show, don't tell.** Instead of telling me you were embarrassed, make me feel it. Back in Chapter 3, I could have told you my music stopped during my pole dancing competition, and I was mortified, then I carried on and won hurrah! This is the exact same information, isn't it? But wouldn't that have been dull? Instead, I took you into the room with me and made you feel what I felt. Don't tell me something was grey-blue; show me it was the colour of the ocean on a stormy day. Let my mind paint the picture.

---

3   Brontë, E. 1847, *Wuthering Heights*, p67.

## Writing With Rhythm

Poetry isn't just for poets; Stephen Fry's *The Ode Less Travelled* is a super book to help you unlock the poet within. Music isn't just for musicians. Rhythm isn't only for drummers and dancers.

You may not be aware of it, but a faster song makes you twitch a little quicker. Your brain synchronises with the music's tempo— and, as neuroscientist Dr Daniel Levitin says, you may not even feel your muscles complain because the music lifts your mood and increases your pain threshold.

A love of music is hardwired into most of us. Watch babies and small children when you play music with a strong beat: they dance, they bounce, they wiggle. (And so do many adults. Read: me. I do that.)

We all march to the beats of our own drums, and we are all influenced by other people's drums.

Watch *Jaws*. Watch the scene where everyone splashes about in the water, shouting and screaming and laughing. Listen, as the famous score starts up:

*Duuuuun dun. Duuuuuuun dun. Duh-dun duh-dun duh-dun da-da-da-da-da-da!*

How does your body react as the rhythm changes and picks up the pace? Pay attention to how your heart rate increases—even though you know it's only a film and sharks rarely kill people.

Now, remember the classic computer game Space Invaders. Can you hear its simple bleeps? They start slow. Easy. They give you time to dodge the bombs and shoot the invaders.

But they don't stay slow; they speed up. They get faster, *faster*, FASTER until you're shooting in a frenzy and yanking the joystick around frantically trying to avoid them until eventually— you're dead.

Do you know why the music does that? So you get more and more agitated. Your heart-rate increases as the beat accelerates. You lose concentration. Then you lose the game—and have to put more money into the coin-operated machine to play again.

Try watching an emotional or action-packed scene from a movie without the score… it's a bizarre, empty experience, like listening in black and white.

## Music To Your Eyes

Fantastic writing contains music: it has **timing**, it has **pace**, it has **rhythm**.

The sentence you just read is paced using the "rule of three", which is an effective way to add rhythm to your writing. The rule of three allows you to express ideas more fully, emphasise your main points, and make your message more memorable.

As you write, imagine your readers are listening to your voice. If you create an audiobook, they may actually be doing so. Wonderful speakers understand that the best speeches are like music; try to capture the sense of compelling oratory in your written words. There are endless ways to do this, so I'll share a few of my favourites—starting with pacing. Vary pace; create space. Listen to the most popular TED Talks, and you'll notice the finest speakers use pregnant pauses and well-placed silences to emphasise crucial points.

You can do similar when writing: bookend long, flowing sentences with short, punchy statements. A long string of protracted sentences is dull. As dull as too many short ones following one after another. You can create speed in your writing with broken sentences—get your reader moving—agitated—excited…

Or… You can slow things down, lower the heart rate, create space for your reader to breathe; a perfectly placed semicolon or a well-curated comma does the trick beautifully.

Match your rhythm to the mood you want to create. If you're writing about a luxury retreat, where one can float languidly in a warm pool, listening to the breeze and the trilling of the birds, let your sentences flow on and on and create the mood.

If capturing anxiety is the order of the day, trap it in sharp, glittering, staccato beats. Breathless words. Over-bright imagery that bites and snaps at your mind.

Vary the number of words in your sentences—not mathematically, not analytically, but naturally, organically. Break all the rules if it serves your purpose. Need to describe a torturous bureaucratic policy? Do it with a run-on-and-on-and-on sentence, drone to your heart's content—then figuratively toss your head at it with a snappy reaction.

Describing a dance? Do it with rhythm, with a beat, with notes—and space between the notes. A tumble down the stairs? Build pace and pressure, write a headlong descent punctuated by bumps, crashes, thuds—and bring your tale to a sudden stop with a concise word.

## Choose More Interesting Words

Seek and destroy most iterations of the verb "to be". Is, was, and any -ing sucks the life from your writing. You may find you write something like, "I was writing to my mother." If that happens, change it forthwith to, "I wrote to my mother." Even better: "I dashed off a note to my ma."

Some sneer at alliteration; not me. I love it. Especially in book titles, chapter titles, and headlines, where they help make key phrases sticky—and they're fun to read out loud. Peruse pop-up picture books for perspicacious ideas. You get my drift.

You're not writing marketing or sales copy now; you're writing a book, and it has a slightly different job to do. Choose words you love. Colourful words, unusual words—but words your reader is likely to understand. Don't make your reader work; but don't make the language you use too familiar, either. Read what you've written aloud. Does it work? Does it flow? Is it fascinating?

English is a vibrant and flexible language: use it fully. Play with the positions of words and phrases. You don't have to introduce the most critical element of your idea first. Where does the headline go in an advert? Or, better: When you write an advert, where's the headline? (Isn't that a better way to ask?)

You may start a sentence with "and". And "but". Ignore your English teacher; he knows not of what he speaks. You may also fragment your sentences[4] if you wish, to add a little colour and flair. Not too much, though. You'll wear it out.

Use contrast, white space, and peaks and troughs of pacing to build up tension or emotion—then add a counterpoint of release. Study films and music: you can't sustain tension for too long; it's too much. Overstimulation of our nerves means we won't tolerate it. And too much languorous chilling gets boring. Crescendos aren't just for music; they're for writing, too.

Rhythm creates a mood. What atmosphere do you want to concoct? Does your writing evoke the feelings you're pursuing? Or does it leave your reader flat, bored, tuned out?

Listen to music. Feel the bass beat, hear the underlying rhythm of the melody, and discover how the vocals weave around them.

Listen to speeches, comedy routines, and scenes from films for inspiration. And, of course, read. Read everything you can get your hands on and read often.

## There's More Than One Way To Build A Castle

Disney-style or motte-and-bailey? Stone keep or concentric? All castles serve a similar purpose: a display of power and wealth, and hopefully, they'll keep the invaders out.

There's more than one way to structure a castle—and there's more than one way to structure your book. I've given you a place to start with the Moxie Book Outline. But consider: is it the best way for you to write your book? Chapter by chapter? Section by section? Probably it is… but consider doing it another way, instead.

Ha-Joon Chang's *23 Things They Don't Tell You About Capitalism*

---

4   A true sentence always contains a subject, a verb, and a complete thought. When you know the rules, you can break them. If you like. ("If you like" is a fragment, added for emphasis.)

is a fabulous introduction to the free market… and it manages to be interesting, too. He's structured his message into twenty-three Things instead of big chunky chapters, and it works brilliantly.

*The Secret Lives Of Colour* by Kassia St Clair is a beautiful book filled, unsurprisingly, with colour. It's structured into colour groups, starting with white and deepening to black.

*Girl, Wash Your Face* is written as twenty-two lies we tell ourselves. And *Eat, Pray, Love* is divided into those three eponymous sections, comprising 108 tales—each representing a bead on the Japamala.[5] Whatever you think of their messages, these books are interesting because they're structured differently. How can you take the usual and make it odd?

## Be Deliciously You

Find the weird angle. The unpopular opinion. The fabulously creative and colourful word. Develop your own vocabulary, one people will associate with you when they hear it. Words and phrases that bring you out of the pages and into people's lives, just for a moment. Write in such a way that your message reaches out of the page or screen, grabs your reader by the eyeballs, and drags them along with you. Write words that move people to action. In that way, we change the world.

You can't outshout your competition… but you can sure as hell outsmart them. Write a book that startles your reader and wakes them up with a jolt. Words to get them thinking and caring. Write a book that lingers in their skull. Tell stories that stick around and wake your reader in the night, so they're thinking about what you can do for them.

You cannot get away with throwing some words together, slapping them between the covers of a book, and hoping it'll sell. It won't. Those days are long gone.

If you want to claim customers from your competitors, if you're going to make real change in your industry and your

---

5   A string of prayer beads used by Hindus, Buddhists, Jains, and some Sikhs for the spiritual practice of japa.

world, you need to be more bloody interesting than everyone else. Figure out what will get your reader's attention and how to write messages that sneak into their brain and stick around.

Finally, and perhaps the most simple tip of all, is to keep a thesaurus[6] on your desk. Along with *Cassell's Dictionary of Slang* (a veritable horde of wondrous words).

This chapter has been all about colouring in your writing. Adding music and flourishes. In Chapter 18, we'll come back to some of these themes when we look at how to edit your work.

First, though, a short chapter on being funny…

## Tiny Beetle Steps

1. Are you cringing as you write? If you are, it's not you; dig in and be more honest.

2. Are you scared to write something? Good—that means it's real. If it scares you, it's worth doing and saying. Say it.

3. Listen to music, to great speeches, to comedy sketches, and learn about writing with rhythm. How does certain music make you feel? What images does it conjure? What mood does it evoke?

4. Make friends with thesaurus.com, because it's a fabulous tool.

5. Go back to Chapter 5 and do the writing exercises again— this time, using what you've learned from this chapter.

---

6   The word "thesaurus" comes from thēsauros, which is Greek for "storehouse" or "treasure". A thesaurus is indeed a treasure trove, and I'm never without mine.

# CHAPTER 17

# To Be Funny, Or Not To Be Funny

*"Life literally abounds with comedy if you just look around you."*

*Mel Brooks*

K nock, knock!
  Who's there?

Moustache.

Moustache who?

I moustache you a question, but I'll shave it for later.

\* \* \*

Okay, "knock knock" jokes aren't the height of sophisticated humour, but this one made me chuckle. Not so long ago, someone wrote to me asking, "If I were to write a book, how do I write with humour—and still hammer home the intent?"

It's a splendid question, and a tricky one to answer—because humour is subjective. One person's hilarious joke may be utterly incomprehensible (or horribly offensive) to someone else. To state the blindingly obvious: everyone's different... and some people don't have a sense of humour at all.

If you write something funny, not everyone will find it amusing. Some people won't get it. Others will be mortally offended. A few may laugh so much they can't breathe.

## Nobody Likes A Preacher

I wonder, though, if my questioner really meant this: "How do I write entertainingly, without talking down to my reader, and still hammer home my message?"

It's all too easy to clamber aboard your soapbox and preach your message to the crowds, but nobody wants a sermon. They can go to church for that. Your reader wants your stories, your experiences, good and bad, funny and sad. It can be tricky to write in such a way that your words take your reader by the hand and carry them with you. It's easier to proclaim from a pulpit.

The last couple of chapters—and this one—are all about stepping down from that platform and joining your reader where they are now.

Here's a quick tip for making your writing less preachy: when you're editing, search and destroy any instances of "should", "must", "need to"—and rewrite accordingly. You'll instantly be more accessible and more entertaining. Then tell real, human stories. Ask questions. Get your reader involved on your level, then you're not bellowing advice at them from atop your soapbox.

But what about comedy? Is it okay to be hilarious?

## Learning To Tickle

Are you funny? Can you make people laugh? Maybe; maybe not. Most people can be amusing sometimes, but unless you're a comedy writer or a comedian, my advice is: don't try to be funny. As soon as you try to be funny, one of two things will happen:

1.   You'll panic and freeze, and nothing at all will dribble out of your fingers, hilarious or otherwise.

2.   You'll be decidedly unfunny because you're trying too hard.

If you're hell-bent on making people laugh, take a class. You can learn to be funny. There are comedy workshops and improv classes all over the place—I know there are because I'm waiting for the next one to start up near me so I can join in. There's an art to comedy; to landing a good joke. I'm no expert, but I know enough to know I don't know what I'm doing. So I'm going to expand my brain and broaden my skills and learn all about comic timing and delivery.

If you want to tickle people into laughter, like anything else, it takes practice. Go and learn. It also takes courage, because I cannot imagine anything scarier than standing on a stage (real or metaphorical) and having to be funny.

## Inappropriate Humour

And how do you know your humour is appropriate? Being funny isn't always a good idea...

I once got an uncontrollable fit of giggles during a christening service in a church. The minister was delivering a fairly ragey sermon—an unusual choice for a christening because it was a bit fire-and-brimstoney—and his voice and delivery were dead ringers for one of the characters from the film *The Life Of Brian*. All I could think about was the scene with the Roman soldiers, where Pilate says, "He has a wife, you know. Do you know what her name is? Incontentia. Incontinentia Buttocks."

At which point all his legionnaires, and my horrified self in this church, collapsed in semi-muffled snorts of laughter.

Here's something to consider: is it appropriate to tell the joke? If you're writing about grief, for example, there's no reason why you can't tell an amusing story... but telling a joke is almost certainly inappropriate. If you're writing about bankruptcy, there might be a funny tale in there—but making a joke may alienate your reader. There's a fine line between being funny and poking fun. Don't make fun of your customers. If you're not sure what side of the line you're on, it's best to avoid joking around.

## Be Yourself: Everyone Else Is Taken

I reckon one of the reasons we want to be funny is we read something someone else has written, laugh our socks off, and think, "Gorram, I wish I'd written that!"

Perfectly natural. It happens to me all the damn time. I wail for thirty seconds, ponder my place in the universe and despair at my lack of talent, then I crack on—because I'm funny in my own way, and I bet you are, too.

We're back to trying too hard again. Another reason we try to be funny is fear. My default response to discomfort in pole dancing classes is to clown around. I've been pole dancing for twelve years—but I only started learning exotic (read: stripper-style) about eighteen months ago. I don't see myself as sexy, so this new style was so far out of my comfort zone I needed binoculars to see that friendly shore… and my go-to reaction to "being sexy" was to go full-on Laurel-and-Hardy-style slapstick comedy.

I'm bloody funny when I do that (one day I'll share my Charlie Chaplin striptease performance). If I can make people laugh, I'm suddenly acceptable to myself again. But clowning around is a distraction. It distracts the audience from my intent, and it distracts me from my discomfort.

If you desperately want to be funny, ask yourself why. Why do you think you need to be funny? Are you afraid? It's okay if you are, but don't let your fear get in the way of your message. Be yourself. If you've a story to help get your message across, tell someone in real life. Do they laugh? Do they smile? If they do and they understand your message, your story is probably funny, and you can use it in your book.

But you don't *have* to be funny to be entertaining. Capture your reader's interest and stick to your main message. Always keep your goal in mind: what's your message here? What do you want your reader to take from your book? What's the chapter about?

Do you have a story to illustrate it? Tell that story. It may be funny, it may be sad, it may be shocking: as long as it helps you get your point across, use it.

Finally, remember this: not everyone will like you. Not everyone will get you. Not everyone will find your funny stories funny. And that's okay. Some will love you. Some won't. So what?

Be yourself, funny or not. Everyone else is taken.

Right: you've written your Shitty First Draft. You know how to take your SFD and make it flamboyant and deliciously yours. The writing part is over! Congratulations. It's time to move onto the next stage: Printing and Publishing, starting with how to edit your work.

First, though, take these Tiny Beetle Steps.

## Tiny Beetle Steps

1. When you re-read your Shitty First Draft, how do you come across? If you're sounding a bit preachy, a quick fix is to search and remove any instances of "you should", "you must", and "you need to". Instant improvement.

2. If you badly want to write comedy, learn how. Otherwise, it'll be forced. Instead, concentrate on being yourself and telling your stories. Re-read Chapters 15 and 16— entertaining is much more attainable than full-on funny.

3. Check in with your progress: how are you getting on? Go back to your outline and see if anything has changed. Do you need to alter your outline and structure? It's okay if you do!

PART III

# The Finishing Touches

*"To be really great in little things, to be truly noble and heroic in the insipid details of everyday life, is a virtue so rare as to be worthy of canonization."*

*Harriet Beecher Stowe*

# CHAPTER 18

# Editing For Victory

*"So the writer who breeds more words than he needs,*
*is making a chore for the reader who reads."*

*Dr. Seuss*

Most writing is boring. Mind-numbingly, tediously, dull. Even if it's on-message, factually correct, selling something genuinely good… it's a big beige blancmange of "meh", extruded from a message machine into a sausage of processed words.

The problem is the deluge of crap. There is so much information available online today and anyone can publish anything, so they do—often by "modelling" (read "copying") what other people have done in their industry—and it all blends together. Even the good stuff is beginning to look familiar. Your book needs to stand out. It needs to be full of you and your personality. It needs editing—which is what we'll do now.

This chapter will help you level up your Shitty First Draft. You'll have to be brutal with yourself. You'll need to be four-gins-in honest. It'll require hard work and patience. But it will be worth it because the most elegant writing is distilled from cracking editing.

When Ernest Hemingway wrote *The Sun Also Rises*, his editor told him to cut out the first two chapters. Hemingway did so, and that book made him famous.

Thomas Wolfe's editor told him to get rid of 90,000 words from his novel *Look Homeward, Angel...* and it became a classic. It was his first novel and launched his career. I know we're not writing novels here, or even fiction—but editing is as crucial in non-fiction writing as it is in fiction.

Even more so, I'd argue, because the writing you and I do must sell our products and services. The problem is, most people have no real idea of how to edit their work—and little inclination to do so. That's not surprising, because editing is a bloody difficult job and the best editors often don't know how to explain what it is they do and how they do it.

Plus, editing takes even more time. You've already written your book, and now I'm asking you to do more work? Ain't nobody got time for that. Except... if you want a book you can be proud of, which lets you reach more people and helps your business thrive, you must *make* time to edit.

Let's take a close look at why editing is a crucial part of writing a book, then I'll show you how to edit your work like a pro. By the way, what you learn in this chapter also applies to articles, blogs, sales pages, emails... everything.

You'll learn how to take your bland book-blancmange and turn it into a sumptuous chocolate lava cake of a read, so more people peruse it, share it, learn from it, are helped—and consequently buy more of your stuff.

Before we start, though, here's a top tip from me: the best way to edit your own work is to pretend someone else wrote it, then rip it to shreds.

## Back To Shitty First Drafts

You might be silently raging at me here. Maybe you think it takes you a bloody long time to write anything, let alone your book—and now I'm asking you to do a proper editing job too?

Damn right, I am. I am *such* a bitch.

But look at it this way: if you've spent sweat, tears, and time writing your book, don't you think your work deserves to be as good as you can make it?

I do.

Otherwise, you're wasting your time.

As I said in Chapter 5, your first draft won't be as good as you can make it. Not even close. The thing about Shitty First Drafts is: they're shitty. *And that's okay.*

Most first drafts are shitty because you frantically vomit words onto the page. Even if you've written an excellent outline—and I bloody well hope you have—your first draft will still be something of a word-salad. If you've resisted the urge to edit as you write, what you write at first is simply your starting point.

Oh, and I know I said this elsewhere, several times, but I don't care. I'm gonna repeat it ad nauseam without apology: **do not edit as you write your first draft**.

That's because, at this stage, we're getting our ideas out as fast as possible before they escape our tiny brains forever. We ramble, we repeat ourselves, we go off on tangents. Our thoughts don't necessarily land in the best order. There will definitely be typos, grammatical oddities, and general verbal shambling. Not really what we want our readers and potential clients to see, is it? Again: it's okay. Because once our first draft is done, we start editing.

Editing is vital because if we put our Shitty First Drafts out there, readers will not be kind to us—and why should they be? If we're not going to put in the effort to do our very best, we deserve a pickling. People take the greatest delight in pointing out typos, grammatical walruses, and inconsistencies in books, articles, emails, and blogs.

Editing is vital because, without it, your work is likely to bloat, float off-stream, and end up in the whirlpool of desolation, spinning into obscurity.

Editing is also vital because you'll sometimes write a line you think, at the time, is worthy of Hemingway… then when you see it in print later, you cringe in shame because you realise actually it's a pedestrian cliché or a pretentious banality that makes you want to cry. If only you'd spent time editing, you could have taken it out—and nobody would have seen your shame.

Shitty First Drafts are a good thing—but it's best if you don't release them into the wild.

First, write for yourself.

Next, write for your reader.

Then polish your work.

The first round of writing is you blurting words onto a page. The second and third rounds are editing. But what actually is editing? For me, editing falls into three stages:

1. **Big picture editing:** does the structure work?
2. **Bonsai editing:** how do the sentences and words work together? How do they feel?
3. **Proofreading:** are there any errors in spelling, grammar, punctuation, or consistency?

All three stages are critical, and I'll go through what you need to do for each. Before I do, though, I have a few more things to say about writing.

## Walk Away From Your Manuscript

After you've written your Shitty First Draft and before you get out the Red Pen of Correction, put down your work. Walk away from it for at least a week, if you can. Leave it to rest. Get some emotional distance from your baby.

This is important because while you're not thinking consciously about what you've written, your subconscious will be digging it over in your mind and planting new seeds for improvement.

After you've given it a little space, read it.

It sounds obvious, but most writers don't sit and read their manuscripts through as if they were their target reader. Don't read it with your editing hat on, read it as if you were the customer. No notes. No editing. Just reading.

Print it out if you can, because you'll see things differently reading it on paper—plus you can make notes on it later. And yes, I do think of the trees—I am a proud treehugger SJW[1] who buys recycled paper and prints as little as possible—but this is important. After all, if your goal is to print 1,000 copies of your book onto pulped trees from a sustainable source, do the trees the honour of giving them the best version of your book.

Once you've let your manuscript marinate and read it as if you were your target reader, it's time to start on the structure, missing sections, and elephant-sized issues.

## Does Size Matter?

"A good speech should be like a woman's skirt; long enough to cover the subject and short enough to create interest."

When Winston Churchill said that, he was (obviously) talking about speeches. But the same principle applies to any writing… including your book.

One of the most common questions I get from aspiring authors is, "How long should my book be?" It's a good question. When we set out to do something as monumental as writing a book, we cast around frantically in search of a playbook or foolproof formula to tell us exactly what to do.

Size seems like as good a place as any to start… but in fact, when it comes to your book, size is not terribly important. It really is what you do with it. I'm talking about self-publishing your business book here, not working with traditional publishers. And I'm talking about non-fiction, not fiction.

Fiction has its own rules, and if you're a brand new, unknown author, it's probably a good idea to follow them. Likewise, if you want to get published by a traditional publisher, it's a good idea to follow their guidelines (and get an agent).

But when it comes to non-fiction, don't worry about word count. I don't want you to make the common mistake many authors make, and stuff your book full of fluff. Many writers

---

1   Social justice warrior. Yep: I want to make the world a better place.

believe their business masterpiece needs to be a big, thick, weighty tome for people to take it seriously. It doesn't.

Writing a book and putting yourself out there is scary. We all suffer from imposter syndrome to some extent—which can lead to overcompensation in the publishing department. We cover our fear with a giant manuscript.

But I have news for you: your worth as an expert does not depend on the size of your book. It depends on your message. Don't fear your message: believe in yourself! Fear leads to waffle; waffle leads to padding; and padding leads to the dark side.

Look at some of the reviews of business books on Amazon, and you'll see what I mean. Look at some of the low-star reviews, and you'll likely find some of them complain the writer could have covered the subject perfectly well in half the pages.

They'll complain about repetition, padding, and overblown writing, which comes from either not knowing your subject well enough to write about it in fascinating detail, or feeling worried that unless you have a big book, you won't be taken seriously.

The truth is, if you have the right amount of junk in your trunk, you don't need any padding.

Your message will speak for itself.

Having said that, keep practicality in mind. If your book is under 100 pages, your printer may have trouble printing your title and name on the spine. One hundred pages are somewhere between 35,000 and 40,000 words.

In 2011, the average non-fiction bestseller stood at 467 pages. In 2017, it fell to 273 pages[2]. It seems like bestsellers are getting shorter… but do not let that dictate your writing.

If your book is under 100 pages, it's not the end of the world! The shortest bestseller came in at 80 pages. You can always print it without anything on the spine. Or you can release it as an ebook edition only. If your book comes out short, but it's brilliant—so

---

2    Scribe analysed a list of every *New York Times* Number One Non-Fiction Bestseller between 2011 and 2017 to find the average length: https:// scribewriting.com/how-long-should-book-be/

be it. Don't pad it just to create extra pages.

Instead—here's an idea—if you feel you need to add more pages, consider what value you could add in the appendices. Can you include examples of what you talk about? Frameworks? Exercises for readers to do so they can put your book into action? Could you include blank pages for your reader's notes (as one of my clients does in her books)? Would your book benefit from a glossary? Or an index? There are plenty of ways to add bulk to a book without destroying your message.

Short books with clear benefits to the reader are better than long ones you have to tunnel into to find the real treasure.

If, as you read through your work, you feel like it's got a bit fluffy, give it a trim.

## Make It More Personal

Beware of the curse of TMI: too much information. Facts are vital, of course, but if your writing is too fact-heavy, it'll begin to read like a textbook or academic research paper.

If you're not writing a textbook or academic research paper, this is a problem. (Actually, I'd argue it's a problem even if you are because I see no reason for educational stuff to be dry and dull, but that's another battle for another book.)

My point is: people want your take on the facts. They can get the bare, dry information anywhere—but your reader wants your interpretation of them. Your point of view. When we understand other points of view (especially opposing judgements) and learn from people we admire, we're better able to form our own opinions and make our own decisions.

If your writing is getting dense, or the book feels devoid of your sparkling personality, add in more of your stories and experiences. How has what you're writing about affected you? Or your clients? Include customer stories and give your writing more than one voice. Make your book personal and make it enjoyable.

Beware, too, of inadvertently plagiarising others. When you're researching your book, you'll inevitably gather information from elsewhere. If, when you read through what you've written, you feel it doesn't sound like you and your voice, you may have accidentally copied something you didn't write.

Don't worry—that's why we edit. Go back and rewrite the passage in your own words. Think about what the story or event means to you, and put it into your personal experience and context. If you can't do that, quote it instead—and credit the original writer. Explain why you've chosen to cite that particular passage and what it means to you, and why you think it'll help your reader. Using other work as influence and reference is fine; copying without credit or reference is not.

## Big Picture Editing

Writing is, I think, the closest we can come to time travel—or even telepathy. Your words enter your reader's brain somewhere else and sometime else—and you almost certainly won't be there to explain what you meant if your reader is puzzled.

If your reader is confused, they'll stop reading and do something else. In future, they'll go to someone who doesn't confuse them. Your job as a writer—as a business owner and communicator—is to make your message as clear as possible, so your reader has no questions or doubts.

The first serious stage of editing involves flow and the big picture, which is where we make sure your message shines through with clarity. Don't worry too much about spelling, grammar, and typos now—we'll catch them later. This is about making your work flow smoothly.

Make your reader's journey through your words effortless. Your writing should be invisible, so your reader glides along a polished pavement, rather than hacks her way through the tangled undergrowth of your ideas. We want people to comment on and remember the message, not the writing.

It may sound like I'm contradicting myself here—after all, I talked about writing beautifully in Chapter 16. There's no contradiction: when I say your writing should be invisible, I mean your reader shouldn't have to work hard at reading it. You don't want your sentences to trip up your reader, or be full of complicated words they have to look up, or long sentences that leave them breathless.

Ask yourself the following questions as you read through your work for the second time:

- **Does your writing flow logically**, guiding your reader along a journey of discovery and transformation?

- **What would make your message stronger?** Are you missing ideas? Examples? Emotional links to your reader?

- **Does your book answer your reader's question** or questions?

- **Is your writing coherent**—does it make sense? Does one sentence flow to the next, and one paragraph to the next, or does it feel disjointed and scratchy?

- **Have you thoroughly explained any thorny ideas?** Are you using jargon without clarifying it?

- **Have you over-explained?** Cut your work brutally, because one or two explanations or illustrative stories are enough.

Speaking of cutting your work, a good rule of thumb is: your second draft should be around 10% shorter. Take out anything that doesn't lead to your point. If you can't bear to delete something, add it to your scrapbook as the basis for an article or blog post. You'll probably find you've repeated yourself in different places, so cut anything you've said more than once.

Reading should be effortless, so make a note of anything that makes you stumble or frustrates you as you read. Remove anything that makes the reader pause. Reading your manuscript out loud will help you identify any clumsy lines.

Have you omitted anything important? Add it now, and check it fits. Don't shoehorn it in; create a flow from one idea to the next, linking each to your central theme.

Write for your reader's language and culture: if English isn't their first language, keep your writing super simple. If your reader is an expert in your field, if they're technically advanced and specialist, use language they're familiar and comfortable with.

For example, one of my Moxie Authors is a translator who specialises in chemical translations. Her clients are chemical companies and experts, so she can and should use complex technical words and phrases because they'll expect it and understand it. But if your readers are novices, seek out and destroy any jargon. If in doubt, assume ignorance and start from the beginning, keeping things as simple as possible.

When you've sorted out the structure, flow, and any significant issues, it's time to get down to the details.

## Bonsai Editing

I call this stage Bonsai Editing because we take tiny nips and tucks, gently altering the look and feel of our writing without changing the overall structure.

I could go into geeky minute detail about the subtler points of writing, but I won't. Instead, I'll direct you towards *The Elements of Style* by Strunk & White—still appropriate to today's writers. Read *Politics and the English Language* by George Orwell, too, in which he rages against confusing, unclear, and obfuscating language, and which contains his six rules of writing well.

I've altered Orwell's rules slightly (yes I am an audacious hussy) because there are always occasions when it's appropriate to break the rules…

1. **Avoid using a metaphor, simile, or other figures of speech you're used to seeing in print.** Sometimes a good cliché does the job perfectly; most of the time, they're tired and dull. If things are familiar, the brain predicts what's coming, so the message goes into your mind unnoticed—filing it in the bin. Think of fresh figures of speech wherever you can.

2. **If a short word will do the job better than a long**

**word, use the short word.** My favourite (or least-favourite) example is "utilise"—"use" is almost always a better option.

3. **If it's possible to cut a word out, cut it out.** For example, you can get rid of the words "that", "just", and "very" 99% of the time without rendering your sentence senseless. In fact, your writing will be ten times better without them.

4. **If you can use the active voice** without butchering your sentence or making it ugly, do so; the passive voice tends to be difficult to read and distances you from your reader. When you write in the active voice, you do things to stuff. When you write in the passive voice, stuff has things done to it.

5. **Never use a foreign phrase, a scientific word, or a jargon word** if you can think of an everyday English equivalent—unless you're writing for a reader whom you know will understand it.

6. **Break any of these rules sooner than say anything outright barbarous.**

7. **And finally, my own last words** on Orwell's rules: good writing—enjoyable, lively, fresh writing—is no place for a dictator. **There are no absolute rules.** If a "forbidden" word or phrase lifts your writing and makes it sing, for heavens' sake, leave it in.

When you're Bonsai Editing, look at sentence structure, clarity, word-use, and grammar. Are there any long, winding, clunky sentences? Anything that causes you to asphyxiate if you read it out loud because it's like drowning under all the words?

## Keep It Simple, Sunshine

You may suffer from a different form of TMI: Too Many Ideas. It's like the writer starts at A, then gets distracted by an exciting avocado, spins off into D, and ends up at 33. All in the same sentence. Keep your writing simple: shorter sentences, one thought per sentence. One idea per paragraph.

If you're not sure how to simplify a sentence, perhaps you don't understand it well enough to explain it—so go back to basics. What's the point you're trying to make? The idea you're trying to get across? Bullet point it. Or draw it. Or explain it verbally to someone, then let them tell you why they can't understand you. Talking it through helps you separate the thoughts in your mind before you put them on paper.

Watch out for unnecessary passive voice atrocities. Like this little gem, written by Aaron Sorkin and delivered by Emily Proctor as Ainsley Hayes in the TV show *The West Wing*:

"I'd like to do well on this, my first assignment. Any advice you could give me that might point me the way of success would be, by me, appreciated."[3]

Lionel Tribbey, her boss, replies: "Well, not speaking in iambic pentameter might be a step in the right direction."

This dialogue is hilarious, especially for a word nerd like me, and especially when you see the show… but I think you'll agree it's a little tough to follow. Tribbey was right about the iambic pentameter, but part of the reason it's a harsh sentence is Ainsley's use of the passive voice. The more active your writing, the more energy it has and the more interesting it is to read. Think of people doing things instead of having things done to them. "I would appreciate it if you could help me." Or, even better, "Please help me." Versus: "Your help would be appreciated by me."

Passive voice isn't just boring to read, it puts up a wall between you and your reader. Using the passive voice distances you from your reader. It makes you sound uncertain about what you're saying as if you don't want to own it. Of course, you can't always flip writing from passive to active, and there are some instances when passive works better and is more elegant. But generally, write using the active voice—it's easier and funner[4] to read.

---

3  *The West Wing* Season 2 Episode 5: And It's Surely To Their Credit.

4  And, yes, it's fine to make up your own words. I do it all the time.

## Make Redundant Text... er... Redundant

Now for even more detail. We're down to the words you're using, which matter. Enormously. Let's start with superfluous nonsense, which creeps into the best writers' work before editing.

Stuff like... 9 a.m. in the morning. If you say "9 a.m." you don't need "in the morning".

Stuff like... at this point in time. Instead, say "now".

Stuff like... at the end of the day, when all's said and done, we ultimately just want to eat biscuits. Say: "All we want is to eat biscuits". Or whatever. You get the idea.

Write tight. Don't worry if you think what you have is a little short: concise is good. Don't worry about being blunt or sounding rude—I'm not suggesting you write as if there's a ration on words. I'm saying, cut the fluff. When you start worrying about your writing being too short, fluff creeps in because you feel the need to pad it.

Check your writing for clarity: is each sentence crystal clear? Does each word make sense? Can your reader understand your message? *Are you sure?*

Get someone else to read it—preferably someone who's not an expert in your subject. If they can understand your book, you're doing well. If they can't, rephrase your writing so they can follow you.

## Avoid Adverbs And Clichés

Another useful and easy way to improve your writing is to delete adverbs. Adverbs modify verbs. Use them sparingly. They don't generally add anything to your writing, and they're lazy.

Let me give you a typical example: "very" is an adverb.

- Instead of saying "very cold", say freezing.
- Instead of "very hot", say scorching.
- Instead of "very tasty", say mouthwatering.
- Instead of "very angry", say furious or outraged.

Don't think you can get away with replacing "very", either. This rule applies to all very's boring cousins: extremely, exceedingly, highly, greatly, truly, pretty, quite…

You can always think up a more exciting word if you make an effort. Preferably a word that paints a picture in your reader's mind. When I read "mouthwatering", for example, I see a watermelon, all ready to eat, on a hot day. When I read "scorching", I see red glows, hot days on the beach, or overheating while running—depending on the context.

Avoid clichés like the plague. (Ahaha, see what I did there?) The problem with overused adverbs, everyday words like "hot" and "cold", and clichés, is they become invisible. Background fuzz. White noise.

They're boring.

If you're stuck for a substitute, pop the word into thesaurus. com and see what comes out. You don't have to use a long, obscure word—pick something that reaches out of the page and pokes you gently in the eye.

Grab yourself a copy of *Words That Sell* by Richard Bayan and keep it on your desk—it'll help you improve your vocabulary and use more persuasive words.

Your Shitty First Draft might contain mountains of adverbs and clichés, and that's okay. This book did before I ripped it a new one. That's what editing is for: get your ideas down first, then make them fascinating.

The final part of Bonsai Editing involves fixing spelling, grammar, punctuation, and consistency. You'll also do this when someone proofreads your work…

## Proofreading

Proofreading is your final check on spelling, grammar, typos, and references (including numbering, page numbers, and what-have-you). Please get a professional proofreader to check it over, or you risk looking like an amateur.

You might be tempted to proofread it yourself to save money—but you'll struggle to do it effectively. Our brains see what we mean to write, not always what we actually write and spellcheckers don't always pick up typos and grammatical oddities.

One of my favourite tools is Grammarly, which does pick up typos and oddities—as well as making suggestions if a word doesn't make sense. The free version is fab, but I pay for the premium version, which gives me all sorts of helpful hints, tips, and recommendations for improving my writing. Go to www.grammarly.com and copy and paste your work into their webpage.

Grammarly isn't a substitute for a professional proofreader, though. It won't catch everything, and it doesn't "read" your work in context. A proofreader will. If you refuse to hire a professional proofreader to check your manuscript before you finally send it to your printer, at least ask a helpful partner, client, or colleague to look it over.

You've now got a good grasp of the basics of editing. If you follow my advice, you'll be able to improve your manuscript enormously. If your budget stretches to it, though, I recommend finding a fantastic editor. They're worth their weight in diamonds and can turn a mediocre book into a bestseller.

## Finding An Editor

If you decide to work with a professional editor, look for someone familiar with your industry. Ask for recommendations and references: talk to authors your chosen editor has worked with before and see if they were happy with them.

Beware of anyone who says they can turn around a full edit in a couple of days; the work they deliver is unlikely to be high quality. Book your editor in plenty of time. The good ones have waiting lists.

Remember you get what you pay for so although you'll probably have a budget and will want to avoid paying over the odds, going cheap may be a false economy. Depending on the type of editing you want, and how long your book is, fees for editing will be somewhere between £1,500 and £10,000 for Big Picture (developmental) and full editing. For Bonsai Editing (copy and line editing) fees will be somewhere between £750 and £2,300. For professional proofreading, fees will be around £300 to £800.

If you really can't stretch to an editor or you're confident in editing your own book, send your manuscript to beta readers, as I've done with this book. Your beta readers will tell you if the structure doesn't work, will point out where your manuscript doesn't flow and will let you know where you need to add more information (or where you need to take out fluff). Beta readers can't replace a professional editor, but they can help you improve your book enormously. At the very least, get a professional proofreader to go through your book before you send it to print.

Always keep the big picture in mind: what do you want your book to do for you? It's not just about shifting copies; it's about using your book to build a solid base of ideal customers who'll be loyal for years. Think of editing and other professional details as an investment that you'll be able to claim back.

## Your Book Is Worth It

I won't lie to you: editing is hard work. It takes ages. And it is compulsory if you want to avoid looking like an amateur. Now self-publishing is so much easier, there are more amateurish books out there—books by people who are "too busy" or too arrogant to rip their baby to shreds. A well-edited book stands out a mile from the dross; it's worth the investment of time or money.

It would be a tragedy for you to go through all the pains and joys of writing your book, only to fall at the last jump and put out a book that's unworthy of you. You're worth the extra effort, and so is your book. Don't sell yourself short.

This chapter was, at its core, all about how to avoid looking like an amateur. But there's far more to being a pro-writer than editing—so read on. The next two chapters are all about competing with the big boys and girls.

## Tiny Beetle Steps

1.  Check your manuscript for padding. Have you repeated yourself or added in unnecessary fluff? Cut it out and put it in the lint trap.

2.  Ask yourself the questions from the Big Picture Editing chunk. Read your manuscript with those questions in mind and a red pen by your side.

3.  Build a team of Beta Readers who'll help you edit your book. You can find more details on how to do this on my blog: www.moxiebooks.co.uk/blog.

4.  Consider working with a professional editor if your budget allows.

5.  At the very least, run your manuscript through Grammarly—and hire a proofreader!

# CHAPTER 19

# Clickbait For Your Covers

*"I never really know the title of a book until it's finished."*

*Mary Wesley*

Every head turned his way when he walked through the door. All eyes were on him. It doesn't get much more compelling than Tom Hiddleston in a perfectly tailored suit… As far as first impressions go, the Hiddleston in a suit wins every time for me.

Imagine you're getting ready for the first date with someone you've had a crush on for ages. You'd make your best effort, wouldn't you? You'd want the first impression to be as good as it possibly could be—your sparkling conversation, your hair, your makeup, your clothes all showing off your personality and your best physical features to their most admirable advantage. And all in the first few seconds of meeting.

Your book cover is like the perfect velvety, rich red lipstick. It's your first chance to make a great impression… and if you don't make a great impression now, you may not get another opportunity.

One of the most stupid phrases in the English language must be "don't judge a book by its cover". Of course, we judge a book by its cover. Until we've opened the damn thing, we've nothing else to judge it by… which is why it's vital your book cover doesn't betray you. **Do not be miserly with your book cover.**

If you're tempted to DIY, remember this: you've poured blood, sweat, tears, and love into writing this book of yours. Are you proud of it? Are you proud of the amount of work you've put in, of how much you truly know about your industry? Has your depth of knowledge surprised you? Do you feel like the expert you are?

Then don't cheapen all your work with a cover that makes you look like an amateur—because if you try to DIY your book cover, you will almost certainly look like an amateur. (Unless you're actually a designer or illustrator—in which case, as you were.)

In this chapter, we'll go through everything you need to create a book cover that grabs attention, hooks interest, and has people fighting their way to the back of the shop to buy it—starting with your title.

## Titles That Tantalise

When it comes to choosing a title for your book, you'll almost certainly want to set fire to everything. I find coming up with titles for my own books an absolute horror show. I'm awful at it. It took me until the second draft of this book to come up with a working title (and even that was awful: *The Book About Writing A Book*).

Go easy on yourself if you struggle with this. You're not alone.

You may have had the title of your book in mind for a long time—some writers do. Some people can come up with a clear idea and nail it down in a title long before they start writing. They find the title the easy part. I am not one of those people.

If you, too, struggle with titles and headlines, don't worry about it yet. You don't need a final title until right at the end.

Sometimes, your title will jump out at you as you write your book. Or perhaps one of your beta readers or your editor will come up with a great idea. Often, writing the introduction and conclusion sparks some great title ideas.

The crucial thing to remember is your title (and subtitle) have one job, and one job only: to get people to buy the book, open it, and read the first line. So don't try to be too smart.

One of my Superheroes once asked me about titles. Should they be clever? Or boringly descriptive? It's a good question because nobody wants to be boring—and boring won't make people want to read your book. But if you try to be "clever", that's risky too: chances are, people won't understand you.[1]

## What Questions Are People Asking?

Your book title should speak to the questions people have in their heads when they're looking for the answers your book will give them. That's how I came up with the title of this book in the end. I remembered my reaction when my mentor told me to write a book.

My first thought was, "I can't do that!" and my second thought was, "How the hell do you write a book?!" I suspect similar ideas have trundled through your mind, too—which is why my book is called what it's called.

The title *How To Stop Your Puppy Chewing Your Christian Louboutins* might sound dull to you—but you're not your reader. To the person whose cherished posh shoes are being nibbled, it's a fascinating title because it promises to solve their costly problem.

Think about effective headlines, search results, and clicks—it's relevant because you want your book title to be searchable and clickable. Your book should pop up in search results when people are looking for the answer to their problem.

There's a reason classic headline formulas are classic: they work. Create clickbait in the most positive sense. Clickbait is sneered at and has a bad name, but all headlines (and book titles) are clickbait. We want people to click on them and read them, for heaven's sake! But don't bait-and-switch.

---

1   In fact, when I asked Drayton Bird to write the foreword to this book, he agreed—but told me to change "Claps For Me" to "Testimonials" because he didn't know what I was on about. He was right. I thought it was cute; it was just confusing.

Bait-and-switch is where you promise someone something with a click-worthy headline, then deliver something else. For example, I might search for, "How to wear high-waisted trousers without looking like a chimney sweep" and Google might serve me an article with that title. But when I get there, the article advertises soft porn involving chimney sweeps in crotchless trousers.

Actually, I wouldn't get there at all, because Google does not like bait-and-switch. Which is my point. If your book title doesn't reflect what's inside your book, you will not get readers. And if by some miracle you do get readers, you'll piss people off because they won't get what your title promised them.

I know you're not going to do bait-and-switch, but you may fall into the trap of wanting to use a "clever" title because descriptive ones bore you. Don't. You must answer the questions people ask. Make clear what they're buying when they choose your book, and what they'll get when they open it.

If you're struggling with this—and you won't be alone, because good titles are damn difficult to write—remember you can also write a subtitle.

Take my first book title, for example, *Business For Superheroes*. On its own, it doesn't mean much—but with the subtitle "from scraping the bottom to six figures in just six months", it gives you a good idea of what you'll find inside. (Don't judge me on the six figures aspect of it, I know every internet marketing idiot says "six figures blah blah". I have much better title ideas now. But it was accurate at the time.)

Here are some other examples of great titles and subtitles:

- *Drunk Tank Pink:* The Subconscious Forces That Shape How We Think, Feel, And Behave.

- *Rewire Your Anxious Brain:* How To Use The Neuroscience of Fear To End Anxiety, Panic & Worry.

- *On Speaking Well:* How To Give A Speech With Style, Substance, And Clarity.

- *The Subtle Art of Not Giving A F*ck:* A Counterintuitive Approach to Living a Good Life.

- *Sleep Like A Boss:* The Guide To Sleep For Busy Bosses.
- *The Brain Audit:* Why Customers Buy, And Why They Don't.
- *The Chimp Paradox:* The Mind Management Programme for Confidence, Success and Happiness.
- *They Ask, You Answer:* A Revolutionary Approach To Inbound Sales, Content Marketing, And Today's Digital Consumer.
- *The Good Divorce Guide*: Facing Reality When Your World Is Upside-Down.

Do you see how they work? There's an interesting title—a hook, if you like, that might not give you quite enough info but makes you want to look closer. Then there's a subtitle (usually) that tells you a little more about what you'll get if you start reading.

What's your core concept? Your Big Idea? Start simple because you can always improve it.

- *Puppies That Chew:* How to stop your bundle of cuteness destroying everything you own with his tiny sharp teeth.
- *Horrible Homepages:* The top 5 mistakes you're almost certainly making on your homepage—and how to avoid them.
- *Flaky Skin:* How to stop shedding on the people you love.

I'm being a little silly, but those daft titles aren't half bad. You know what you're getting when you read them, which is the most important thing. Think: hook and promise. Catch your reader's attention, then promise them something interesting, useful, and/or entertaining to read. And remember to choose an easily readable typeface. Speaking of typeface, we're getting into design territory here—so let's move onto to your cover design.

## The Red Lipstick

Your book cover can be as simple or as colourful as you like— the crucial thing is that it's eye-catching, readable, and gives your reader an idea of what to expect inside.

Some of the most successful business books have simple, graphical covers—just the title and subtitle writ large and proud, easy to read, standing out like a flamingo at a penguin party.

Others have beautiful illustrations or cover images (like this one, thanks to the fabulous Julia Brown at Brown Owl Design). It's your book, so it's your choice. Just make sure the design is easy to read and understand.

Having said that, there are a few guidelines you'll want to stick to. Publishers understand which book covers sell, and which don't. Here are some of their secrets:

1. **Use lots of space.** Simple is best, and many book covers are too busy; there's too much going on, and the eye doesn't know what to pay attention to. If you do want to include lots of elements—as I did on the cover of this book—tie it all together with a smooth background colour and make sure the most critical elements jump out.

2. **Make it "pop".** This is a vile phrase meaning: use contrast. Consider a strong light-to-dark transition, or contrasting colours—opposites on the colour wheel. For example, orange and teal green is a visually pleasing combination. Blues and greens—think peacocks—look beautiful and striking. In fact, if you're stuck, look to nature: the most beautiful and brightly coloured animals are splendid inspirations.

3. **Use a subtitle or tagline** and tease your reader, especially if your title isn't immediately obvious (like my first book *Business For Superheroes* or *Made to Stick* by Chip and Dan Heath).

4. **Use a smart image:** non-fiction appeals to the brain because we're in learning mode when we look at business books. A solid colour background is a good idea, and a gimmicky image can work well. On the cover of *Made to Stick*, the cover designer used gaffer tape, which is cool.

5. **Bold, easy-to-read typeface:** don't use anything too fancy or it'll be unreadable. Avoid using a free font on your

cover, because it'll be overused. Find something that ticks all the readability boxes, but stands out. Get a designer to help you with the kerning—the spacing between the letters—because poor kerning is an obvious sign of an amateur designer. You'll know poor kerning when you see it; you don't notice it when it's done well.

6. **Put a human on the cover**, but beware of being cheesy. We're drawn to faces in images; it's programmed into our genes to recognise faces. Just look at how fascinated babies are with people's faces. Were you drawn to my cover? If you were, I'll wager one of the reasons you like it is because my face is on it.

7. **Fit your words together beautifully.** Look at the book covers on your bookshelf: some of them will be uniform; others won't. On the cover of *The Chimp Paradox*, for example, the word "chimp" is slightly larger than the others, drawing attention to itself. Small words like "in, of, the, and" can be physically smaller to fit between larger words.

8. **If in doubt, keep it simple.** Simple covers usually outsell complicated ones.

If you work with a book cover designer or illustrator, choose someone who understands books and publishing. Ask to see previous examples of their work, and see how the design elements work with the title and the contents of the book.

If you use an image for your cover, don't pick a random picture with no connection to your title or message. Pick something to enhance your writing and give your reader an idea of what they might encounter when they open your book. Make sure the image is high-resolution, or it'll look fuzzy when it's printed. And for the love of all that is holy, don't use a coloured border around your image, even if you think it looks nice. It doesn't. It looks like an amateur book, and people will assume you're an amateur because of it.

According to famous book cover designer Hobie Hobart, people spend eight seconds looking at your front cover, and fifteen seconds looking at the back cover, so you don't have long to get and keep someone's attention.[2]

Top tip: mock up a handful of book covers and create Facebook adverts for people to pre-order your book. Use the cover design that gets the most pre-orders.

## The Blurb On The Back

I have a confession to make: I loathe writing the back blurb for my books. I put it off and put it off and put it off until my cover designer starts sending up smoke signals. In fact, it's such an unfavourite job of mine, I even forgot to write about it in this book when I wrote my first draft.

It's kind of crucial, though, so here we go.

The blurb on the back is the third most important part of the cover after the front cover design and the title. Why? Think about what you do when you're considering buying a new book. The cover catches your eye, so you read the title and subtitle. They hook you and pique your interest, so... you flip the book over and read the back, right? Then you decide if you want to buy it.

Your back cover blurb isn't a synopsis (a detailed outline of the book). It's not a blurb (a short endorsement by a celebrity or someone prominent in your industry which goes on the front cover). It's not a review. And it's not a book description (although it may form part of the description you put on Amazon and other sales sites).

The back cover blurb is a sales pitch for your book, so it must be persuasive, captivating, and make the reader want to read on. And it must do all that in around 200 words. Easy, right?

Wrong. I would have loved a step-by-step instruction manual for writing my back blurbs, but there wasn't one. So I made one. Here it is:

---

2    The same article states that a literary agency has a three-second rule: if the cover doesn't grab them in three seconds, they pass on it. From: https://www. huffpost.com/entry/8-mistakes-that-will-abso_b_1017230

1. **Look at the bestsellers in non-fiction** and read their back blurbs. What similarities do they share? What makes them compelling? What makes you want to read on? Make a note of the structure so you can adapt it for your book.

2. **Put yourself in your reader's shoes.** You're writing non-fiction, so your reader has a problem to solve or a goal to reach. Start there. Richard Bayan's *Words That Sell* back cover blurb shows you immediately that if you struggle to find words that sell your products and services, his book will help you: "More than 6,000 words and phrases that make the difference between "yadda-yadda-yadda" and copy that sells".

3. **Make it easy to scan.** Most readers will give your back cover blurb around ten seconds to convince them to buy, so it better be easy to read. Bullet points are fantastic for this: pull out your book's main benefits—three to five is plenty—and pop them on your back cover.

4. **Write a killer first line.** Easier said than done, I know… but check out other non-fiction books for inspiration. Look outside your industry for inspiration. I love this one from Professor Steve Peters: "Your inner Chimp can be your best friend or your worst enemy... this is the Chimp Paradox". His back cover is intriguing, scannable, and contains celebrity endorsements. Winning!

In short, your back blurb should set out the question, challenge, or problem your reader faces. It should promise answers. And it should let your reader know what they'll get if they read the book.

## Your Book Must Sell Itself

Remember: your book cover is the red lipstick—it must get attention, hook your reader, and persuade them to invest money and time in reading your message. Your cover isn't the place to go cheap—it would be tragic to waste all the time and effort you've put in writing your book by sabotaging it with a crap cover.

Invest in a good cover designer, one who understands the principles behind sales and marketing as well as gorgeous design. Put time and care into choosing your title. And make sure the back of your book is a well-written, compelling advertisement that'll hook your reader in and persuade them to buy.

Now you know what needs to go on the covers, let's take a look inside because good writing isn't enough—you must make sure your book's innards are professional, too.

## Tiny Beetle Steps

1. Take photos of book covers that catch your eye. Trawl Amazon and save the covers that jump out at you. Note down ideas about what you want your book to look and feel like. What colours do you want?

2. Find a fantastic book cover designer. I recommend Julia Brown at Brown Owl Design. She creates all my book cover packages and is marvellous. She understands books and publishing, and she understands the principles of using design to sell, rather than just making pretty pictures (although she makes pretty pictures, too).

3. Scribble down 100 title ideas, and let your mind go wild. Come up with titles that are as bad as you can possibly make them, as well as splendid ideas. Give yourself permission to come up with rubbish. You never know where a good idea will come from.

4. Write the blurb for the back cover of your book. Follow my four steps and look at other non-fiction books for inspiration.

CHAPTER 20

# How To Avoid Looking
# Like An Amateur

*"Amateurs don't show up. Amateurs crap out. Amateurs let adversity defeat them. The pro thinks differently. He shows up, he does his work, he keeps on truckin', no matter what."*

*Steven Pressfield*

Are you an amateur? That's a rhetorical question because if you're reading these words, you most certainly are not an amateur. Amateurs don't write books. They don't even consider doing so.

Amateurs give up at the first sign of trouble; pros give it their best shot and make sure their book is the absolute best it can be.

You are an expert in your field. You help change your clients' lives for the better. You run a dynamite business that helps people. You go above and beyond to deliver a spectacular service. You show up, and you do the work. Right?

If that's true—and I hope it is—your book must reflect that. If your book looks amateurish, your readers and prospective clients will assume *you're* an amateur. If your book is sloppy, people will think *you're* careless. It might seem unfair, but that's the way it is.

This chapter is all about the details. The little touches that make all the difference, that will help lift your book from good to fabulous. If you go the traditional publishing route, your publisher will take care of this for you. Indeed, you'll have little input into how your book looks—unless you're extremely influential in your

---

CHAPTER 20

# How To Avoid Looking
# Like An Amateur

*"Amateurs don't show up. Amateurs crap out. Amateurs let adversity defeat them. The pro thinks differently. He shows up, he does his work, he keeps on truckin', no matter what."*

*Steven Pressfield*

Are you an amateur? That's a rhetorical question because if you're reading these words, you most certainly are not an amateur. Amateurs don't write books. They don't even consider doing so.

Amateurs give up at the first sign of trouble; pros give it their best shot and make sure their book is the absolute best it can be.

You are an expert in your field. You help change your clients' lives for the better. You run a dynamite business that helps people. You go above and beyond to deliver a spectacular service. You show up, and you do the work. Right?

If that's true—and I hope it is—your book must reflect that. If your book looks amateurish, your readers and prospective clients will assume *you're* an amateur. If your book is sloppy, people will think *you're* careless. It might seem unfair, but that's the way it is.

This chapter is all about the details. The little touches that make all the difference, that will help lift your book from good to fabulous. If you go the traditional publishing route, your publisher will take care of this for you. Indeed, you'll have little input into how your book looks—unless you're extremely influential in your

237

industry and in the publishing industry.

You'll probably go down the self-publishing route—which is no reason to end up with a book that looks amateurish. Gone are the days when self-published books looked like a maniacal toddler went at them with potato stamps, cheap paper, and glue. It's relatively easy to create a professional book yourself now.

In the previous chapter, we looked at what makes a fascinating book cover, so over the next few pages, we'll go through what typeface to choose; how to lay out your book, and why it matters; and we'll consider your options for printing and binding.

You've done all the hard work. All the sculpting and toning, all the thinking, all the learning and writing and rewriting and editing. Now it's time to dress up and pay attention to the details.

## Typeface

Nerdfact: printers used to hand-set type, and they had to pull actual metal letters, numbers, and symbols out of a box. The collection of characters in the box is called a "font".

The typeface is the look and feel of all the characters in the font. So when we talk about Times New Roman or Arial, we're talking about typeface. The individual symbols are the fonts.

You might be tempted to skip this section because it's about the technicalities of what the words look like, but please don't. Apart from anything else, typography and design are fascinating—honest! It's so exciting, there's a whole feature-length documentary film available called Helvetica.[1]

Let's talk about typeface because what you choose isn't just crucial for readability and comprehension, it's also an expression of who you are. (No, really.)

The typeface you select for the interior of your book will probably be different from the one on your cover.

Most importantly, your typeface should be easy to read (please do not choose a dragon typeface—which actually does exist). You

---

1   You can watch it on Amazon Prime if you like. It's cool!

don't have to be unusual and, in fact, you shouldn't be: your book should sit well with other books on a shelf. Your typeface can and should reflect your personality, but only in the sense that it suits you and your book. You're the only one who'll notice it: it should be invisible because you want your reader to see your message, not the black and white words.

Choose a serif typeface—that's the typeface with the little tops and tails on the letters. It's thought the tops and tails lead the eye, and make the text easier to read.[2] This typeface you're reading now is serif. Old-style typefaces work best in books—tried-and-true examples like Garamond, Caslon, Minion Pro, Baskerville (which this book is set in), and Palatino.

It's not just readability that's important, though; it's vital your reader understands what you've written—and the typeface you choose has a significant impact on reading comprehension. A study tested 224 participants who read material printed in serif type and sans serif type. Here are the results[3]:

- Serif body type: 67% of readers showed good comprehension of the text, and just 14% poor.

- Sans serif body type: 12% of readers showed good understanding, and 65% showed poor comprehension.

If you want your readers to be able to read and, crucially, understand your book, choose a typeface that's easy to read and encourages comprehension.

Some typefaces come free with Windows and Apple computers; others you can buy if you want. Don't spend a fortune on this detail, but do choose something you like. The most important thing is your book is easily readable, and you like the typeface. That's for body copy—for the main blocks of text.

For titles and headings, you can use a basic sans serif, so it

---

2 Interestingly, sans serif typefaces are more readable for people with dyslexia and some other learning difficulties. However, unless you're writing a book specifically aimed at people who have reading difficulties, use a serif typeface. For more information on dyslexia-friendly printing, visit: https://www.bdadyslexia.org.uk/

3 Wheildon, C. 2005, *Type & Layout*, The Worsley Press, p47.

contrasts with the body text. In this book, I chose a typeface called Roboto. It's easy to read in short sentences, and stands out, helping you find your place.

A good place to find fonts and typefaces, free and paid-for, is www.dafont.com. There are loads of lovely, free fonts out there to choose from.

If you can't decide, flip through some of your favourite books. Take a look at the colophon or the copyright page, and see if they've mentioned the typeface there. If not, take a photograph and upload it to www.whatfontis.com, which identifies different fonts. It's a pretty nifty site, actually, because you can do this for more unusual typefaces on book covers.

Spend some time thinking about the size of the typeface you want to use. It doesn't matter for your ebook version because you can make the words bigger on your e-reader. But size does matter in print. How old are your readers? The older they are, the bigger your words need to be. Do they have dyslexia or other reading difficulties? Consider this before you choose your typeface and font size. Eyes aged forty and older start to deteriorate. As I'm editing this, I'm forty, and I'm starting to notice. In fact, it was like I turned forty and suddenly became a person who has to hold things out in front of me to read them. I'm writing this in Scrivener at 175 per cent size because of my ageing eyes.

The main body text must be at least 11 points. Compact-width typefaces like Times New Roman look best in 11 or 12-point. Wider typefaces like Palatino look best in 10 or 11-point. "Large print" books are set in a minimum of 14-point type.

Always keep in mind what will make your book easy for your ideal reader to read and understand.

## Readability, Layout, And White Space

Can you use sub-headings to make your book clearer and easier to read? To enhance the sense of rhythm you're building with your words?

Consider paragraph size: big blocks of text are off-putting, even in books. You want your writing to look friendly and easy to read, with plenty of white space, and sentences and paragraphs of varying lengths. Long paragraphs are fine, but break them up with shorter paragraphs and subheadings.

Illustrations and photographs help, too. If an image or diagram will help your reader understand what you mean, use one! If you find an image that will underline a vital point, include it. When you use an image, make sure you use a caption. Captions always get read because people look at pictures. It's an excellent place to hammer home an important point or encourage people to take the next step.

Think about how involved your reader is in your work. Could you ask more questions and get people reading actively? (Almost certainly yes.)

I see first-time authors make three main mistakes with book layout:

1. **Not enough space** between lines and paragraphs, and between elements like the headers, footers, page numbers, page edges, any images, and titles.

2. **Boring headers or chapter designs.** You can have a little fun by adding a graphic element, like my quill pen and tiny beetle icons.

3. **Too much decoration** inside the book, or inappropriate fonts that are difficult to read or don't match the subject matter.

Generally, the first page of a chapter doesn't have headers, footers, or page numbers, and the first paragraph has no indent. You can choose to have a page number on the first page of a chapter if you like; there are no real rules, just guidelines.

Some authors pop a drop-cap (an initial capital letter that takes up more than one line) on the first line, which can look groovy. Some writers capitalise the first six words or so, which you can choose to do if you like.

I like to start my chapters about halfway down the page, and

I start them on a right-hand page, leaving the left page blank if necessary—but that's my personal preference. You can begin your chapters at the top and on a left-hand page if you want to.

You might want to introduce a simple design element on the chapter page, as I've done with my quill pen icon—or you can leave it very simple. Don't try to do too much, though, because too many flashy baubles will distract your reader.

Indent the first line of each paragraph because it makes reading easier. Your reader can easily see where to go to start the next paragraph. Leave enough space between your lines—at least 1.2 line spacing, and a couple of millimetres after each paragraph. Leave a little space before and after numbered and bulleted lists, so they don't look crowded.

Make sure your paragraphs are fully justified—equally spaced from left to right. First-time authors sometimes make the mistake of using ragged-right text. Don't do this, because it looks a right mess and it's difficult to read.[4]

Whatever writing program you use to design your book's interior—Scrivener, Word, Pages, Indesign, Vellum—turn off the hyphenation function, or you could find words split over pages. Some authors don't mind hyphenation, but I think it looks messy.

Study the layout of books you like. What works? What doesn't? What could you incorporate into your book?

## Numbers, Headers, And Footers

I like to use running headers and footers when I'm designing my books to help reader navigation. If you do that—and I recommend you do, to make your reader's life easier—pop the book title on the left-page header, and the chapter title on the right-page header. Leave plenty of space beneath the headers before the main text begins. Where you put your page numbers is up to you: at the top or bottom, in the centre, or in a corner. Leave plenty of space above the page number, so it isn't crowded.

---

4   This is good practice online as well as in print.

Top tip: if you have a blank page, for example, if you want your new chapters to start on an odd-number, right-hand page, make sure the blank page doesn't show a header, footer, or page number. A blank page should actually be blank.

## Index

Do you need an index? You don't have to have one, but an index can help readers if they might want to refer back to parts of your book often.

If you decide to include an index, find a professional indexer. It's a skill in and of itself, and you'll find it tough to do yourself. Also, it will take you forever and likely make you want to set fire to the world. Leave plenty of time for this, because a good indexer will read the manuscript several times. The indexer I work with is a treasure because she also points out typos and grammatical oddities if she finds them.

The best place to find information about indexing is the Society of Indexers at www.indexers.org.uk.

## Printing & Binding

My paperback books are perfect-bound, which means glueing the pages into the spine. This method works well for most books, as long as the page count is between around 40 and 700 pages.

You do have other options, though. Saddle stitching is good for magazines and short pamphlets, but not proper books. Wiro-binding can be suitable for workbooks—or for advance copies for beta readers. I sent wiro-bound copies out to my fabulous Launch Team to get their feedback. Then there are hardback books: great for special or limited editions, and fantastic for coffee table books or art books.

Your paperback cover should be at least 250 gsm, or it'll feel flimsy and cheap. You can choose a matte or gloss finish, it's up to you. When I printed *Business For Superheroes*, my first edition was gloss, and the second edition was matte. I prefer the matte. This book cover is matte. If you have details on your cover, you can ask for distinctive printing elements like spot-gloss or metallics, which can look fantastic—but they'll add to the printing cost. If you want to produce limited edition print runs, such details can help to make them unique.

Hardback books are heavy cardboard covered with cloth, buckram, or sometimes leather—and often have a dust jacket. Underneath the dust jacket, you can have richly coloured plain fabric—or a printed design to complement what's on the dust jacket. Chip Kidd shows some wonderful examples of how you can use dust jackets to great effect in his delightful TED Talk.[5]

I've popped a downloadable cover dimensions PDF in the resources area on the website—this will help you and your book cover designer when you're working on your cover. Your book printer should be able to help you with cover dimensions, too.

Use the best paper stock you can afford, or you risk your book feeling and looking cheap. I recommend using cream, off-white, or natural paper. I think it looks better and more professional than white—and, crucially, it's easier on the eye and more comfortable to read because of the lower contrast.

Use high-opacity paper, or you risk being able to see through to the print on the other side—which is the classic hallmark of a cheap book. You want at least 80gsm for a black-and-white book and at least 100gsm for colour, so you don't get bleed-through. Use uncoated paper for a matte finish, and coated for high-art or photography book. If you're writing a "normal" book like this one, opt for an uncoated matte finish.

Finally, I want my books to be as eco-friendly as possible. I use FSC-certified paper, vegetable-based inks where possible, and check the eco-credentials of my printer. In an ideal world, I'd use fully recycled paper—but that's not usually practical, and the quality can be variable. Hopefully, technology will improve, and I'll be able to attain full tree-hugger status one day.

5  https://www.ted.com/talks/chip_kidd_designing_books_is_no_laughing_matter_ok_it_is

## Fact Checking And References

Every time you make a claim, include a statistic, or state a fact, check it. Are you correct? In the first edition of *Business For Superheroes*, I forgot to check one "fact" and found out later it was nonsense.

I'm still embarrassed by it, but at least it's no longer mocking me in the second edition or the Kindle edition. Check your facts and figures. Dig up evidence to reinforce what you're saying—which may be scientific research, stories from other experts, or testimonials from your clients.

Do you have a list of all your references and facts? Here's my advice which you ignore at your peril: make a proper note of any information and quotes and where you found them, as you see them. Do not leave it until the end and think you'll do it then. It will be a total nightmare, and you'll hate the process. If you have all your references handy as you go along, you'll love yourself for it when it's time to publish. Trust me.

## Five Common Rookie Mistakes

The five most common layout mistakes that newbie authors make.

1.  **Using ragged-right composition.** Almost every book you have read uses justified composition, so the text forms a rectangle on the page, and the lines are flush at the left and right margins. Ragged-right means the edges are only flush on the left margin, and the right margin is ragged because each line is a different length. Ragged-right is difficult to read, so don't do it.

2.  **Running headers on blank pages.** Blank pages are supposed to be blank[6]. If you have a blank left-hand

---

6   This is a publishing convention, and it matters because of our expectations of what a "proper" book should look like. When people talk about books looking amateurish, but they can't put their finger on why, it's often because of a detail like this.

page, make sure there are no page numbers, no running headers, and no navigation aides.

3. **Keep an eye on your odd and even pages.** This is one of the gnarliest layout mistakes you can make, especially if you're working with lots of different documents. If you're working in Word or Mac Pages, things can get messy. It's a little less worrisome in Scrivener because Scrivener compiles everything for you—but keep an eye on it anyway and check everything after you've finished. When you open up any book, page one (an odd-numbered page) is always on the right. So all your odd-numbered pages will be right-hand pages, and all your even-numbered pages will be left-hand pages.

4. **Make sure you don't have any blank right-hand pages.** Start your chapters on right-hand pages—and if you have to, put a blank page between them. A blank right-hand page screams amateur so check carefully.

5. **Page numbers help your reader navigate, of course, but they don't belong on every page.** Take them off the copyright page, the title page, the half-title page, and any other display pages within the book like part-openers. If you've got part one and part two, or any advertising pages, take the page numbers out. Page 1 starts on the first right-hand page after the Table of Contents.

## Make A List And Check It Twice

Over the years, I've made mistakes. I've learned from every one of them, and from those mistakes has emerged one of the most essential weapons in my book project box: my Final Checklists.

Once all the writing, editing, proofreading, and designing has happened, and you have a proof copy in your hands, you'll want to send your book to print. But wait! Now is not the time to rush.

I know the last thing you want to do is delay your print run, but trust me—spend a couple of days running through some final checks. Stuff like, is the ISBN correct? Does it match the barcode?

Are there any errors on the cover? On the title pages?

There's a lot to think about, so I wrote it all down. Do what I do: do not press "go" on your book printing until you've checked and ticked off everything on your list, then signed it and dated it. Yes, I know you're not doing this for a client, but act as if you are your own client. Check it. Sign it. Date it. *Then* send it to print.

## One Final Thing...

You'll probably work with a handful of experts to get your book written, designed, and printed. What I'm about to say should go without saying, but I need to say it anyway. Which gives me a sad face. Pay people. Pay them on time, and pay them the amount you agreed to pay.

You may be shaking your head and scowling at me: how dare I suggest you wouldn't pay a supplier! I'm not suggesting that, not for a moment. But I am including it in my book because you'd be amazed at how many business owners *don't* pay their outside experts. Or pay slowly. Or pay them less than agreed.

Word gets around. If you're a wonderful client who pays on time, every time, people will recognise you as a fabulous client, and they'll fall over themselves to work with you. Behaving like a professional is all about courtesy, not wearing a suit; and it'll set you apart from all the amateurs out there.

## Oh My Gosh... Are You Done?

And with that... you've written your Shitty First Draft, you've tidied it and polished it, you've had it edited and proofed... and you've laid it out beautifully.

Oh my gosh, you have written a book! Flamingo, this is huge.

You. Have. Written. A. Book!

You are an author. Crack open the bubbles, do the Snoopy Dance, and congratulate yourself.

We'll move onto the publishing part soon, but before we do, I want to cover a couple of crucial points first—including how to deal with criticism. Because it's not just your inner voice you'll have to deal with. Other people will have Opinions, too. I don't want criticism to cripple you, so take these Tiny Beetle Steps, then read on...

## Tiny Beetle Steps

1. Look closely at typefaces in books. Which are easy to read? Which do you like? Choose your typefaces and try them out.

2. Have you used plenty of white space and subheadings to break up your blocks of text and make your book easy to read? Can you turn any big lumps of copy into easy-to-read bullet points?

3. Decide on your layout: page numbers, headers, footers, navigation aids, graphics, and any other design details. Look at other books for ideas.

4. If you want an index, go to the Society of Indexers website and find someone with the experience you need: www.indexers.org.uk.

5. Check your references and facts: are you missing anything? Do you need to add footnotes and citations?

6. Get a printed proof copy sent to you. Do not skip this step to save a few quid. You'll need your proof copy to check for any mistakes...

7. Download and print my Final Moxie Book Checklist from www.moxiebooks.co.uk/moxie-book-resources and use it.

# CHAPTER 21

# Criticism Hurts—How To Take The Sting Off

*"I much prefer the sharpest criticism of a single intelligent man to the thoughtless approval of the masses."*

*Johannes Kepler*

Dita von Teese once said: "You can be the ripest, juiciest peach in the world, and there's still going to be somebody who hates peaches."

True dat.

Some people will love your book. Some will hate it. So what?[1] Once your book's out there, what people think of it—and you—is beyond your control.

But what about when you're wallowing deep in the editing stage of writing your book, and it's time to get some feedback? What then? How do you deal with criticism with grace and gratitude, and how do you turn it into something helpful?

I thought about sticking this chapter in with Chapter 3—but this isn't about your Inner Dickhead. It's about Outer Voices poking your Inner Voice until it cries. So this short section is all about what other people think—and how to deal with it.

---

1  My wonderful mentor, Peter Thomson, calls this the Chelsea Principle: SW3. Some will, some won't, so what?

## Asking For Feedback

My primary weapon in defence of my ego and self-esteem is to get in there first. I ask for feedback from my beta readers often and early—and here's why: I want my book to be the best it can be. So do you, right? You've poured weeks, possibly months, of your skills, knowledge, passion, tears, and experience into creating this book. You've written it because you want to reach more people and help them improve their lives in some way. And of course, you want your book to be the best it can be.

No good book is written alone. (Plenty of bad ones are, though.) It takes a group of dedicated, caring weirdos to write something worth reading.

You have clients, customers, email subscribers, colleagues, and peers who are willing you to succeed, so bring them into your book writing adventure. Create a group of beta readers and ask them to read your book, piece by piece. Ask them for feedback. What works? What doesn't? Does it flow well? Was there anything that tripped you up, or you didn't understand?

Ask detailed questions and make it clear you're after constructive criticism as well as praise.

We all love to hear that what we've written is fabulous and moves people… but pure praise with no substance, while lovely, isn't useful. Criticism, on the other hand, is like uncut diamonds: somewhere in there is treasure you can turn into a tiara.

You and I both know criticism can hurt. It's hard to hear you've created something that's not up to scratch. It's tough to realise you're not done yet—especially if you're tired and you can see the finish line. But criticism—constructive criticism—is crucial if we want to write better books.

## Receiving Criticism

My advice, to soften the blow, is to remember three things:

1. **You've asked for the feedback** so you can make your book as good as it can be—use it.

2. **This isn't about criticising you as a person**, it's about improving the book you wrote. Separate yourself from your art (because it is art, even if it's non-fiction).

3. **Receive the criticism, allow yourself five minutes to grumble or cry or swear**—then read it objectively and in detail and figure out how to use it.

Most of your critics want you to succeed. They want to help you. Let them. You don't have to listen to everything they say, and you don't have to agree with it all—but pay attention and evaluate it. Do they have a point? If so, make changes to your book. Improve it. If they don't have a point—thank them and ignore it.

If someone gives you unsolicited negative feedback, you can ignore that, too. Only ask people for feedback if you know they will be honest but kind. Only invite feedback from people whose opinions you value.

## Giving Feedback

If you're lucky enough to be asked to critique someone else's book, remember this: it's a great privilege. Someone trusts you enough to ask your opinion on their work of art. That's huge. So be kind.

Start with what works well. We're a fragile lot, writers. We bruise easily. Tell your author friend what you love about their book, how it moves you, and why. This is helpful because when they're editing, they'll be able to incorporate more of what you like into their writing.

Then, and only then, move onto criticism—and be constructive. Telling someone their writing is clumsy or amateurish or just not good, and leaving it at that isn't just unhelpful, it's mean. Instead of focusing on what the writer has done, look at how they can improve in the future.

We get defensive when people tell us something we've done is shit (and even if you don't actually say something is shit, that's how we often hear it). If we hear suggestions for how to make something better in the next round of editing, though, it's positive. Suggestions for future improvements are not connected to us and what we wrote in the past. It's about what we've not yet written.

We have a negativity bias: we're far more likely to remember negative feedback than positive, so we focus on the negative and forget we're also amazing.

Suggesting where a writer can rephrase sentences and paragraphs, or cut out words, or use more fascinating descriptives, is much more helpful—and it's kind. If you have a specific criticism, pair it with a suggestion.

Mix your feedback up: include positive and constructive criticism—and when you give positive feedback, explain why. Why did this paragraph work? What moved you about the end of that chapter?

## Who Really Matters?

Finally, I'd like to remind you about Brené Brown's Post-It note trick, the one I shared with you way back in Chapter 3. Grab a Post-It note or a small square of paper, and write down on it the names of all the people whose opinions matter to you. People you admire. If you get negative feedback from anyone and it upsets you, check your list. Is their name on it? If not, screw them. They don't matter. Ignore it. If their name is on the list, though, remember why you admire them and remember they'll undoubtedly have your best interests at heart. So perhaps this is feedback you should pay attention to.

Finally finally, remember this: you are skilled. You are talented. You want to create something outstanding that'll make a real difference in the world. Let people help you do that, and ignore those who can't or won't be helpful and kind.

Right. Now you're prepared for people's Opinions, it's time to say thank you to everyone who's helped you…

But first, you know the drill: take these Tiny Beetle Steps.

## Tiny Beetle Steps

1. Prepare detailed questions about your manuscript that you want your beta readers to answer for you. You can find the questions I asked my beta readers in the resources area on my website: www.moxiebooks.co.uk/moxie-book-resources.

2. Set aside time to read and reflect on the feedback you get.

3. Sort it into positive praise, and constructive criticism—then divide it into comments you agree with and will use to make changes, and comments you don't want to use.

4. If you didn't do the Post-It note exercise I suggested in Chapter 3, do it now. Put your list somewhere prominent in your writing space. Look at it whenever someone or something upsets you.

CHAPTER 22

# How To Thank People

*"Gratitude turns what we have into enough."*

*Melody Beattie*

Every morning, I write down three things I'm grateful for. Every evening, I do the same. A few people have mocked me for it, but I don't care—because I know my days are happier and more fulfilled when I take a few moments to think about what I'm thankful for.

I'm often thankful for the people who help me every day: my ever-patient and supportive husband, my clients, my friends, my trapeze coach, and recently, my beta readers. I'm even more thankful when I'm writing a book because—as you now know—writing a book is bloody hard work. It's emotionally draining, and we need all the support we can get. So I want to thank my lovely tribe in writing.

I take this part of creating a book pretty seriously, which is why it has a chapter all on its own. It's not a tick-box exercise; it's my opportunity to sincerely thank the people who've helped me make my book better, not as a sterile list, but as part of the story.

You might be wondering if you have to include acknowledgements; if it's compulsory. It's not. Of course, it's up to you. Your book; your rules. I won't think any less of you if you choose not to include them. But if even one person has helped you, wouldn't you like to thank them? In fact, it'll undoubtedly be more than one person. It takes a village to write a great book.

The best place to show your gratitude is in the acknowledgements of your book. Take it from me: it's utterly thrilling to open a book and see yourself thanked for helping. It's a real privilege. But how do you go about it? What really is the acknowledgements section, and where does it go?

## What Are Acknowledgements?

Unsurprisingly, your acknowledgements are where you acknowledge anyone who's helped you write your book, either directly (like an editor or cover designer) or indirectly (like a long-suffering partner who made you endless cups of tea and stroked your hair when you just wanted to explode the whole thing).

It's your opportunity to thank people explicitly for what they've done for you.

I love to detail how people have helped me and tell a little of their story as part of my story. I want people to read my acknowledgements, so I make them enjoyable to read; it's never merely a list of names. My thanks are part of my book journey, so they need details to bring them to life. My thankees are splendid human beings (and sometimes cats and chickens and TinySheeps) and deserve to be three-dimensional.

## Whom To Thank

You can thank anyone you like—most thanks fall into these categories:

- Family (spouse, kids, parents, pets, brothers and sisters).
- Friends.
- Teachers and mentors.
- Colleagues.
- Editors, proofreaders, and beta readers.

- Designers and illustrators.
- Printers.
- Publishers.
- Agents or managers.
- Contributors and advisors.
- Sources of inspiration.

In my books, I've thanked family, friends, mentors, colleagues, beta readers and proofreaders, designers, printers, advisors, and inspirational people.

## Where Do Acknowledgements Go?

You can put your thanks wherever you like—but by convention, they form part of the front matter or back matter. If there's a lot of stuff in your front matter, you may want to balance it out by putting your thanks at the back; and vice versa. I put my thanks at the end because it finishes off my story and gives readers a little inspiration as to where they can find help with their book, should they need it.

If your book is research heavy and you've used some space thanking a person or institution in detail for their help, you may want to put it at the front to give some context to your book. If your thanks are informal and don't include material research, they may sit better at the back. There are no rules. But there are some guidelines...

## How To Write Your Acknowledgements

Every time someone does something—anything—that helps you write your book note down who they are, what they did, and when. It's easy to forget vital help you've received, and you will be mortified if you publish your book and discover you've forgotten someone important. Categorise people so you'll be able to see more easily if someone is missing.

I use Scrivener to write my books, so I just open a document within the book file and call it "thanks", and fill it with names, dates, and details.

If you write in Word or Pages or similar, create a folder for everything to do with your book and make a document called "Thanks". Save all your helpers in there, so you don't forget them.

## Be Delightful

How many times have you read a book and skipped over the acknowledgements because they were dull? Because the author had obviously thrown them in there fast, without much thought to the story behind them? Wouldn't it be fantastic if you could write acknowledgements people thought were as compelling as the rest of the book? Put thought into the story behind the thanks and take care of the details. Check and double-check you've spelt people's names correctly! Nothing says, "I don't care about you" louder than getting someone's name wrong.

Thank people specifically for what they've done. When you start writing, bring the story to your mind. Rather than simply list out names and deeds, weave your thanks into a story. What were you struggling with? How did your helpers help? What did you feel and what did they think? Give us an insight into who they are, and help us step into your shoes.

This isn't specific: "Thanks to my husband Joe for all his help."

This is specific: "First and foremost: Joe Fraser, my ever-patient husband, who didn't mind me going away yet again to "get some writing done". I actually did the writing this time. Thank you for reading my Shitty First Draft and helping me make it better. Thank you for making me endless cups of tea and prising me away from my laptop with the promise of a delicious meal. Thank you for always being there and supporting me on my latest hare-brained scheme."

This isn't specific: "Thanks to my beta readers."

This is specific: "Thanks so much to all my beta readers for taking the time and making an effort not just to read my draft book, but send detailed comments and feedback. This book is far better thanks to you. Special thanks to…"

## Don't Worry About How Long It Is

Like everything else, your acknowledgements should be long enough to cover everyone and everything you want to thank them for. They can be as long as you like. If your reader gets bored, that's cool—they can skip it.

But for the people you're thanking—which is the whole point—they deserve the details. You can't unprint a book that's missing someone crucial, so thank everyone and don't worry about the length.

## Keep It Real

If you can't be sincere in your thanks, don't write acknowledgements at all because you'll sound fake. Remember: you don't have to include this section, so if you don't feel like adding it, that's cool. On the other hand, don't go over the top, either. You're not accepting an Oscar here, so keep it real. Be meaningful. Be sincere. Be personal.

And a word of advice: if you're not sure the person being thanked will thank you for including them, ask them if they mind. Especially if they don't know you well, or at all.

Finally: have fun! This is another chance for you to inject a little more personality into your book, outside of its content.

The acknowledgements are pretty much the last thing you'll write, so take a moment to realise what you've accomplished before you move onto the next phase: publishing.

Chin chin!

Right. Now let's get you published.

## Tiny Beetle Steps

1. Open a document where you can note down everything people have done to help you.

2. Check your list and make sure you haven't missed anyone out.

3. Contact anyone you're not sure about and ask if they're okay with being included in your book.

# CHAPTER 23

# The Publishing Part

*"In my experience, what every true artist*
*wants, really wants, is to be paid."*

Sir Terry Pratchett (Soul Music)

If images of enormous cheques are waltzing before your eyes, courtesy of a big publishing house, I'm afraid this chapter will be like a bucket of cold water in your face.

Writers like J.K. Rowling, Tony Robbins, and Stephen King get the kind of royalty cheques that can buy a yacht; the rest of us... well, let me paint you a picture. A dreary, disappointing picture of how the publishing world really works.

Typical book publishing royalties are between 10-12% of the retail price of the book, and an advance is usually around one-third of the total royalties. Let's say your book costs £20. You negotiate a royalty rate of 10%, so for each book sold you receive £2. If your print run is 5,000, and they all sell, your total royalties will be £10,000.

Which means your advance, around a third of your total royalties, will be £3,330. And the rest will drip in as and when your books sell. Not really enough to buy that yacht, is it?

Now, before you start weeping into your typewriter, I have good news for you. You don't need a publisher to make lots of money from your book. You don't need to be a big name. You don't even need to become a *New York Times* bestseller or sell a gazillion copies. Gone are the days when you had to grovel to the big publishing houses to get your book out there. The power no longer rests with them; the internet and Amazon have levelled the playing field (which is a double-edged sword, if I'm honest— it's never been easier to publish a book; but it's also never been easier to publish a crap book).

As I hope you now realise, becoming rich purely off the back of this book you're writing is not the purpose of what you're doing. We'll talk more about what you can do with your book in the next chapter (and on my blog).

First, though, you have to publish. Let's run through all your publishing options. You have three of them: traditional publishing, hybrid publishing, and indie-publishing (self-publishing). This book is really about indie-publishing, but let's glance briefly at the modern publishing world.

Before we do, though, sear this into your brain: book promotion is now your raison d'être. Doesn't matter whether you go the traditional route or the indie-publishing route: you are responsible for your own success. (Good rule for life, that.)

## Traditional Publishing

If you've ever read a book, you'll be familiar with at least some of the big names of the publishing industry: Penguin Random House, Hachette Livre, HarperCollins, Faber and Faber, Pan Macmillan, Bloomsbury, Simon & Schuster, Oxford University Press, and Wiley.

Your chances of being published by one of these guys are— let's be honest here—slim. But they're not your only option in the trad-publishing world.

There are several smaller, independent publishers like Hurst Publishers, founded in 1969 and specialising in non-fiction. Or there's Alma Books, which rejects the "capitalist approach to publishing" and advocates a specialist focus. Then there's Cillian Press, which specialises in fiction with contemporary, young adult, and adult novels. Persephone Books publishes "neglected" out-of-print works from the 20th century, mostly by women. I've been to their shop and have a few of their books, and Persephone's whole set-up is delightful. Harriman House specialises in business, trading, investment, and other financial-type books.

There are other independent publishers, too, and if you really want to go down the traditional publishing route, find a publisher who specialises in your field and whom you get on with.

If you do want to give it a go—and particularly if you want to try for one of the big publishers—you'll need an agent, and you'll have to learn to write a book proposal. I'll come to the agent in a moment because I want to warn you about the book proposal. It's a beast of a thing, and it'll feel like writing your book all over again. It might even be worse.

Your book proposal will be around 30-40 pages long and will need to include the following:

- A description of the market for your type of book and how the market looks at the moment.
- What makes your book different from the others.
- Your expertise: what makes you the expert on your topic?
- A summary of your book.
- One or two sample chapters.

Still interested? Go and learn everything you can about how to write a book proposal[1], and study hard.

Okay, let's talk agents. You need an agent if you want a traditional publisher because if you send your manuscript without an agent, it'll probably get thrown away. Or returned without being looked at. They're called unsolicited submissions. If you're incredibly, lottery-winner lucky, it may make it to the slush pile and get read by a hungover intern. Possibly. I don't blame the publishers, really—they'd be buried under a mountain of manuscripts if they didn't put gatekeepers in place.

---

1  You can download a book proposal from Harriman House's website at www.harriman-house.com/proposals. This is a useful document that'll get you answering valuable questions.

Your chance of success in traditional publishing without an agent is microscopic. So go and find an agent—look online, go to events and conferences, use social media—then pitch them.

Agents get tons of pitches from wannabe authors, so you need to get noticed. If you don't get the chance to dazzle an agent in person, you can write what's known in the industry as a Query Letter. Your query letter should tell the agent who you are, why you're contacting this agent in particular, what your book's about (in no more than a couple of paragraphs), and why you think your book will sell well in the current market.

Find an agent, read a book about the process, study it, then get pitching.

## A Word Of Warning

There are, without a doubt, many advantages to being published by a publishing house—especially one of the big ones. The more famous an author you are, the bigger the benefits.

But if you're a typical business owner like me and a publisher publishes your book, remember: that paltry royalty advance is likely to be the last money this particular book makes you.

Your book will probably wither away on bookshelves because a few months after you've published, your publisher will move onto the next book. They'll be promoting someone else's baby, not yours.

*And there's nothing you can do about it because your publisher owns everything.*

That's the big, huge, giant downside of traditional publishing when you're a business owner. When you sign a contract, you sign away all your rights of ownership to the book, and you have no creative control over the title, cover, blurb, or anything else. But they'll still expect you to do most of the marketing. Imagine you want to produce a second edition… but you can't, because the publisher isn't interested. Imagine the publisher pulps your book! Your book will be a massive wasted opportunity.

## Hybrid Publishing

Back in the day, hybrid publishing was—somewhat spitefully—known as "vanity publishing". Some people still call it vanity publishing, which makes me smile because it's pure, vicious snobbery.

The tables have turned, and—for those who want to make a real living from writing books or from creating a book to help you grow your business—the real vanity today is wanting the kudos of a big-name publisher on your book cover. Don't misunderstand me: it'd be fantastic to get an amazing book deal with a big publisher if that's best for your business. But for most, traditional publishing is not the best option.

So, what's hybrid publishing? Unlike traditional publishing, you don't get an advance from a hybrid publisher.

Instead, you pay the publisher. Wait. What? Yes, that's right.

With traditional publishing, the publisher takes all the business risks. They edit, design, print, publish, and (if they're betting big on your book) market your book for you—and gamble that they'll sell them by sending you an advance on your royalties.

With hybrid publishing, you split the risk. There are a bunch of different formats for hybrid publishing, but essentially you pay for publishing and printing, and maybe some marketing too.

Your partner publisher will make sure your book looks like a "proper" book, has a professional cover, is professionally edited, and is printed at high quality. That's what you generally get for your money. In return, you usually retain ownership of your work and can do what you like with it.

A good, trustworthy hybrid publisher won't take on your book if they don't feel it has a decent chance of at least making your investment back. They'll know how to get your book into places that will sell it and will have contacts you almost certainly won't in the publishing and bookselling industry.

But they may not understand the principles of direct response marketing, and all the cool stuff you can do with your book once you've written it. Some hybrid publishers—those who specialise in books for small businesses—do understand direct response marketing. They know there's far more to a business book than just making your investment back through selling copies (more on that later).

Hybrid publishing may well be the best option for you—if you've got the money to invest up-front and are willing to do what you need to do to promote, sell, and use your book.

## Indie-Publishing (Or Self-Publishing)

Finally—and most commonly for today's authors—there's self-publishing or, as I prefer to call it, indie-publishing. Which is what I and Moxie Books can help you to do. Self-publishing implies that writing is a hobby—and there's nothing wrong with that. But I work with top-quality professionals to produce my books, and this is my business. I'm an independent author business owner, and I help other business owners and authors to publish independently.

It has never been easier to write and publish an honest-to-sprouts book, and that's brilliant. It allows everyone to get their message out—an opportunity they may never have had if their only option was traditional publishing.

However, indie-publishing also allows everyone who wants to, to write and publish a book. Just because it's easy and relatively inexpensive to publish your own book doesn't mean you should do it on the cheap. The biggest mistake small business owners—and other organisations and individual writers—make when they're self-publishing is doing an amateur job of it.

Do not scrimp on the details. I cannot emphasise that enough, so I'll say it again, in italics.

*Do not scrimp on the details.*

Do not think you can do this without investing in some experts.

If your cover looks amateurish, potential readers will assume your book is unprofessional and, by extension, you and your business. If it's typeset in Comic Sans and looks like it's been laid out by an overenthusiastic primary school receptionist, potential readers will assume you are as amateurish as your book looks.

If it's riddled with typos and run-on sentences that threaten the very structure of the English language, readers will give up on it and assume—yep, you've guessed it—that you and your business are amateurish. Do not underestimate the damage you can do to your reputation by cutting corners here.

I've written long and lovingly about the Shitty First Draft in this book, and you do need to embrace it. But what you release into the world should be worlds away from that first draft, which is why I wrote Chapter 20: How To Avoid Looking Like An Amateur. Go and reread it, but let me reiterate the most important points.

1. **Hire an experienced and talented cover designer** to create an eye-catching, professional, and beautiful book cover.

2. **Hire an experienced editor and proofreader** to polish your manuscript and make sure it's as good as it can possibly be.

3. **Get beta-readers to read your manuscript.** They'll be able to tell you if there are any gaping holes or if there's anything your ideal reader is likely to misunderstand.

4. **Consider hiring an interior book designer** if you're worried about creating a professional layout.

5. **Find a printer that specialises in books,** like Bill Goss at Elite Publishing Academy. Don't go to your local brochure printer and expect them to be able to turn out a professional book; in most cases, you'll be bitterly disappointed—it's not their area of expertise.

Just because you're an indie-author doesn't mean you have to look like an amateur. Okay? Good.

Now we can move onto the magnificent benefits of indie-publishing, which I can sum up in one word: **control**.

You don't have to give up your rights to your work. You don't have to let someone else decide on the cover, the title, and what happens to your book once it leaves the printers.

You keep control of everything: final wording, design, selling price, reprints, release date, printing style, format, marketing—everything. Which is splendid, because you can do what you like with it—including creating ebook versions for the Kindle and other e-readers, creating an audiobook, printing limited edition hardback copies...

But with great control comes great responsibility—financial responsibility, that is. You bear all the costs of printing and publishing. (I have more good news for you on that front, though, as you'll find out in the next chapter.)

You'll need to pay your printer, and for a good quality book, you can expect to pay at least £1.96 per copy. At the time of writing, my printer Bill charges the following:

- 250 = £ 2.43 per copy
- 500 = £ 2.27 per copy
- 1,000 = £ 1.96 per copy

So, if you order 1,000 copies of your book, costing you £1,960 in total and send them second class as large letters at £1.64 postage, you could get your book into someone's hand for £3.60. If you're charging £20 for your book, suddenly it doesn't look so expensive.

Assuming you sell all 1,000 copies at £20 each, you'll make a total of £20,000—with a profit of £16,400. That's just for selling the books. But remember: what your book leads to is where the real profits lie. You'll also need to pay for an editor, a cover designer, and an ISBN (if you go with a printing package from my printer Bill at Elite Publishing Academy, your ISBN is included in the package price—as is a printed proof copy, legal deposit copy, and delivery charges).

If you decide on short-run printing, as I do through Bill's service, talk to your partner, housemate, mum, or other cohabitees... because you'll need space to store your books. Don't underestimate how much space 1,000 books take up. Or even 250 books[2]. If you order lots of books all at once, ask your printer if you can print them in batches when you need them. Some printers will do that for you, or store your books for a fee.

Independent printers and short print runs aren't your only option, though. There are many choices for print-on-demand—like Amazon's Kindle Direct Publishing (which replaced CreateSpace) and Lulu.com. These services hold your electronic file and print your books only when someone buys them. This is usually a little more expensive per copy, but it's a good solution if you're short on storage space.

## Getting an ISBN

You definitely need an ISBN. ISBN stands for International Standard Book Number, and every edition and variation of a printed book needs one. A paperback, hardback, and ebook edition of the same book would each have a different ISBN.

If you're a publisher, and you are if you self-publish, you must send a copy of your book to the British Library within one month of publication. Other legal deposit libraries may also request copies from you. Your printer may include this service in their package—mine does. This requirement has been part of English law since 1662, and it's brilliant. The British Library collects our country's biggest ideas and puts them safely away as our heritage.

You can sell your printed book yourself—or you can get a third-party like Amazon to do it for you—or you can do a combination of the two. Amazon will issue you an ISBN for "free", but you must list them as a publisher, and you can only use that free ISBN to sell through KDP or Amazon. Read the fine print before you take up any enticing offers. If your printer or publisher doesn't provide an ISBN for you, you can buy them individually or in batches from Neilsen[3]. At the time of writing, a single ISBN costs

---

2   With around 40 books per box, if you order 250 books, you'll probably have 7 boxes. Enough to build a small fort. 1,000 books means 25 boxes—which will happily fill most of a reasonably sized garage.

3   www.nielsenisbnstore.com

£89 and a batch of ten costs £164. If you think there will be a second edition, and you're creating an ebook (and of course if you want to write more than one book) it makes sense to buy ten ISBNs. Check your printer can produce a barcode for your ISBN, or you can get one online[4].

## Print Or Ebook?

You might be wondering if you can skip the expense of printing your book and go straight to creating an ebook. Of course you can if you want to. However, you'll miss out on a huge opportunity. A printed book has the Wow Factor. There's nothing like turning up at an event, having someone ask you for your business card, and telling them, "Oh I don't have business cards. But here's a copy of my book." It knocks their socks off.

People don't throw books away; they keep them and refer to them. It's not as easy to dip in and out of an ebook, and ebooks are quickly forgotten. So, please, print your book.

Then, once you have a printed book in your sticky mitts, you can turn it into an ebook and an audiobook. Give people as many opportunities as possible to read your book: some prefer paper, some prefer electronic books, some prefer audio—and some will want to buy all three formats. The more formats you have for your book, the more readers and the more revenue you'll create.

The best-known ebook format is Amazon's Kindle, and you will definitely want to put your book on there. It has the biggest audience, and most of your readers are likely to be there.

One of my past students, Julian, has created a Kindle publishing empire that brings him in around £1,000 a month. He creates the books and puts them out there, and they make him money while he's busy running his business[5].

Format your book for Smashwords, too, so you can sell it on iBooks and other e-readers. A side benefit is Smashwords lets

---

4   buybarcodes.co.uk/isbn-barcodes

5   If you want to know exactly how he's done this, and how you can too, you can sign up to my 90 Day Moxie Book Course Online.

you sell your book as a paperback through large booksellers like Waterstones and Foyles. If you do put your book on Smashwords (or anywhere else), fill in the synopsis and author information to give yourself the best chances of selling your book.

It's relatively simple to create an ebook version of your printed book yourself—do a little tweaking and formatting, then upload it to Kindle and wherever else you want it to appear. I've found Scrivener to be a bit of a pain when it comes to formatting.

Or, you can outsource it to a specialist ebook formatter, which is what I used to do until I discovered Vellum.

Vellum is now one of my favourite pieces of software. It's only available for Mac at the moment, but you can download it for free to play with it, and you only pay when you're ready to export the file for ebook or printing. At the time of writing, Vellum costs $199.99 for ebooks only, or $249.99 for print and ebooks. I got the full version, and it's already paid for itself in saved time and saved fees from sending books out.

## Audiobooks

You may feel reluctant to create an audiobook. After all, you'll either have to talk it out yourself or pay a voice actor to do it for you. But you'd be a fool to avoid it altogether. Just ask this fool, who—at time of writing—*still* hasn't turned her first book, *Business For Superheroes,* into an audiobook. I'm on it though. After I've audiobooked this one.

There can be a lot of money in audiobooks, and you're leaving cash on the table if you ignore them. Not to mention the fact that not everybody likes to read books; one of my Superheroes gets through a lot of books, but she rarely reads them. She listens to audiobooks. She's not alone.

You have two options: pay someone to do it all for you, or do it all yourself. There are pros and cons to each approach, and I've written articles on this topic that you can find on my website.

Briefly, though, if you hire a voice actor to record your book for you, your fees will start from around £200 per finished hour. So your total will be anywhere from £500 to £3,000[6].

ACX is "a marketplace where authors, literary agents, publishers, and other Rights Holders can connect with narrators, engineers, recording studios, and other Producers capable of producing a finished audiobook. The result: More audiobooks will be made."

If you want to do it yourself—which helps you further build relationships because your listeners will hear your voice telling your story, plus you keep more revenue and won't have to pay a voice actor—there are a few things to consider. Audible and other audiobook providers have strict quality standards, and rightly so: poor-quality audio is one of the most infuriating things ever. I have turned off podcasts and poor-quality audiobooks before because I will not waste my energy trying to decipher them.

Invest in high-quality equipment: a decent microphone at least, which you can get for around £100[7]. Find an appropriate space that gives excellent sound quality: big empty spaces create terrible-quality recordings, but you don't need a professional recording studio. You can get top-notch sound by building a blanket fort. (Which is also just fun.)

You'll need to find a sound engineer to master your recording, so it meets the standards. And you'll need time. Voice actors are used to talking for a long time; most of the rest of us aren't. Your audio should be as close to perfect as you can get it. You'll definitely be able to do this, but don't underestimate how much hard work and time it will take. Once you've done it, though, it's done—and you can release it into the wild to make money for you while you get on with the vital business of business.

## What Does Indie-Publishing Cost?

Although indie-publishing isn't enormously expensive, it's *not*

---

6   Rates from https://www.voquent.com/rates/#example

7   I use the Blue Yeti, which is top-notch and also looks like R2D2, which is a fun bonus.

cheap if you want to do a professional job—but think of this as an investment.

Done right, this whole book-writing project is just the start of a long-term marketing strategy that will repay you in great clients, higher fees and prices, and a more enjoyable business.

Remember, it's not just about paying other experts to help you with your book: there's a time investment, too. It will take you a fair chunk of time to write your book, so factor that into your expenses.

Let me do a quick run-down of what you might expect to pay:

- Developmental editing: from £1,600, depending on word-count.
- Proofreading: from £300, depending on word-count.
- Cover design: from £100 at the cheapest to £1,600+ at the top end (I always choose top-end—Julia at Brown Owl Design).
- Interior book design and layout: from £500, depending on page-count.
- Indexing: from £200, depending on word-count.
- Printing:[8] from £1.96 per copy, depending on quantity.

Creating a professional-quality book isn't cheap, as you can see. Expect to invest a few thousand pounds in it. But always keep your eye on the end goal: you will make your investment back and much more if you promote your book and sell it, and use it to build your business and credentials.

If you pre-sell your book before you print it—and you definitely should—you may find you make enough money from these early sales to cover some of these costs. When I wrote *Business For Superheroes*, I sold around 100 copies before I printed it, which paid for my print run.

My client Kenda Macdonald sold 180 copies of her book as

---

8   You can find out everything you need to know about printing your book on my blog. You'll also get expert information straight from the printer's slab here: https://www.elitepublishingacademy.com/billys-blog/

VIP pre-orders. Her full book price is £17.99, and she offered a discount for pre-orders, making the price £12.99. So those 180 sales made her a total of £2,338.20—which more than covered her first print run. But that's not all writing a book did for Kenda. Read on…

## This Is Just The Tip Of The Profit Iceberg

This might all sound pricey, and it can be. But selling books is only the start of your profit. Remember why you're doing all this: to boost your credibility, open doors and create opportunities, and find and win higher-paying clients. Not to mention all the other cool—and profitable—things you can do with your book once you have it. The money you make on the books themselves isn't the point. It's the tip of what can be a vast iceberg of opportunity.

Take Kenda. On the day I edited this chapter, I had a conversation with Kenda, and she told me what she's been up to since publishing her book *Hack The Buyer Brain*. So I'm adding this in to show you what's possible:

- She did a book signing at an event, where the organiser bought 50 of her books and gave them to the audience. People queued for 45 minutes to meet Kenda.

- She won the outstanding contribution to her field award from the Content Marketing Academy because the judges said her book made her the obvious winner.

- Two universities want Kenda to lecture for them, and they want to put her book in the curriculum.

- The Content Marketing Academy has made her book required reading.

- Because of her book, Kenda has an average of two interviews per week for the next few months—which will get her name and credentials out to a far wider audience.

- A potential client watched Kenda speak, bought her book, read it the next day, then contacted Kenda asking to talk about a project. She closed him on a £9,000 project on the call. "No fuss, he knew what his problem was and how to solve it, just wanted us to do it."

- She closed a £12,000 contract off the back of the book, too.

All within two-and-a-bit months of publishing. So if you're wondering if writing a book is worth the investment, I hope this spurs you on. You must do the work, of course—but without the book, these opportunities may never have come up for Kenda.

Whatever publishing route you decide to go down, there's one thing you absolutely must do—no excuses and no exceptions. You must build a platform from which you can launch your book. That means a website, social media presence, and other marketing gubbins.

Even if you're going the traditional publishing route, you will still need to do this because even if your publisher loves you, they're never going to be as invested as you are. It's a requirement these days for all traditionally published authors to have a reliable marketing platform. Look at people like J.K.Rowling, Steven Pressfield, and Stephen King, and you'll see they have well-oiled marketing machines in place.

Build a platform, do it now, and start working it.

Chapter 24 will walk you through how to get started. But before that, take these Tiny Beetle Steps.

## Tiny Beetle Steps

1.  Decide which publishing route you want to go down, and start preparing. Go back to the plan you made in Chapter 2 and tweak it if you need to.

2.  Find an editor and proofreader (and indexer if required) and book them as far in advance as possible (this has the added advantage of giving you a hard deadline to work to—which I need if I want to get anything done, ever).

3.  Find a cover designer and start working on your cover.

4.  Find a printer and make sure you'll have your ISBN covered.

5.  Start building a platform now: remember, book promotion is your new raison d'être.

# CHAPTER 24

# Being Relentlessly Helpful

*"You will get all you want in life, if you help enough other people get what they want."*

*Zig Ziglar*

Hopefully, you've realised by now that once you've written your book, the hard work isn't over. The success of your book—and your entire business—is all down to you. Writing a book is a fantastic achievement. I can't even tell you how excited I am for you, and how proud I am of you. It's bloody difficult.

But I'm afraid writing the thing is just the start. Because you, my fabulous Flamingo, must build a platform and get comfortable with shameless self-promotion. Are you ready?

Maybe not. Because shameless self-promotion isn't really what we're doing, so let me reframe it for you. What we're doing here is being relentlessly helpful. If you're still struggling with the idea of self-promotion, let me remind you of a thing and ask you a thing.

Reminder: nobody will blow your trumpet for you. Apart from you, me, and your mum, nobody really cares if your book is a success. So you will have to shout about yourself and big up your book.

Question: are you proud of what you do? Are you proud of your book? I hope the answer to those questions is a resounding "yes". If you *are* proud, why on earth wouldn't you shout about it?

Think of it this way: you wrote your book to help people solve a problem and improve their lives, right? If those people never hear about your book, it can't help them. If you don't shout about your book and promote it at every opportunity, your potential customers won't ever hear about it. And keeping it to yourself is rather selfish, don't you think? Don't you have a duty to help as many people as you can?

And finally, if you're worried about sounding arrogant when you market your book, don't. There will always be people who want to knock you down, who'll call you arrogant for promoting yourself and your book.

Ignore them. You're not arrogant, and they don't matter.

Self-confidence is incredibly attractive, and the confidence to shout about your book will attract just the kinds of people you want to work with. Let me point you to Brené Brown (again). Read *Daring Greatly*. It will help you with your confidence issues.

Once you've got your head around it all and you've made the scary but brilliant decision to promote your book at every opportunity, it's time to get cracking. Right now.

Start building anticipation for your new book immediately— even if you haven't finished it yet. I sold about 100 copies of *Business For Superheroes* before I even finished writing it, and I had no idea what I was doing back then. I just had an email list and spaniel-like enthusiasm.

Pre-selling your book has another benefit, by the way: all those people who pre-ordered and paid for my book before I'd finished writing it helped pay for the printing costs. Good, eh?

And we do it all by… *whispers*… *marketing*.

## Marketing is NOT a Dirty Word

When you think about marketing, what image pops into your head? Probably the same thing as pops into a lot of people's heads… shiny-suited liars pushing you to buy stuff you don't want, noisy ads trying to sell you things you don't need and take money you don't have, and the used-car salesman pushing the hard-sell, who just wants to sell you the most expensive car on the forecourt.

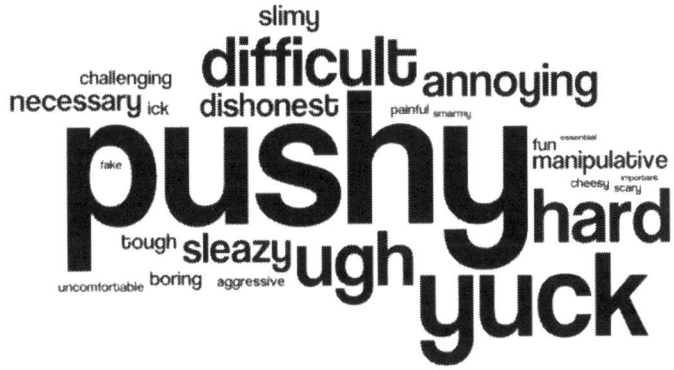

Author Daniel Pink conducted a survey to help him write his best-selling book *To Sell Is Human*. He asked people to state the first word they thought of when they heard the words "sales" or "selling". A whopping eighty per cent of the twenty-five most common words had negative connotations, as you can see from the word cloud[1].

It seems most people believe sales and marketing is pretty grim, that it's all about pushing people into buying things they don't want with money they don't have. Well, I have a secret to tell you. That's *not* what marketing is all about.

Marketing is, at its core, solving problems for people. Helping them to overcome obstacles. Giving them a hand to change their lives for the better. If that sounds like weasel-words from a marketing professional, I understand. I know there are awful scoundrels out there giving sales and marketing a bad name. I'm not naïve. But I also know how *I* approach marketing, and how I teach my clients and authors to approach marketing: keep your customers' best interests in mind.

---

1   Image from https://www.danpink.com/wp-content/uploads/2012/12/Chap-3-Word-cloud-1-fixed.jpg

Who would you rather encounter: the car salesman who wants to sell the most expensive car at any cost, because he'll get a big fat bonus? Or the car salesman who listens to what you want and need, looks at your budget, and gets you the best possible deal for what you can afford?

I know who I'd rather meet. And I know what type of marketer I am. I'm the same kind of marketer you are: someone who wants to help people improve their lives, with the best deal for everyone. A win-win marketing situation.

My friend, you must get comfortable with marketing if you want your book to be a success—so remember what marketing really, truly is. It's your way to help people get what they want. Ethically, honestly, and trustily.

Marketing is about trust. Business is about trust. Selling and using your book is about trust. Trust is what building a platform is all about. And how do we start building a platform? We start with the obvious…

## Your Website

Hopefully, you already have a website for your business. I'm going to assume you do. If you don't, though, your book is now your reason to create a website. Whether you have a business website or not, you'll need a website for your book too. (And one for every book you write.) But don't panic: I don't expect you to run and manage 53 different websites. Instead, I'd like you to buy the domains you need for your book website, then you can ask your webmaster to set up a redirect for you.

When you visit howthehelldoyouwriteabook.com, the browser redirects you to moxiebooks.co.uk/howthehelldoyouwriteabook. And my *Business For Superheroes* book site redirects to moxiebooks. co.uk/businessforsuperheroes.

I don't want a bunch of different websites to manage, but I do want to make it easy for people to find me from my books. When you've decided on your title, choose a URL that makes sense, then get it redirected to your chosen website address.

A website is critical because it's the first place people will go to find out more about you if they love your book. Keep the website simple: allow people to buy your book from this page, and give them an opportunity to sign up to your email list if they already have your book or aren't ready to buy it yet. Your website is more important than your social media presence, and here's why: you do not own your social media platform. Social media is important—but only to get people from there to your website and onto your contact list.

If you rely on someone else's platform—be that Facebook, LinkedIn, Medium, or anything else—to build your business, you could lose the whole thing overnight if your "landlord" makes the wrong move. Squatting on someone else's platform is called digital sharecropping. These platforms have every right to shut you down if they want because your social media presence is there at the sufferance of the big social media companies. They don't work for you; you work for them. You and I are the product.

And what if one of those social media companies shuts down or everyone stops using it? Remember MySpace?

Create your own platform, your own real estate, and nobody can take it away from you. Buy your domain—spend a few quid a year on it—and build a website. Then send people to your website from your book, from your social media accounts, and from everywhere else. Once you've done that, your primary objective is to get their contact details.

## Your Email List

The next most important thing to do is gather and collect people's emails so you can contact them often. Every day, preferably (but however often you email people, be consistent).

You might be thinking two things: "I have a social media platform! I don't need no stinking emails!" and "Every day? No way, you lunatic. Nobody wants emails from me every day."

I have two things to say to that: you're wrong on both counts.

Social media's fine and good but, as I said before, you don't own the platform. If your account gets canned, you're stuffed. You have no way of contacting all those "fans" again. Not to mention the fact that when you post on Facebook, just one percent of your audience sees them (unless you pay for advertising). Which means if 1,000 "fans" like your Facebook page, just ten people will see each post. Not looking good, is it? But if you have your own email list, you can contact them all as often as you like and, as long as you follow email deliverability best practice, you know your emails will land in their inbox.

As for daily emails—I've been emailing my list every day (more or less) for the past six years. It's how I've built my business. It's how I sell my books and products and courses. It works. If you give someone a reason to opt in to your list—by offering them something valuable—then you show up in their inbox regularly with entertaining, useful, valuable messages, they will be happy to receive your emails.

Build an email list, because you'll need it to launch your book. If you have people's contact information, you can build anticipation and excitement about the book you have coming out soon. You can get feedback on what's inside the book. You can ask people for ideas about what to include. And you can sell your book before you've even finished writing it.

Before you get overexcited and start emailing the entire world from your email account, though, hold your horses. You can't do it like that, because your domain will almost certainly be blacklisted. And it's illegal. You need permission to send people marketing emails, and you need a system to help you do it all.

I use Infusionsoft by Keap, which is much more than just an email system, it's an entire customer relationship management system. It's also pretty pricey. I do not recommend you dive into Infusionsoft if this is your first foray into email lists. Start small and inexpensive—or even free—with something like MailChimp, Convertkit[2], Drip, Campaign Monitor, or Aweber. Keap now

---

2  Convertkit was created especially for authors, so if your primary business is writing books, this is worth looking into.

does a low-cost starter version of Infusionsoft. Shop around and see what suits you. Book some calls with their sales team, explain what you want from your email system, and see which one's right for you.

Then build your email list—and contact them regularly. The easiest way to build your list is to offer people something simple and useful that solves a problem and ask for their email address and name in return. We call these things lead magnets. There's tons of information about how to create a lead magnet and build an email list—including on my blog. Go forth and learn.

Keep things simple. Find one thing people want and offer it. Get them onto your list. Email them regularly. If you refuse to send emails every day, send them *at least* once a week. More important than daily is to send them regularly. If you send emails every Friday, be consistent. People will expect your message to land in their inbox on Friday and will look forward to it.

Once you've set up your own platform and email list, look at using other people's "real estate" because there's nothing wrong with using platforms that aren't yours. Just don't rely on them.

## Using Amazon

Amazon is one of the most underused and underrated book sales tools in the world. There is an enormous amount you can do to harness the mighty power of Amazon to help you sell your book and ultimately sell your products and services.

Remember: you don't own the platform, so using Amazon is not a substitute for creating and maintaining your own website and list. But getting involved with Amazon is vital if you want your book to serve you well.

Once your book goes live on Amazon, you're eligible to create an author page. Head over to Author Central at https://authorcentral.amazon.com/ and claim your page—and spend some time on it. Follow their online instructions.

Here's why you need an Amazon author page:

- An effective Amazon author page will increase your search rankings in Amazon and Google search results.

- If you have more than one book, you can connect them all via your Author Central profile and increase your page views on Amazon.

- You can connect your blog posts to your Amazon Author Central profile using your blog's RSS feed—and increase traffic to your website, where you have control over what your reader does next.

- If you organise a complete list of all your books for sale on Amazon on your Author Central page, where readers are just two clicks away from buying your book, you'll make it easier for readers to discover and buy your books.

- You'll be able to see customer discussions about you and your books on the Amazon customer forums.

Setting up your Author Central profile is not optional—I left it far too long to set mine up, and I suspect it's cost me dearly in book sales and follow-on business. Take a look at my author page to see how you can you do it: amazon.com/author/vickyfraser. Follow your favourite authors and watch what they do.

Once you've created an author page, start jazzing it up. Make it interesting. Turn it into a page people find interesting, useful, and persuasive. There are several ways you can do this:

- Add RSS feeds from your blog or social media accounts—encourage people to go to your website, where you control the action.

- Showcase events you're involved in, including workshops, training events, speaking gigs, and bookshop appearances.

- Add up to eight photos of yourself (which you can update any time)—a great opportunity to feature your next book, upcoming promotions, workshops and products based on your book, or even awards you've won. When you start selling your books, you'll find you start gaining fans—and fans love seeing this type of thing.

- Upload videos—have you been interviewed? Use that. Do

you have a book trailer? Get it up there. How about you talking about your book at an event? Perfect for this page.

Once you've got your Author Central page up on Amazon. com and Amazon.co.uk, head over to Amazon France, Japan, and Germany and claim your author pages there, too. If your budget allows, get a professional translator to translate your bio. At the very least, though, if you know someone who speaks French, Japanese, or German, ask them to help you translate your bio rather than running it through Google Translate. Writers often find their reach is amplified—sometimes considerably—by author pages in different countries.

Author Central is massively underused as a sales tool. Claim yours and fill it with goodies. Even if you haven't put your book live on Amazon yet, you can plan your author page now. Write your bio, choose some photos (or have some professional photos taken), and start creating some blog posts and videos to include.

## Using Goodreads

Have you ever visited Goodreads? It's a social network for authors and readers with more than 20 million members. Goodreads is one of the most visited websites in the world—and no wonder, because it's like Spotify for books. It helps people find the next book they want to read—whether that's space opera, Mills & Boon-style romance, or the next book about how to do pilates or start a dog-walking business or write a book. If you aren't on Goodreads, you're missing a trick.

Another good reason to set up your author page on Goodreads is to secure your books. One of my clients, Sarah, found someone else had claimed her book as theirs. She had to prove to Goodreads that she was the correct author and get her book assigned correctly. Whether the other Sarah had done this deliberately or accidentally is irrelevant—if someone else claims your book, it could damage your reputation.

Here's how to get started:

1. **Set up your author page.** Go to https://www.

goodreads.com/author/program and find out how to join the Goodreads Author programme. Follow their instructions.

2. **Ask your readers to list your book on Listopia**—a Goodreads list for every kind of book you can think of. Go to www.goodreads.com/list to find out more.

3. **Investigate if it's worth using Goodreads's advertising programme,** which allows you to target people who rated specific authors highly. For example, I might target people who rate Dan Kennedy highly.

4. **Give books away on the Goodreads book giveaway.** Do your homework and find out all about Goodreads latest best practice, but this can be an effective way to get your books in front of people.

5. **Connect your blog to the Goodreads website.** If you do this, Goodreads will email your fans all your new blog posts once a week. You get integration as a perk when you join the Goodreads Author Program.

6. **Start a Q&A discussion group about your book.** You can be as involved as you want: start a conversation, stoke it, then let your readers take it from there. It's a great way to get people talking about your message and helping each other... and it can turn casual readers into passionate raving fans.

7. **Ask your fans to review your book on Goodreads.** Books get featured based on the number of reviews they have—and don't worry about negative reviews. The key is the number—the more you have, the more popular it looks, and the more people will buy it.

## Get The Word Out

Your website, email list, social media, and services like Amazon and Goodreads aren't the only way to build and grow your platform. The online world is crowded, so jump offline and scoop up readers your competitors won't even think about.

- **PR:** your chance to build a reputation and trust among an audience you may not otherwise get an opportunity to reach—and build your email list, too. Many small business owners and authors mistakenly believe PR is just for celebrities, big business, and charities—but it's not. PR is for everyone, whether you're a lone wolf entrepreneur or you have 50 employees. The fact you've written a book is interesting to people, and it'll be attractive to journalists.

- **Direct mail.** I'm a huge fan of email marketing (obviously)—but it's not all I do. I also go offline and produce print newsletters (which you'll be familiar with as the owner of this book), direct mail campaigns, postcards, and letters. Most business owners these days do not bother with direct mail, which is a huge opportunity for you.

- **Article marketing.** Write lots and lots of content answering the questions your readers and customers ask. Be there with helpful information when people turn to Google asking for answers. If you're the person people see being helpful, who do you think they'll turn to when they need the products or services you provide? (You.)

- **Put on events.** Get out there and meet people face to face. Speak at other people's events and take your book with you. Put on your own events—a book launch and a tour, for example—because you can't beat meeting people in real life and building relationships in person.

- **Do interviews on popular podcasts and radio shows.** Piggyback on other people's audiences and speak to people you may not otherwise be able to reach. Look for industries that serve the same clients as you, and offer to write articles or do interviews to help out their customers.

- **Create a referral scheme.** Kenda offers rewards to people who share her book and increase her sales. If you refer a certain number of people to her, you get an exclusive t-shirt only available for referrers. Make it easy for people to pass on your book.

You don't have to do all of these things, and you definitely don't have to do them all at once, so please don't panic. Do consider them, though, and add them to your marketing repertoire gradually.

## Get Comfortable Self-Promoting

All this is by way of saying: you must get comfortable with self-promotion. Build your platform and be all over the place. Everywhere your customers and potential customers go, they need to see your face talking about your exciting and fabulous upcoming book.

Every time you see friends and family, ask if there's anything they'd like to see specifically in your new book. Ask if they'll help you promote it (most of the people who love you will love to help you). Believe in yourself and your ability to help people live better, funner, safer, happier lives.

This is by no means all there is to marketing your book—I've barely scratched the surface. I wanted to give you enough to start you down the marketing road. In my next book, I'll walk you through how to launch, market, and use your book and there'll be much more detail about all these options.

For now, though, focus on writing and publishing your book, and start to build a platform so you can launch it.

Do the Tiny Beetle Steps on the next page, then move on. We're almost at the end of your book-writing journey, and I'm so excited for you!

## Tiny Beetle Steps

1. Buy the domain(s) you need for your book website. I use 123reg.com, but there are lots of domain registration services to choose from.

2. Start blogging about your book: talk about why you're writing it, how you're writing it, and start dropping hints about selling it.

3. Choose some email software and build your list.

4. As soon as your book goes live on Amazon, set up your author page on Amazon and Goodreads.

5. Start shouting about your book on social media: get your Facebook page, Twitter account, YouTube channel, and Instagram roaring.

# CHAPTER 25

# YAY YOU!

*"Writing is like driving at night in the fog. You can only see as far as your headlights, but you can make the whole trip that way."*

E. L. Doctorow

As I write this final chapter, gin and tonic in hand, I have a huge grin on my face. Massive. I look like Jack Skellington[1] after he discovered Christmas is a thing.

Because *I am so frickin' excited for you.*

You're writing a book—and I cannot thank you enough for trusting me with your Big Idea. For believing my book will help you write yours. If you take it steadily, step-by-step, piece-by-piece, and do the things I've urged you to do, you will be holding your shiny, amazing, life-changing book in your hot little hands in no time.

I'm excited because I know what a book can do for you and your business. I know what a game-changer it can be—not just for your bank balance, but for your confidence. I understand—intimately—how it can draw your kind of people to you, wrap them in the essence of you, and turn them into true fans. And I know you'll be a different person—a better, wiser, more patient, and more confident person—when you're finished.

---

1    If you've never seen *The Nightmare Before Christmas*, you need to rectify this situation immediately.

I cannot tell you how wonderful it feels when your first ever published book arrives in its box. The racing heart as you pull the tape off and scrabble among the packaging. The feeling like your heart might burst in your chest because—hey—you made this.

With tears, oaths, love, and excitement, you made it.

You thought it up.

You wrote it, over days and weeks and months.

You published it.

And now you get to send it out into the world so it can help people do what you can do.

If you're still doubting your ability to Write A Book, remember this: everything happens in Tiny Beetle Steps. You're not sitting down to write a book.

- You're having an idea.
- You're deciding who you want to help.
- You're fleshing it out.
- You're writing some notes.
- You're telling stories.

I have some fantastic clients who've written their books and done extraordinary things with them: Dom Hodgson, who's on book number four at the moment and has enormous plans. Kenda Macdonald, whose book netted her two five-figure clients within two months of publishing—not to mention more speaking gigs than she can shake her tail feathers at. Julian Northbrook, who wrote a book then created a Kindle publishing empire that made him a grand a month while he did other things. Teresa Payne, who's changing the face of family law and making the legal world accessible to us all.

None of these people are superhuman (although they are all fabulous humans). They're just like you and me.

They had an idea. They decided whom they wanted to help. They fleshed it out. They wrote some notes. They told stories. Then they published their books.

You can, too.

And you don't have to do it alone: you've got me on your side. You bought my book, so you're part of the Moxie Authors. You can email me at any time at **1000authors@vickyfraser.com** and ask me a question. I promise I'll answer it. I answer all my emails—not always immediately, but I do answer them.

Go join my 1000 Authors Group on Facebook here: **bit.ly/ VixBookFB**. You'll get approved once you've answered three simple questions. I'm in there often. Join an extraordinary community of business owner authors, and write your book. Find out what's possible when you do.

When you've written your book, will you send me a copy, please? Tell me how you did it. How long it took you, what you struggled with, and what I could have done differently in this book to help you. My address is:

Superheroes

PO Box 120

Leominster

HR6 6BZ

Oh, and your first book?

That's just the beginning.

# What's Next?

*"Progress is made in Tiny Beetle Steps. Don't fret
about the big picture: figure out where you're going,
then put one foot in front of the other."*

*Me*

I wrote this book so you can write yours. Everything you need
to create and publish a life-changing, earth-shattering book is
in here. But I also know, from painful experience, how hard it
is to do it alone. If you've made it to this point and now you're
thinking, "I can write a book. I will write a book. But doing it
alone is terrifying!" I hear ya, grasshopper.

Which is why, if you're committed to this Big Book Adventure,
I've made sure you don't have to do it alone. Start by joining my
1000 Authors Facebook Group here:

**bit.ly/VixBookFB**

It's full of people who've read *How The Hell Do You Write A
Book* and want to write their own—or who have taken my book
courses or coaching programmes in the past.

Whenever you get stuck, pop in there and tell us what you're
struggling with. Post up anything you want feedback on. Ask
questions. We'll help keep you on track when you'd sooner tile
the bathroom than write another damn word.

And if you'd like more structure, virtual butt-kicking, and the
odd awkward virtual cuddle, book onto my self-study course.

## The 90 Day Moxie Book Self-Study Course

It is possible to write and publish a book in 90 days. A *good* book. I know, because I've done it. So I created a course to help you do it, too. Although you don't have to do it in 90 days, of course. Most people won't, and that's a-okay. This is a 12-week online self-study course, structured so you plan, outline, and write regularly, so you make actual progress on your book.

It's a mix of videos, downloadable and printable fun-sheets, audio, regular emails, and written material that walks you through every Tiny Beetle Step you need to take to get your finished book into your hands. You get access to me via the Facebook Group above and in an exclusive private Slack Group for Moxie Book Students, so you can ask me anything about the writing and self-publishing process at any time.

You also get support and feedback from your fellow Moxie Authors, so you can share struggles, wins, setbacks, and triumphs. We'll lift you up when you're down, and cheer with you when you're winning. Find out more about The 90 Day Moxie Book Self-Study Course here:

**moxiebooks.co.uk/90-day-course-online**

## The 90 Day Moxie Book Course: Live!

Once a year, I run a live version of The 90 Day Moxie Book Course. It's a 12-week group programme following the structure of the online course, but with my input and input from your fellow students every weekday.

Yes: five days a week. Make no mistake: this is an intensive programme, and it's hard work—but we work in Tiny Beetle Steps. You will never be asked to do anything overwhelming.

With a maximum of 20 people at a time, you'll work on your book with a small group of fellow business owners. Every Sunday, you'll get your week's assignments broken down into bite-sized pieces. Each day, you submit your assignment for my feedback—and for your fellow students' feedback. By the end of the course, if you do the work, you'll have—at the very least—your not-so-Shitty First Draft written.

This course is application-only, and places go fast. To find out more and apply to join the waiting list, go here:

**moxiebooks.co.uk/90-day-book-course-live**

## The Moxie Book Coaching Programme

If like me, you tend to invest in a course with all good intentions but ultimately know you'll need more hands-on guidance, my 12-week book coaching programme is ideal for you.

You get access to The 90 Day Moxie Book Self-Study Course—plus a weekly 45-minute coaching call with me to keep you on track, answer any questions you have, and help you overcome any challenges.

I also give you access to my Indesign book template and the accompanying mini-course, so you can design and create your own professional book, with my guidance, when you've successfully completed the programme. Plus, I walk you through how to set up your Amazon author pages, your book listings, and start selling through Kindle and Amazon.

By the time you've finished the coaching programme—if you do the work—you'll be a published author with your book on its way.

I only work with three authors at a time, so apply to join the waiting list for The Moxie Book Coaching Programme here:

**moxiebooks.co.uk/moxie-coaching**

## Luxury Moxie Book Retreats

If you're seriously committed to getting your book written and published, and want to do it in one of the most beautiful places in the world with your every need looked after, apply to join me on my annual Luxury Moxie Book Retreat.

You'll join me and a small, select group of fellow business

owners and Moxie Authors in a top-secret location for a week of intensive writing, editing, rewriting and celebrating. This is for a maximum of eight people, and (aside from your flights) it's all-inclusive: world-class coaching, accommodation, meals, drinks, and entertainment.

You'll receive preparation work to do before you arrive, so when you get there, you're ready to go. The retreats are divided into writing workshops and coaching sessions, private writing time, and feedback and editing sessions.

By the time you go home, you will have written your book and be ready to publish and launch. This is not for the faint-hearted—but it is a lot of fun, and you will go home a changed and more excited human.

Join the VIP list, and be the first to know when and where the next retreat is happening:

**moxiebooks.co.uk/luxury-retreats**

## Got Questions?

If you have any questions about writing your book, or about any of my exciting Big Book Adventures, please get in touch.

And please let me know how you're getting on with your own Big Book Adventure! Drop me an email here:

**1000authors@vickyfraser.com**

# Where To Find More Of My Brain

If you're looking for more of the stuff that pours out of my head, I lurk all over the place—online and off. Here are a few places to find me:

- *Business For Superheroes:* my first book, available from my website or from Amazon, in print or Kindle format. And—at some point—available on Audible.
- **The 1,000 Authors Show:** I sat Joe down a few years ago, poured him a gin and tonic, and made him do a podcast with me. 191+ episodes later, it's still not dead. You can find it on iTunes, Spotify, or wherever you get your podcasts. (It used to be called The Business For Superheroes Show.)
- I write regular articles on my website at **moxiebooks. co.uk/blog** and at **medium.com/@Word_Nerd_Girl**.
- I write the **best daily emails in the entire multiverse** (fact-checked and found to be TRUEISH), which you can get at **moxiebooks.co.uk** (I promise to entertain you).
- I have a YouTube channel, which you can find at **youtube. com/c/VickyFraserMoxieBooks**. I share music I love and I make videos answering your questions. There's Flamingo Friday, where I call out something sensational in the business world and show you how to stand out, too. And sometimes I share videos of me doing trapeze-stuff and trying to train my TinySheeps to do agility courses.
- Join my Facebook group and get to know fellow authors at **facebook.com/groups/1000authors**.
- Follow my aerial antics on Instagram **@treefrogtoe**.
- You could follow me on Twitter **@word_nerd_girl**, but I don't do much. I'm not a tweeter.
- Connect with me on LinkedIn at www.linkedin.com/in/ moxieauthor.

## Get The Moxie Books Newsletter

I send out a monthly printed newsletter to all my readers, clients, and authors. It's all about how to write, self-publish, and market a book for your business, filled with advice and stories from real business-owner-authors just like you.

If you'd like to receive a copy of it, please email me at 1000authors@vickyfraser.com with a copy of the receipt for this book and tell me your postal address.

That'll get you into the Club.

# With Endless Gratitude

*"To give thanks in solitude is enough. Thanksgiving has wings and goes where it must go. Your prayer knows much more about it than you do."*

*Victor Hugo*

Sorry, Victor Hugo, I don't agree. I want to thank people personally. I always get sweaty-palm nervous when I'm writing my acknowledgements. I'm terrified I will miss out someone who needs to be thanked, then massively overcompensate when I see them and give them an awkward, sweaty hug.

If I miss you out, please know it wasn't intentional. I'm just a bit of a cranefly.

Apart from the first thankee, this list is in no particular order. I love you all.

First and foremost: Joe Fraser, my ever-patient husband, who didn't mind me going away yet again to "get some writing done". I actually did the writing this time. Thank you for reading my Shitty First Draft and helping me make it better. Thank you for making me endless cups of tea and prising me away from my laptop with the promise of a delicious meal. Thank you for always being there and supporting me on my latest hare-brained scheme. And thank you for helping me build a life I love.

The Lanzarote Posse: Kenda Macdonald, Jennifer Murgatroyd, Mike Browne, who came to a volcano with me and made me write. I don't know if this book would be here without you guys. I know for sure it would have taken much longer without you. Thank you for the company, the solitude, and the horrific three-euro fizzy blue wine.

Mum and Dad, for always assuming I could do whatever I set my mind to and for never telling me to aim lower. And for coming to The Dingle and helping us get stuff done, so I can spend more time writing.

Noodle and Whiskey, for purring on my knee and calming me when my brain goes into frantic overdrive. Bronson, Kernic, and Picard: the three bestest TinySheeps a writer could wish for. There are few things more delightful than being greeted by your little woolly faces when I go outside to take a break.

Mandie Shilton-Godwin, for writing me a beautiful letter 22 years ago. I'm doing what I do partly because of you.

Peter Thomson, my first mentor and the man who told me to write a book in the first place. "Really? A book?" Thank you <3 This is all your fault.

Julia Brown, for the beautiful and fabulous cover designs and illustrations.

Misty Mozejko, my sista-from-another-mista who always cheers me on and comes up with great names for my stuff, and goes along with my ludicrous ideas (and drags me on hers). What's the most unusual place we can break bread? Let's find out.

Bill Goss of Elite Publishing Academy for doing a beautiful job of printing as usual, and for putting up with my last-minute panicky shenanigans. You rock.

Dom Hodgson—my good buddy, who kicked me into focusing on this shizzle. And for not rolling your eyes too hard when I finally realised what everyone else had known for ages. Thank you for including me in your business adventures.

Yinka Ewuola, my beautiful, wise, kind friend and one of the strongest women I know. Thank you for always believing in me even when I didn't.

Harriet Randall, my beautiful assistant and burlesque star extraordinaire, thank you so much for everything you do for me.

I promise I'll let go of more stuff too. Soon. Honest.

Jon McCulloch, the Evil Bald Genius, for years of support, mentoring, and kicking. Thank you for making me stand in front of a roomful of people and declare my intention to write a book four years ago.

James Daniel, for the chicken story and general writerly encouragement.

Ann Sheybani, for your beautiful writing and inspiration. And for making me want to be better and do better and write better.

Sophie Morgan for the perfectly snapped author photograph (from my *I Put A Spell On You* trapeze performance).

Teresa Payne, for trusting me with your words and for showing me what women in business can achieve with grace, kindness, and compassion.

Drayton Bird. Etiam si omnes, ego non. Thank you so much for writing my foreword, and for everything you've taught me over the years (even if you didn't always know it).

Mark Setch, who dragged me out of the swamp of comparison and gave me the tools to improve myself.

My buddy Mark Cottle for listening to me be indecisive every week for the past few years and for calling out my bullshit when I needed it.

Sean and Renuka D'Souza for the storytelling workshop, the cartooning course, and endless inspiration and support and the odd delicious chocolate bar.

Suzi Hoare for the term "brain tornado".

James Clear for the Nichelle Nichols story and for giving me permission to use his story in my book.

Wendy Baskett, who's done a fabulous job of indexing.

My clients, for trusting me with their messages and ideas.

My Superheroes and my Flamingos, for doing amazing shizzle with their businesses and lives, and for always having my back.

The authors I have coached, for doing what most people won't.

## My Beautiful Beta Readers

Thank you to everyone who was part of my launch team: Dani Moore, Sarah Silva, Jill Robinson, Yinka Ewuola, Jane Mann, Carol Clark, Graham Butcher, Julia Brown, Tanya Smith Lorenz, John Holcroft, Mark O'Loughlin, Nicky Salazar, Terri Williams, Mike Garner, Natasja Lewis, Rob Middleton, Morag Heirs, Martin Bailey, Jamie Veitch, Kathryn Reid, Sandra Williamson, Kelly Cordell-Morris, Janice Cumberlidge, Abby Popplestone, Carrie Stuthridge, Joy Ainley, Heather Stevens, Kat Smith, John Cleary, Louise Blackburn, Dennis Kelly.

Special thanks go to a few beta readers who went above and beyond all expectations and far beyond the call of duty.

John Holcroft, for your incredibly detailed videos and for the time you've spent talking to me about my ideas and what I want to achieve. I couldn't have done this without you, and I am grateful beyond measure. Plus, you sent me a flamingo cup, which is just marvapotamus.

Sarah Silva, for writing your book! And for being so excited about this one. Thank you especially for the extra notes on ebooks and audiobooks. That chapter is much better thanks to you.

Julia Brown, for loads of stuff—not least making sure I don't get sued into orbit by one of the world's largest organisations…

Jamie Veitch, for the extremely detailed feedback and a couple of suggestions which have made this book immeasurably better.

I appreciate you all more than you will ever know.

## Last, but definitely not least…

And finally, thank you, dear reader, for choosing me. Without you, there's no point. Now go and write your book.

# APPENDICES

# APPENDIX I

# Moxie Book Roadmap

**Thinking about writing a book but not sure it's a good idea for you?**

Read Chapter 1.

**Wondering about how to get started?**

Read Chapter 2.

**Struggling with confidence?**

Read Chapters 3, 5, 14, and 21.

**Got stuck on the Blank Page Of Doom?**

Read Chapters 2, 4, 5, 6, 7, and 9.

**Want to improve your writing skills?**

Read Chapters 5, 12, 13, 15, 16, and 18.

**Struggling with structure?**

Read Chapters 8, 9, 10, and 11.

**Finished writing your first drafts and need to polish it?**

Read Chapters 18, 19, 20, and 22.

**Ready to publish?**

Read Chapter 23.

**Wondering what to do with your book once you've written it?**

Read Chapter 24.

# APPENDIX II

# The Writer's Toolbox

It's time to choose your weapons. I won't go into minute detail here about every writing tool available to you. There are too many. Instead, I'll tell you what I use and how they help me.

## Analogue Tools

I love technology and digital tools, but I start with my trusty old pen and paper. I never go anywhere without a notebook and pen, because you never know when a brilliant idea is going to fight its way out of your head. In fact, I recommend having two notebooks and plenty of things to write and stick in them. Some people are one hundred per cent digital, but I find the act of writing stuff down on paper helpful. It helps my thought processes, especially when it comes to outlining.

- **My Bullet Journal**. I used to use separate notebooks for different things, but I ended up with a confused pile of scribbles on books and random pieces of paper. Now, my whole life lives in my BuJo. Take a look at the resources area on the book website if you want to know how I use my Bullet Journal and other productivity tools.

- **Pentel EnerGel 0.7mm ball pen.** I know it sounds daft, but this is the only pen I use to write with. It's the next best thing to a proper fountain pen, but less messy.

- **Conté Colouring Pens.** I use felt-tip pens when my notes need a splash of colour.

- **Post-It notes.** These are invaluable to me for the editing process. When my book comes back from the beta readers, I get busy with my sticky notes.

- **Books.** One of the most important tools in your writer's toolbox is other books. Good writers are great readers. If you want to improve at writing, read more. Make a note of what you love—and what you hate. Pay attention to what's easy to read, what's difficult to read, and figure out why.

## Digital Tools

As for digital tools, I love those too. Here's what I use:

- **750words.com.** These are my Morning Pages, inspired by Julia Cameron. I write three pages of nonsense from my brain—give it a try. All those thoughts swirling around and demanding your attention: imprison them in pixels so they can't distract you. Got to get more chicken food? Write it down. Need to remember to pay the milkman? Write it down. Ruminating over a row you had with your employee or your mum? Write it down. Get all that crap out of your head and onto paper, then it won't destroy your day. Don't edit. Don't hesitate. Don't worry about spelling, grammar, or even if it's legible. Just write (electronically or on paper). This exercise does two things: it gets you used to writing without editing, which is vital; and it clears your brain of rubbish so your creative neurons can fire. And you might even get some post-modern poetry out of it, too. (Kidding. Or not.)

- **Scrivener.**[1] This is my go-to writing tool. It's a piece of software created especially for authors—although I use it to write email sequences, newsletters, blogs, and articles as well as books. It does have a steep learning curve if you want to use all its features, but it's a marvellous tool, and it'll format your work for print and e-publishing, too. Scrivener allows you to keep all your chapters, notes, and research in one place, so you can dip in and out of it,

---

1  You don't have to use Scrivener. Although I adore Scrivener, it can be intimidating — and the last thing you need if you're trying to write a book is a piece of software waiting around the corner, ready to scramble your brain. I want to remove as many obstacles as I can for you, so you can get on with writing.

and shuffle things around with ease. You can't do that with traditional word processing programs; you may find something like Microsoft Word leaves you with a huge pile of confusing stuff.

- **Microsoft Word or Apple Pages** (other word processing programs are available). If you think you'll struggle with the act of writing, use a tool you're familiar with. Do you write regular blogs or articles in Microsoft Word or Google Docs? Then use Word or Google Docs to write your book. It'll take longer to pull it all together at the end, but that's okay. It's crucial to do the writing, or there won't be anything to pull together.

- **Vellum.** Having said I love Scrivener—which I do—I find it wildly frustrating to format documents for print and ebooks. I used to outsource that... until I found Vellum. It's another piece of software developed specifically to help authors get the most out of ebooks. It helps you build box sets if you have a series of books, connect to social media, add links to help readers buy more from you, and generate ebooks for Kindle, Apple Books, Kobo. I paid $249.99 for the software, and it's already saved me time and money. I love it. Note: Vellum is only available for Mac OS at the moment.

- **Trello** is a free online organisational tool, which I use for practically everything. I find it particularly useful for planning book launches, email sequences, and client work (because you can add due dates and times)—not so much for writing, although I imagine it would be splendid for creating your outline because you can move cards around.

- **Grammarly** is brilliant for initial proofreading and writing suggestions—but it's no substitute for a human proofreader before you send your book to print.

- **Thesaurus.com** is always open on my desktop because otherwise, I spend a lot of time staring out of the window with my mouth open, failing to remember that cool word that's right on the tip of my brain.

- **Evernote** is my go-to scrapbook: every time I find an article online, or an interesting website, or an image, or a video, or a sound clip—they all go into Evernote and get tagged so I can find them again.

- My **iPhone voice recorder**: if I can't write something down—if I have an idea while I'm driving, for example— I'll speak the note into my phone then upload it to Evernote.

- **Nuance Dragon.**[2] If you're dyslexic, developing RSI (repetitive strain injury), or simply don't like writing or typing, you may find software like Dragon Dictation valuable. You don't have to use a pen or typewriter to be a writer…Drayton Bird dictates everything he writes and has it typed up. Speak your truth into a recorder, and either have the recorder transcribe it, or send it to a human to transcribe it for you.

- **rev.com.** I use this service to transcribe my podcasts and other audio material, and it's excellent value, with a lightning-quick turnaround ($1 per minute). Once you have your transcript back, you simply edit it. You can do the same for your book.

- **Freedom.** I have little impulse control when it comes to digital candy like Facebook, so I've installed an app on my MacBook to limit access.

---

2   Used to be called Dragon Dictation. They do two versions: Dragon Home for £139.99 and Dragon Professional for £349.99.

# Example Book Structures

## Company Of One by Paul Jarvis

In the front matter, Jarvis includes:
- Praise for his book on the very first page.
- About the author followed on the second page.
- Title page.
- Copyright page.
- Dedication.
- Epigraph.
- Table of Contents.
- Prologue (basically a preface).[1]

In the back matter, he includes:
- Afterword.
- Another epigraph.
- Acknowledgements.
- Notes (notes can be footnotes, as I've done, or endnotes, which—as the name suggests—all go at the end).
- Index.
- Publisher's message (from Penguin Randomhouse).

## Atomic Habits by James Clear

In the front matter, James Clear includes:
- Half title page.
- Author name page with a grey background.
- Title page.

---

[1] Prologues aren't usually included in non-fiction books—but as I keep saying, it's your book, and you make your own rules.

- Copyright page.
- Epigraph (actually a definition of the words "atomic" and "habit").
- Table of Contents.

In the back matter, Clear puts everything together under a section called "Appendix" and includes:

- What you should read next.
- Little lessons.
- How to apply what you've learned to business and life.
- Acknowledgements.
- Notes.
- Index.

Clear doesn't include an explicit "about the author" section, but his introduction is called "My Story".

## On Speaking Well by Peggy Noonan

Peggy Noonan's front matter includes:

- Half title page.
- Other books by Peggy Noonan.
- Title page.
- Copyright page
- Dedication.
- Epigraph.
- Acknowledgements.
- Introduction.

Note: Noonan doesn't include a Table of Contents... but it's a book of anecdotes, mostly, so perhaps it doesn't need one.

The back matter includes:

- Summing up.
- A note to writers.
- Index.

# The 4-Hour Work Week by Tim Ferriss

Tim Ferriss includes in his front matter:

- Praise for *The 4-Hour Work Week*.
- Half title page.
- Title page.
- Copyright page.
- Dedication.
- Table of Contents.
- Preface.
- FAQ.
- My story and why you need this book.
- Chronology.

And in his back matter:

- Last but not least—a section with his back matter.
- The best of the blog (snippets from his blog).
- Living the 4-hour work week (case studies, tips, and hacks).
- Restricted reading (Ferriss's recommended reading).
- Bonus material (getting you onto his website and his email list, gameified by getting you to find Easter Eggs and passwords hidden in the book).
- Acknowledgements.
- Index.
- About the author.

You can see different authors make different decisions depending on what they want to include. You can do the same.

# APPENDIX IV

# Typeface & Layout

In case you were wondering about the typeface and layout of this book, I've included all the details below.

- The typeface on the cover is Black Diamond.
- The main body of this book is set in Baskerville 11-point.
- Chapter titles are set in Roboto 18-point, centred.
- Subheadings are set in Roboto 14-point.
- The first line of each paragraph is indented at 5 mm.
- My line spacing is 1.2 with a 1 mm space after each paragraph.
- Page numbers go in the footer, in the centre.
- Printed book size is Demy (138 mm x 216 mm).
- Margins: Top = 25 mm, Bottom = 18 mm, Inside = 22 mm, Outside = 16 mm.

## APPENDIX V

# The Final Print Checklist

Do not send your book for the print run until you have ticked off every single item on this list. Use the proof copy your printer sends you and run it through my checklist. Do not be tempted to send it to print without getting a proof copy! You never know quite what it'll look like until it's in your hands.

I have created this checklist thanks to years of making painful—and often expensive—mistakes. I've made those mistakes, so you don't have to.

## The Cover

- ☐ Correct title
- ☐ Correct subtitle
- ☐ Correct spellings on front cover
- ☐ Correct author name
- ☐ Correct typeface
- ☐ Image is high-quality and non-blurry
- ☐ Spine text is correct
- ☐ Correct spellings on spine
- ☐ Text and images are in the correct position on the spine
- ☐ Correct version of back blurb
- ☐ Back blurb spellcheck
- ☐ Back cover is clear and readable
- ☐ Correct ISBN for edition
- ☐ Does the ISBN match the barcode? (Scan it)
- ☐ Correct price
- ☐ Are you using the right cover art version?
- ☐ Is the book cover finished as you want—gloss or matte?

## The Interior

- [ ] Correct paper weight
- [ ] Correct paper colour
- [ ] Is the trim tidy?
- [ ] Does the ISBN on the copyright page match the cover?
- [ ] Correct copyright information
- [ ] Correct edition on copyright page
- [ ] Odd page numbers on the right-hand page
- [ ] Are blank pages blank?
- [ ] Do chapters start on the right-hand page?
- [ ] Check interior spine margin doesn't crowd the text
- [ ] Check all margins leave enough white space
- [ ] Header and footer space: check they don't crowd the text
- [ ] Are running navigation headers correct for each chapter?
- [ ] Correct typeface for headings throughout
- [ ] Correct typeface for main text throughout
- [ ] Are your chosen typefaces easily readable?
- [ ] Images: are they clear and easy to read?
- [ ] Check all footnotes/endnotes are present and correct
- [ ] Bullets and numbered lists are tidy and consistent
- [ ] Have you had the final version proofread?
- [ ] Check index hasn't changed
- [ ] Does the table of contents match the actual contents?

# Bibliography

## Books Mentioned Or Recommended:

*101 Naked Confessions of a Gay Hairdresser* by Kat Smith

*23 Things They Don't Tell You About Capitalism* by Ha-Joon Chang

*A Technique For Producing Ideas* by James Webb Young

*A Whack on the Side of the Head* by Roger von Oech

*Atomic Habits* by James Clear

*Bird By Bird* by Anne Lamott

*Cassell's Dictionary of Slang*

*Commonsense Direct And Digital Marketing* by Drayton Bird

*Company Of One* by Paul Jarvis

*Creative Mischief* by Dave Trott

*Daring Greatly* by Brené Brown

*Decisive* by Chip and Dan Heath

*Deep Work* by Cal Newport

*Digital Minimalism* by Cal Newport

*Drunk Tank Pink* by Adam Alter

*Eat, Pray, Love* by Elizabeth Gilbert

Everything by Neil Gaiman

Everything by Sir Terry Pratchett

*Furiously Happy* by Jenny Lawson

*Girl, Wash Your Face* by Rachel Hollis

*Hinch Yourself Happy* by Mrs Hinch

*How To Eat The Elephant* by Ann Sheybani

*How To Sell A Crapload Of Books* by Tim Vandehey & Naren Aryal

*Living Forward* by Daniel Harkavy and Michael Hyatt

*Losing My Virginity* by Richard Branson

*Marketing Insights and Outrages* by Drayton Bird

*Ninebarrow's Dorset* by Jon Whitley and Jay LaBouchardiere

*On Speaking Well* by Peggy Noonan

*Perennial Seller* by Ryan Holiday

*Politics And The English Language* by George Orwell

*Rewire Your Anxious Brain* by Catherine M. Pittman & Elizabeth M. Karle

*Self Comes To Mind* by Antonio Damasio

*Sleep Like A Boss* by Christine Hansen

*Start With Why* by Simon Sinek

*Telling True Stories: A Nonfiction Writers' Guide* by Mark Kramer and Wendy Call

*The 12 Week Year* by Brian P. Moran

*The 12-Week Year Field Guide* by Brian Moran

*The 7 Habits of Highly Effective People* by Steven Covey

*The Art Of Asking* by Amanda Palmer

*The Artist's Way* by Julia Cameron

*The Brain Audit* by Sean D'Souza

*The Bullet Journal Method* by Ryder Carroll

*The Chimp Paradox* by Professor Steve Peters

*The Complete Nonsense of Edward Lear* edited by Holbrook Jackson

*The Copywriter's Handbook* by Robert Bly

*The Easy Way To Control Alcohol* by Allen Carr

*The Elements of Style* by Strunk & White

*The Founding Fathers: Quotes, Quips, and Speeches* by Gordon Leidner

*The Go-Giver* by Bob Burg

*The Good Divorce Guide* by Teresa Payne

*The Little CBT Workbook* by Dr Michael Sinclair & Dr Belinda Hollingsworth

*The Miracle Morning* by Hal Elrod

*The Ode Less Travelled* by Stephen Fry

*The Power Of Habit* by Charles Duhigg

*The Secret Lives of Colour* by Kassia St Clair

*The Subtle Art Of Not Giving A F*ck* by Mark Manson

*The War Of Art* by Steven Pressfield

*They Ask, You Answer* by Marcus Sheridan

*Through The Looking Glass* by Lewis Carroll

*To Sell Is Human* by Daniel Pink

*Tribes* by Seth Godin

*Type & Layout* by Colin Wheildon

*Walk Yourself Wealthy* by Dominic Hodgson

*We Are All Weird* by Seth Godin

*Wired For Story* by Lisa Cron

*Words That Sell* by Richard Bayan

*Workin' It!: RuPaul's Guide to Life, Liberty, and the Pursuit of Style* by RuPaul Charles

*Write. Publish. Repeat.* by Sean Platt, Johnny B. Truant, & David Wright

*Wuthering Heights* by Emily Brontë

## Podcasts I listen to:

99% Invisible

Akimbo by Seth Godin

BBC Inside Science

Cafeteria Christian

Freakonomics Radio

Getting Curious With Jonathan Van Ness

Hidden Brain

Philosophize This!

Planet Money

Psych Insights For Modern Marketers

Published by Greenleaf Book Group

Radiolab

Terrible, Thanks For Asking

The Copywriter Club Podcast

The Daily Bugle

The Guilty Feminist

The Infinite Monkey Cage

The Memory Palace

The Moth

The Self Publishing Show

The Story Grid Podcast

The Three Month Vacation

Writing Excuses

You Are Not So Smart

# Really Did Run Away
# With The Circus...

How does one accidentally end up with three TinySheeps? Answer: be in the wrong place at the right time, and come home with a surprise wonky lamb.

Not a joke. This is my ridiculous and delightful life.

This isn't one of those About The Author pages where I tell you my rags-to-riches story. I've never been poor (for which I am incredibly thankful), and I don't sit on a pile of gold (yet). I don't measure riches in £-signs, although a big pile of dosh certainly helps things along.

Also, I don't think you want my CV, do you? How dull is that?

Instead, I thought I'd open the window into my brain. Just a crack, mind. If I open it too wide, all the weird will pour out and swallow the world, kind of like VANTA black (look it up, it's fascinating).

I'm not only a writer and teacher; I'm also a collector of small, cute animals, horrifying bruises, inappropriate facial expressions, and colourful socks.

And I did, in fact, run away with the circus. Kind of.

After my ever-patient and totally awesome husband Joe and our animal friends, and my love affair with writing, the other big love of my life is the circus and aerial arts. Specifically, trapeze, hoop, and pole dancing. Just don't ask me to juggle; it rapidly turns into chaos and lethal projectiles.

# 24 Things About Me

1.  I started out as a direct response copywriter and marketing bod, so when I tell you I can help you sell and market your book, I'm not bullshitting you. (I've spent years not just learning from the masters, but writing sales copy that gets results for me and my clients.)

2.  I love, *love*, LOVE helping business owners gain the confidence to be more bloody interesting—and seeing them tell their stories in their books.

3.  I've been pole dancing for more than 12 years—and, yes, I do the exotic stripper-style proudly (and often ineptly), mo-fos.

4.  I love my cats more than is socially acceptable.

5.  Ditto, my TinySheeps and my Beaky-Face chickens and Maisie Snake Fantastico.

6.  Ditto, cheese and gin. I have more half-drunk bottles of gin than you can shake a stick at.

7.  My addiction to buying books and leggings is totally under control.

8.  I have a short hairtenntion span (it's currently blue and silver).

9.  I legit ran away with the circus (I'm a trapeze artist, and I do actual performances on a trapeze onstage. I have the scars and bruises to prove it).

10. I send an email to my email list subscribers every single day—and they make me money (if you want to sell and use your book, you should do this too. Ask me how).

11. When I decided struggling and working 18-hour days and having no weekends sucked big hairy donkey balls, it took me just six months to make my first £100k. I'm pretty damn proud of that because it means we're now living in our dream cottage in the country. The only downside is, we can often see the outside through the walls. And I don't mean through the windows.

12. Random ability: I can read and write ancient Egyptian hieroglyphs (although I'm a little rusty these days).

13. I once made Drayton Bird scream (true story—ask him). And that led to an exciting opportunity...

14. I once rendered Dan Kennedy speechless for a few moments (also a true story).

15. I'm learning to draw cartoons, and I'm occasionally competent at it (I started cartooning so I could illustrate my own blogs, articles, books, and other marketing gubbins).

16. Once, when I was a teenager, I was in a band. We played at a pub, and they gave us free drinks. We drank so many free drinks, they cancelled our next gig and banned us.

17. My aim in life is to accept only excellence from myself. Occasionally I fall short because I'm human.

18. If you touch or attempt to touch my belly button, I will cut you (it's nothing personal, it's a reflex reaction: google omphalophobia).

19. I love words. *Love* them. Love the feel of them as they roll around in my mouth and the sound of them as they caress my eardrums. I love how they go together, of course, and the things you can do with them... but I love the words themselves.

20. I am learning patience through growing my own vegetables (did you know you can't harvest asparagus for the first two years?)

21. I have discovered that "nice" isn't valuable or helpful... but kindness and grace will get you a very long way.

22. I live by JFDI (just fecking do it). Sometimes more forethought would be helpful.

23. I spend more time than is probably sensible or sane working on my Zombie Plan (look, you never know what's around the corner, okay?)

24. One of life's tiny pleasures, for me, is putting on socks in the wind. It's like a hug for your feet.

So now you know more about me than you probably ever wished to. Sorry. I'd like to know all about you now.

Tell me *your* story. Write it in your book.

Share it with the world. People are interested, I promise.

# Index

# Index

Made in the USA
Las Vegas, NV
28 October 2021